Managing Major Sales

For more information please contact:
Huthwaite, Inc.
Wheatland Manor
15164 Berlin Turnpike
Purcellville, VA 20132
U.S.A.
Tel: (540) 882-3212
Fax: (540) 882-9004

MANAGING MAJOR SALES

Practical Strategies for Improving Sales Effectiveness

Neil Rackham
Richard Ruff

HarperBusiness
A Division of HarperCollins*Publishers*

Printed in the United States of America

Library of Congress Cataloging-in-Publication Data

Rackham, Neil.
    Managing major sales : practical strategies for improving sales effectiveness / Neil Rackham, Richard Ruff.
      p. cm.
    Includes index.
    ISBN 0-88730-508-3
    1. Sales management. I. Ruff, Richard, 1941– . II. Title.
HF5438.4.R34   1991
658.8′1—dc20   91-8563
                                        CIP

01 CC/HC 20 19 18 17

This book is dedicated to
the many sales managers who
have patiently given us a practical
education in the perils of sales
management.

Contents

Introduction

Several years ago we were in Philadelphia giving a keynote address to the annual conference of the National Society of Sales Training Executives. Our topic was research into major account selling. Towards the end of our address, we complained about how little research attention selling receives compared with marketing. "Why is this?" we asked. "Surely selling deserves better?" At discussion time, a member of our audience stood up and offered an explanation. "It's because marketing is a true profession," he began, "while selling still isn't there yet." As you might imagine, this wasn't a popular position to take at a meeting of an organization of sales professionals. There was a chorus of dissent, but the speaker stuck to his guns. "Let me explain," he said. "A profession like engineering, medicine, or marketing is based on a *technology*—a special body of knowledge and techniques that the profession has accumulated. The more technology a profession has developed, the more research it stimulates. The reason why selling isn't a true profession yet is that we don't have enough technology, and as a result, selling doesn't attract research. Marketing, however, *does* have a technology in areas like market research and advertising. That's why it attracts researchers." This further explanation gained no new converts for his position and the discussion moved to other issues. We never discovered the speaker's name, but in retrospect, we have to confess that we think he was right. Selling is becoming a true profession fast, but it still needs to develop much more technology in terms of models, methods, and systematic knowledge before it can compete on equal terms with most of the older, more established, professions.

During recent years, that new technology has started to emerge in some areas of selling. We've learned more about selling skills, for example, in the last five years than in the 50 years before that. Our knowledge of major account selling and sales strategy has made significant strides forward. Selling is growing and maturing professionally, but how about sales management? Who is helping sales managers keep up with this tide of change? Where's the sales management technology?

The fact is, it's only very recently that researchers like us have started systematically to focus their attention on sales management. This book is the first ever that's specifically written to help managers whose business is to manage major sales—the most exciting, most challenging, and fastest changing area of selling. We've drawn on our own research and on the experience of the many major account sales organizations we've worked with during the last 20 years. To the several thousand sales managers we've trained, argued with, and learned from during these years, we owe thanks for the genesis of many of the ideas we cover here. In particular, we'd like to thank Howard Kleinert, Laird Matthews, and Doug McNair for their comments on the draft manuscript. We'd also like to offer gratitude to John DeVincentis and our many other friends at McKinsey and Company. Their consistent intellectual integrity has provided us with a much valued sounding board for some of these concepts. Most valuable of all has been our understanding team of colleagues here at Huthwaite whose help and patience has made this book possible. We'd especially like to thank Joan Costich who, as Operations Manager, has provided a business environment that has allowed this effort and John Wilson who contributed to many of these ideas. We must also thank Ken Webb and Jack Fagan who took workload from us at crucial times during the writing. Outside of work, a special thank you to Quincy Rackham and Janet Spirer who reviewed our progress and encouraged every step of our efforts.

Managing Major Sales

1

A DIFFERENT KIND OF ANIMAL

The Sales Manager in Major Sales

When we first made public our research on selling skills, we upset a lot of people. It didn't matter that our work was based on the largest research study of selling in history—a scientific analysis of the selling skills used in 35,000 sales calls. It didn't matter that it took our team at Huthwaite 12 years, working in 23 countries, to check and double check our data. People were upset. If we hadn't already realized how controversial our findings would be, we certainly had no doubts after a national conference we addressed in Los Angeles. At the end of our session we were surrounded by a little lynch mob of angry trainers who protested in loud and hysterical terms that we were undermining everything they had been teaching in their sales training programs. When we finally escaped from them and turned to pick up the overhead projector slides we'd used in our presentation, we found that every one of our slides had been damaged or defaced. A couple of years later we had a contract with a major publisher for a book based on this sales research. When the manuscript was sent to reviewers for comments their reactions were a replay of the group's reaction in Los Angeles. "A trash heap," wrote one reviewer, "combining arrogance with ignorance." As a result, the publisher canceled our contract. What was it, you might ask, that made these ideas so offensive that they couldn't be calmly presented or published?

Our main findings were simple enough. We had shown that the skills which make you successful in small sales can actually hurt your success in larger ones. The small sale normally involves just one face-to-face meeting between a single salesperson and a decisionmaking customer. This is significantly different from the major sale, which requires a series of meetings spread over many months, involves several people in the selling effort, and often allows little or no direct access to the decision maker. Although we use the same word *selling* to cover both small sales and major sales, in reality we're talking about two very different processes, each needing a different set of skills for success. We found, for example:

- The closing techniques that succeed in smaller sales will actually *lose* you business as the sale grows larger. Most of the commonly taught closing techniques just don't work in large sales. Our research showed that there were much better and more sophisticated ways to obtain commitments from customers in major sales.

- The classic questioning methods of open and closed questions may suffice in smaller sales but are not going to help you much in bigger sales. From the analysis of several thousand sales calls, and from watching some of the world's top salespeople in action, we were able to discover some alternative probing methods that were more business centered and brought better results in major sales.

- In major sales, objection handling skills contribute only marginally to sales success. Instead, effective salespeople in larger sales concentrate on objection prevention rather than on objection handling. Our research analyzed how successful major account salespeople prevented objections from their customers.

- Traditional wisdom suggests that it's better to sell through benefits than through features. Our research found that some kinds of benefits that succeeded in small sales were actively counterproductive when used in larger sales. From an analysis of the types of benefits offered by successful major account salespeople, we were able to isolate the kinds of benefits that have most impact on the major sale.

Why should innocent sounding findings like these cause such antagonism? The answer is not unconnected with the vested interests of the billion-dollar-a-year sales training industry, which had been making a comfortable living from teaching that selling was selling, whether the product was a door-to-door vacuum cleaner or a multimillion dollar computer system. Research like ours was bad news, showing that major sales required different skills. Traditional sales training models, unfortunately, were based on what succeeded in smaller sales. We were raising an awkward point. If the research was right, corporations whose businesses involved major sales were wasting a great deal of time and money teaching their people models and programs that, frankly, didn't work for their kinds of sales. No wonder we weren't making many friends in the one-size-fits-all climate of sales training that was current at the time.

Our Debt to Sales Managers

But this is a story with a happy ending. Gradually, interest in new models for major account selling grew. The first champions of these newer ideas were practicing sales managers who were dissatisfied with the training that their people were getting. Even before our research, thoughtful managers in major sales had been concerned about the relevance of some of the sales training offered to their people. "Existing training just doesn't apply to our sale," one of our early supporters told us; "we send our new people on programs that teach them selling's about going straight to the decision maker, overcoming a few objections, and closing the business. When these kids go out in the field and try to behave that way, they get slaughtered. There's got to be a better way." Managers like this one found, in research on major sales, data to support their need for more sophisticated and more appropriate selling skills models. Thanks to the encouragement of major sales practitioners, acceptance for these new ideas grew. Our rejected book was published by a different publisher, McGraw-Hill, under the title *SPIN® Selling* and, in true fairy-tale manner, quickly became an international best seller. Many of the world's leading sales forces began to adopt major sales models based on radically different thinking about what it takes to succeed in major sales.

In just a few years, the climate has changed completely. It's no longer considered daring to suggest that major sales are different and require different skills and strategies. There are books and training programs available specifically designed for major account selling. We can't claim much of the credit for this welcome change. It happened because practicing major account salespeople and their managers demanded something better. Nevertheless, it's been exhilarating to have played an active part in making these changes happen. We find it very satisfying that we're now on the side of the majority. Few thoughtful people today would quarrel with the once controversial message that major sales are different and that success in major sales rests on a unique set of skills.

Is Major Sales Management Different?

Although the battle over major sales has been won at the salesperson level, it still remains to be fought at the level of the sales manager. If selling skills and selling strategies are different in major account selling, isn't it plausible that sales management is different too? During recent years we've become much more sophisticated in our understanding of what it takes to sell successfully to large accounts, but how well do we understand major account sales management? What are the special skills and abilities needed to manage major account salespeople? There's ample evidence that managing major sales *is* different. For example:

- There are many well-documented cases of people who have been outstandingly successful as sales managers with a low-end sales force. When promoted to management positions involving major sales they have failed dismally. Why? The most likely explanation is that the skills that helped them manage small sales well were no longer useful for managing larger sales. It's probable that managing major sales required some unique skills that these people didn't have.

- Some of the techniques that have proved remarkably successful for increasing productivity in small sales have turned out to be much less effective when used with larger sales. Activity management, as we'll see in detail in the next chapter, is a classic case in point. In most small sales, one of the best tools for increasing productivity is tight management of activity, such as call rates. The same activity management techniques that increase productivity in small sales can often be demonstrated to *reduce* productivity if they are used to manage major sales. Again, the inference is that major sales need to be managed differently.

- Selling skills and strategies, as research in recent years has so clearly documented, are different in small sales and in large. It's therefore almost inevitable that managing those strategies and skills will be different too.

If the major sale requires different management skills, what are they? Where can major sales managers turn for advice? Not to any of the books on sales management that we've come across. Ten years ago, we were complaining that books on selling failed because they didn't recognize the difference between small sales and large. Exactly that complaint can be made today about books on sales management. The fact is, it was only very recently that researchers and writers started to realize something that practical sales managers had known for a long time. Managing major sales requires special and different skills. This is the first book that specifically sets out to describe what some of those skills are and what it takes to be a successful major sales manager.

Some Initial Research

Our research into big-ticket sales had convinced us years ago that managing major sales involved a unique and complex set of skills. We had only to look around us during our research to find examples of some very effective—and some much less effective—

managers in action. What were the effective managers doing differently? Our first thought was that they were using a different *style* of management. We believed that if we could analyze the management style used by successful major account sales managers, then the problem of how to manage major sales would be solved. Full of the certainty and enthusiasm that only afflicts the blissfully ignorant, we persuaded a large telecommunications company to let us study their successful major account sales managers to find the magic management style that we believed successful managers were using. Armed with nothing more than questionnaires and structured interview schedules, we set out to explore the management style used by the 50 most successful major account managers in the company. It didn't take long to discover that our quest was, to put it mildly, somewhat naïve. Successful managers didn't have just one management style. We found that, in this telecommunications company at least, successful major sales managers used widely different styles. Three successful styles stood out, each showing significant differences in how a manager behaved.

- *Entrepreneurs* were successful managers who behaved as if they were running a small company of their own, treating their accounts as a marketplace of business opportunities to be seized and exploited. These managers tended to use a *hands-on* approach to selling. They were more directly involved in face-to-face selling than either of the other successful types of sales manager. They tended to become particularly involved in face-to-face meetings with customers whenever they felt an obstacle was holding up business or there was an important transaction to be closed. These managers often competed viciously for internal resources, some going as far as stealing sales talent away from other managers in their own company. They inspired their sales teams to act. Their offices were invariably busy. In addition to a strong business sense and a good understanding of figures and sales profitability, they had a sense of their own contribution to the bottom line compared with other sales managers. One of the Entrepreneur managers we interviewed kept a large wall chart—updated weekly—that showed how much revenue he was generating compared with other sales teams. When he was ahead, the chart was prominently displayed on the wall for all visitors to see. Our visit occurred at a time when he had temporarily slipped into third place, so, for the time being, the chart was discreetly tucked behind a file cabinet.

- *Coalition Builders* were successful managers who built careful networks of contacts and friends, both in customer accounts and within their own company. These managers were less active in face-to-face selling. They spent less time face-to-face with the customers than the Entrepreneurs. Instead, they worked behind the scenes, using their network of contacts to help them and their salespeople surmount any obstacles in the selling cycle. Their meetings with customers were most likely to focus on relationship building. Frequently they would be meeting outside of the formal work environment—at trade shows or on the golf course. These managers always knew somebody who knew somebody who owed them a favor, and as a result, they could quietly make astonishing things happen.

- *Competitive Strategists* were successful managers who were particularly skilled at outthinking and outmaneuvering their competition. Again, they spent less face-to-face time with customers than did the Entrepreneurs. Their strength lay in the way they helped their people plan and form competitive strategies. When they were with customers it was most likely to be during the competitive stages of the sale where, for example, there were competitive capability presentations to be made. Many of the Competitive Strategists we met were clearly bored by *safe* routine business. "I'm a hunter," one of them told us; "I'd like nothing better than to unload all my safe accounts on a bunch of customer care farmers, so I can go out and kill a few competitors." In general, Competitive Strategists put great emphasis on the importance of *timing*. They told us how important it was for a manager to become involved in the selling effort at the right moment in order to gain a competitive advantage.

In addition to the differences among these three types, we found an interesting similarity. All the successful managers emphasized the importance of *coaching* as a management tool for improving the performances of their people. To them, coaching wasn't just traditional coaching of selling skills. By coaching, they also meant working with their people on account strategy.

Each of these three styles of management is clearly very different, and each has different strengths. These types exist in most successful major account sales operations. If you think of the effective managers you know, you'll probably have no difficulty slotting most of them into one of these three types. However, interesting as these findings are, they spelled bad news for our attempt to find an *ideal* style of management for major sales. Long experience as researchers warned us that if we picked out three types of successful managers from a single study in a single organization, chances were that we were just scratching the surface. Further work in other places and in greater depth would almost certainly reveal other types and a whole bunch of complications. The only definite conclusion we could draw from this study was a negative one. There is *not* one successful style of management that works best in the major sale. However, this study did give us some important clues about what it takes to be a successful manager in large sales. For example:

- From the *Entrepreneur* we can see that the successful manager in major sales runs a *business* rather than just managing salespeople.
- From the *Coalition Builder* we can see how important it is in major sales to build and use a network of contacts, inside and outside the organization, in order to make things happen.
- From the *Competitive Strategist* we can see how useful it is to have a keen awareness of competition and a sense of timing that lets a manager intervene in a sale at the point of maximum competitive advantage.

Perhaps most important of all, Entrepreneurs, Coalition Builders, and Competitive Strategists all agreed on the importance of coaching for successful management of major sales.

How Managing Smaller Sales Is Different

For us, the most interesting results of this study were the things we *didn't* find. Let's imagine for a moment that we had been conducting this study in a classic sales organization that was involved in small sales. In all probability, if the traditional theory of sales management is anything to go by, we would have found that successful managers had these characteristics:

Strong activity management: In small sales it's common to find successful managers who closely manage and monitor their people's activity levels. They introduce and use call reporting systems, and they take steps to ensure that their people have a high call rate. They ensure, in other words, that their people are working *hard.* Before we carried out our study we had assumed that if it was important to manage people's activity levels in small sales, it would be even more important to do so in large ones. After all, we reasoned, in the small sale people are forced to work hard even without close activity management because, if they slacken, it's immediately visible in their results. In contrast, with larger sales, if someone decides to work less, it may take many months before any slackening of activity becomes noticeable in terms of results. For this reason, we had anticipated, it might be more important for managers to give attention to activity levels in large sales than in small. Consequently, we were surprised to find that very few of the successful managers we interviewed made any mention of classic activity management issues such as call rates. At the time we found this curious, but we didn't have any convincing explanation of why successful managers seemed so uninterested in how hard their people were working. Since our initial research we've come to understand the reasons much better. In large sales, as we'll see in the next chapter, techniques for making salespeople work harder tend to backfire. Traditional activity management brings with it some crippling disadvantages in major sales. There are well-documented cases that show how, following the introduction of activity management systems in major account sales organizations, sales volumes actually fall rather than increase.

Focus on territory management: Most books on sales management have whole chapters devoted to the importance of territory management. To judge from the published literature, effective territory management is likely to be a key ingredient for success in managing any sales force. Again, there was a curious absence of concern in this area among our successful major account sales managers. In this case, at least, the explanation wasn't hard to find. In smaller sales it's usual for salespeople to each have several hundred customers and prospects in their territory. Efficient management of sales territories becomes vital to ensure coverage of such large numbers. However, this becomes a nonissue in most major account sales organizations where salespeople usually have fewer customers and sometimes don't even have geographic territories. It's therefore less important to manage coverage efficiently. For this reason, we'll not be giving the usual space to territory management that seems obligatory in sales books. In fact—and we're sure that many readers will sigh with relief at this—we won't mention territory management again.

The manager as motivator: Traditional sales management has put great emphasis on the role of the manager as a motivator. For years, writers on selling have emphasized that selling is the loneliest job in the organization. In most other organizational functions, such as manufacturing, administration, or finance, people work together with their peers and receive motivation and support from this peer contact. Salespeople, in contrast, not only work alone, they work in an environment where rejection is a daily fact of life. Under these circumstances, say traditional writers, sales managers have an essential role as motivators. This role is all the more important because, so these writers claim, there's a direct link between motivation and results. By increasing the motivation of salespeople, you increase sales. We therefore expected that our sample of successful major account managers would put great importance on their role as motivators. To our surprise, motivation was rarely mentioned in our interviews. As we'll see later, we had stumbled on a very significant difference between small sales and large. In chapter 7, we'll discuss some case studies that show how motivational techniques that are highly successful in small sales will fail as sales grow larger. We're not suggesting that motivation is unimportant in major sales, but we shall be saying that effective motivation in large sales requires a very different kind of approach. This exploratory study gave us our first clue that traditional approaches to motivation might not be appropriate to major sales.

The key role of coaching: In one area, our successful managers appeared to confirm the conventional wisdom. There was general agreement among our three types of managers that coaching played an essential role in their success. In this respect, our results seemed to uncover a common factor between management of both large and small sales. Coaching, despite the fact that it's often neglected or done badly, is perhaps the most important single sales management skill. It's hardly surprising that it should emerge so prominently in our study of success. However, our interviews did reveal another contrast between large and small sales in the coaching area. In small sales, most coaching is intended to develop people's selling skills; in larger sales, coaching often has a different focus. In particular, we found that our successful major account managers spent a good deal of time coaching in the area of account strategy. At the time, we regarded this as a relatively minor issue of emphasis rather than as a significant difference between small and large sales. After all, we thought, coaching is coaching. It's reasonable to suppose that a manager who is a good skills coach will have little difficulty in putting those same coaching skills to work in the strategy area. Since then, we've found that it's not so simple. Skills coaching and strategy coaching are very different. We've often found good skills coaches who are mediocre at strategy coaching and vice versa. A likely explanation is that different skills are needed for each type of coaching. One factor, of course, is how well the coach understands the subject matter. We recall, for example, one manager who had come into sales from a marketing position. His background gave him an excellent understanding of strategic elements such as pricing or competitive differentiation, and as a result, he was well equipped to coach certain areas of strategy. However, because he hadn't sold before, he knew very little about selling skills, which was a severe disadvantage when it came to skills coaching. But there's a lot more to being a good skills coach or strategy coach than understanding selling skills or account strategy. For example, you can only coach skills by actually watching how your people sell. That means going out in the field with people, being present with them on customer calls and—yes—letting them do the selling while you observe. Strategy coaching, in contrast, can effectively be carried out without ever going near a customer. There are several other significant differences that would be important for any effective major sales manager to understand. These differences have led us to include two chapters on coaching: one on strategy coaching and one on skills coaching.

Initial Conclusions

Although our early work on sales management failed in its objective of finding the *ideal* managerial style, we came away with some conclusions that started us thinking. It was abundantly clear that managing the major sale required a different approach from managing smaller sales. Equally clear, conventional approaches to sales management contained in books and training programs seemed much more relevant to small sales than to large. It was déjà vu all over again. Ten years earlier, we had found that approaches to selling skills were derived from small sales and didn't apply to the larger sales we were studying. Now we were finding the same problem in the sales management area. Nobody had recognized the unique set of issues which constituted major sales management—or, if they had, they were keeping very quiet about it. In our work we would frequently be asked by sales managers for things they could read which would help them manage large sales more effectively. We knew of nothing. We searched the literature, and as a reward for our efforts, we came up with less than a dozen or so not-very-helpful articles. In the end we decided to tackle the problem ourselves.

This book is the result of our efforts. It's the first book to focus on the unique issues that face managers of major sales. Because nothing quite like this has been written before, it may be helpful for us to give you a preview of some of the issues we'll be covering in depth in the chapters ahead.

Productivity in Major Sales

The methods that achieve sales productivity in small sales are generally less effective in large ones. Putting the issue at its very simplest, you could say that in most small sales you can increase productivity by making people work *harder*—for example, by increasing the number of sales calls that people make. In larger sales, you're much less likely to get an increase in productivity from working harder. Sometimes, a work-harder orientation towards sales productivity in major sales can seriously backfire. In the next chapter we quote the case of a Chicago-based company where sales *fell* after measures were introduced to encourage major account salespeople to work harder. As many cases exist where pressure to work harder has failed to improve sales results, and even hurt them, it's important to understand what goes wrong. Fundamentally, small sale thinking encourages managers to believe in the simplistic formula, *more calls = more sales.* There's good evidence, which we'll examine in depth in the next chapter, to show that this formula holds true in many smaller sales. In one low-end sales force we studied, for example, we found that by pushing the sales force to work harder, managers were able to double the number of sales calls their people were making. New business sales rose almost in proportion, showing a 90 percent increase. Clearly, here was a case where the *more calls = more sales* formula turned out to be valid. However, when we've studied attempts to apply this kind of thinking to major sales, we've generally seen very disappointing results. Why? There's certainly room for working harder—for making more calls—in most major sales organizations. Surely, even if more calls don't bring a proportionate increase in sales, it doesn't hurt to encourage your people to work hard. Unfortunately, it's not so simple. Pressure to work harder usually brings with it some unintended side effects in major sales. To take one example, when salespeople are pressured for higher activity levels, we've found that they tend to focus on making smaller quick-hit sales at the expense of larger strategic ones. We tracked one company that introduced an activity management system to increase their call rates. We found that, after the introduction of the system, calls increased and so did the number of sales. However, the increase was almost exclusively in terms of smaller one-off sales. Large sales fell after the system was introduced and, overall, sales revenue dropped.

Efficiency and Effectiveness

If working harder isn't the answer, what is? At the risk of oversimplifying the points we'll cover in the next chapter, in major sales success comes from working *smarter* not harder. Consequently, any attempt to increase sales that focuses only on working harder is likely to have little impact on overall productivity. It's useful to think about sales productivity in terms of two components:

- *Sales Efficiency:* which is about how to get in front of customers for the right amount of time at a minimum cost
- *Sales Effectiveness:* which is about how to maximize sales potential once you're there

Broadly speaking, though with some important exceptions that we'll be explaining, efficiency is about working harder, while effectiveness is about working smarter. In smaller sales, a focus on sales efficiency usually brings productivity gains. However, in larger sales, sales efficiency is not normally the answer. Knocking on more doors, for instance, is more likely to lead to increased business in small sales than in large ones. In contrast, it's what you do after the door has been opened—what we're defining here as sales effectiveness—that has most influence on your success in major sales. The methods that increase efficiency are very different from the ones that increase effectiveness. Many sales organizations have run into severe problems because they have tried to apply efficiency solutions to effectiveness problems, and vice versa. In particular, we're disturbed at how often major sales managers damage their own success and the success of their people by intentionally adopting *selling harder* solutions for *selling smarter* problems.

The Manager's Selling Role

Another area in which managing major sales is different from the traditional theory of sales management lies in the manager's own selling role. A perennial management disease in smaller sales is the manager who, after a successful selling career, is promoted into sales management and continues to behave like a super salesperson. As the sales vice president of one large insurance company put it, "We promote salespeople to sales management as if being good at selling qualifies you to be a manager. All we are doing is creating managers who can't let go of the selling role. When will we learn? Selling and managing are two separate professions, and as far as I'm concerned, the further apart we keep them the better." He speaks a great truth. We carried out a study of successful sales management in a division of a company that sold simple low-end products. We found:

- The most successful managers did no selling themselves, concentrating instead on managing the activities of their sales teams.
- Less successful managers, in contrast, played a much more active role in face-to-face selling. It seemed that they couldn't let go of their selling role.
- Salespeople hated it when their managers became directly involved in selling to customers.

This study and others like it, convinced us that classic sales management theory was right. Managers should manage and leave the face-to-face selling to their people. But, although this may be true in smaller sales, it's an unworkable concept for major sales. You can't manage very large sales without playing an integral part in every facet of the sales process, including face-to-face selling. Playing a face-to-face role in major account selling, however, can easily go wrong unless that role is carried out in accordance with some simple but important principles.

Principles for Involvement in Face-to-face Selling

We believe that there are five fundamental principles to guide any sales manager's face-to-face involvement in a major sale.

Principle #1: Only become involved in face-to-face selling when your presence makes a unique difference.

Principle #2: Don't make sales calls on a customer unless your salesperson is with you.

Principle #3: Before any joint call, agree on specific and clear selling roles with your salesperson.

Principle #4: Be an active *internal* seller for your salespeople.

Principle #5: Always have a withdrawal strategy that prevents any customer from becoming dependent on you personally.

In chapter three we explore these principles in more depth and show how to use them to avoid some of the traps that face-to-face selling involvement creates for the unwary manager.

Sales Effectiveness Models

Most of the basic concepts about how to sell that appear in books and training programs are derived from small sales. In the 1920s, E. K. Strong—a pioneer in our understanding of the one-call sale—introduced such ideas as features and benefits, open and closed questions, objection handling, and closing techniques. For more than 60 years, these concepts have played a central role in the way people have thought about selling skills. However, as we now know, simplistic concepts like these are little help when it comes to complex multicall sales. In order to understand, manage, and coach selling skills in large complex sales, you need to have an effectiveness model. Let's define what we mean by *effectiveness model* and explain why we think it's so important to have one. A model is a simple way to define the elements of a complex real-world problem and to describe how those elements relate to each other. So, for example, economists use econometric models in an attempt to understand the messy and confusing interrelationships that cause them to fail to predict the timing or severity of recessions. Meteorologists use climate models to predict the weather. Doctors and dentists use models, engineers use models, even (heaven help us) lawyers use models. Whenever any profession faces a set of interrelationships that are complex and difficult to predict, it creates models as a simplified way to understand the components and how they fit together. A model becomes an essential tool whenever reality is too complex, or too messy, to easily understand. In the nineteenth century, when engineering, economics, medicine, or other sophisticated professions of today were much simpler, it was possible to survive without the simplifying framework that models provide. As each of these professions became more sophisticated, models came to play an ever more important role.

In selling, we're now at the same point that many other professions reached a hundred years ago. At the simpler end of selling—the one-call sale—it's still possible to survive as a manager without formal models because the sale is not very complex. It's possible, in theory at least, to understand the one-call sale using your own experience without additional help.

However, in larger sales, as the complexity of the sale increases, it becomes much harder to understand what it takes to be effective. Figure 1.1 illustrates how the need for a model grows greater with the increasing complexity of the sale. Since the time of Socrates, people have known that, in order to persuade others, it's more effective to ask questions than to give opinions. In any sale, it's good advice to ask the customer questions. This hardly deserves to be called a model, but that's what it is. It's the oldest,

FIGURE 1.1

Example of an effectiveness model for probing skills

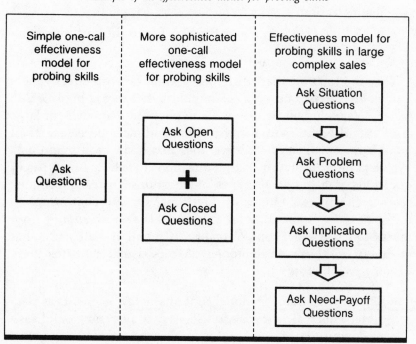

and the simplest, sales-effectiveness model in existence. In 1925, E. K. Strong gave this model a new twist. He suggested that it's not enough just to ask questions—you have to ask both open and closed questions. Now the model begins to get a little more sophisticated, raising issues such as when is it appropriate to ask each type of question. However, in major account selling, it's clear that just asking open or closed questions isn't an adequate effectiveness model. A major sales probing model derived from research suggests there are four types of questions that successful people ask:

- *Situation Questions:* about facts and details of the customer's present circumstances. These provide a background that leads to

- *Problem Questions:* about problems, difficulties, and dissatisfactions the customer is experiencing which you can solve with your products or services. These lead to

- *Implication Questions:* about the consequences or effects of the problems that could make them urgent or severe enough to justify action.

- *Need-Payoff Questions:* about the benefits to the customer from solving the problems.

This model, together with other examples of effectiveness models for larger sales, is explained in detail in our book *SPIN®️ Selling.* We include it here as an example of how models for large sales are different, more sophisticated, and more necessary, than models for small sales. "Where does this end?" you might ask. We've gone from simply asking questions to asking two types of questions to asking four types of questions. In really complex sales, aren't there 20 kinds of questions? Or 50? That brings us to the next point about models. A model is a *simplification,* it's not meant to be an exact copy of reality. After all, if reality was that great we wouldn't need models. A model exists to delicately balance two factors:

- *Simplicity:* so that the model contains as few elements as possible. This makes it easy to use, easy to remember, and easy to communicate.

- *Validity:* so that the model is as near to the truth as its simplified elements allow.

There's a desperate need in complex sales for more and better models that combine simplicity with validity. In chapter 4 we'll be showing you techniques for creating effectiveness models of your own.

The Importance of Coaching

The fact is, every major sales manager uses models, whether they come from a manager's own experience and observation, from books, or from training programs. Each of us has a set of ideas about what works and what our people should do to be more effective. Whether or not we call them effectiveness models, these ideas play an important role in managing salespeople and in improving their performances. If you have a good model—which we've defined as a set of ideas about effectiveness that combines simplicity and validity—then you have an essential first step for improving your people's sales effectiveness. The next step is to translate those ideas about effective performance into action. That's where coaching comes in. We suggested earlier that there are two distinct types of coaching, skills coaching and strategy coaching, each of which plays a key role in building sales effectiveness. In small sales, skills coaching is the more important, because there's generally little need for strategy and, in consequence, little need for strategy coaching. In major sales, both skills coaching and strategy coaching are equally important. We'll be devoting a chapter to each type; there coaching issues will be covered in depth. For now, we'd like to make a few general points about effective coaching.

In Coaching, Less Is More

Coaching often fails because the coach is overambitious. Whether we're talking about skills or strategy, coaching is a time-consuming process and it's easy to take on more than you can handle successfully. We've found that the most effective coaches tend to work on fewer things in greater depth. In skills coaching it's important to recognize that people learn skills slowly and in small increments. The good skills coach will

- Choose to coach a few people in depth, rather than superficially coach the whole team.
- Work with each person on one skill at a time, rather than working on several skills at once.

Good strategy coaching requires a slightly different approach from skills coaching. For example, to ensure the depth of coaching that's needed to have an impact on performance, effective strategy coaches will limit the number of *accounts* they coach, rather than the number of people. In this way, the coach can get to know each account in the detail that's required to participate in forming and reviewing a workable account strategy.

Strategic Coaching Is Iterative

Another special characteristic of strategy coaching is that its real value comes from the coach having a *repeated* involvement in the account strategy. Too often, managers put disproportionate coaching effort into initial strategy meetings. They work with their people in great detail, setting account objectives and deciding on elaborate strategic plans for how these objectives will be achieved. Then, once these plans have been created, they have less involvement as the sale progresses. Good strategy coaches, in contrast, don't spend all their time making long detailed initial plans. Instead, they spread their coaching effort across a number of sessions as events unfold and the seller's knowledge of the account increases. The reason is straightforward. In the initial stages of account planning there are usually too many unknowns to let you form a realistic detailed strategy. It's better to start with a quick and dirty initial strategy and then refine it by repeated iterations as more information about the account, the players, and the competition becomes available.

Coaching Is a Neglected Motivational Tool

In small sales, salespeople can quickly see the results of their actions. Let's assume, for example, that a seller decides to change some element of selling style. By the end of the week, if the change is a good one, it may already have led to increased sales and to increased income for the seller. In larger sales, however, any changes—even changes that are clearly desirable and effective—may need many months before they lead to a visible impact on sales results. The immediacy of results helps motivate people to change in small sales. It's relatively easy to motivate salespeople to try something new if, within days, they can see tangible effects. It's an entirely different matter asking someone to try something for several months before the change is visibly rewarded by results. This is an area, as we'll see in chapter 7, where coaching has an important motivational role to play in major sales.

Motivation in the Major Sale

Motivation is a complex area. In general, most motivational tools such as incentive payments, prizes, or motivational speakers, do a much better job of helping people work harder than helping them work smarter. We might, for example, persuade you to put in an additional hour a day, or to make five more sales calls per month, by offering you double your present salary. By using money in this way as a motivational tool, we can probably motivate you to work harder. But whether we double your salary or quadruple it, we're unlikely to cause you to work smarter. Many people could, if they chose, work harder—but most people are already working as smart as they know how. Unfortunately, except in rare cases, working harder isn't the answer to productivity problems in major sales. Because of this, many motivational techniques fail to work in larger complex sales. Yet, as we'll see in chapter 7, there *are* motivational tools that you can use to help your people to work smarter.

The Future of Management in Major Sales

In the last 10 years, selling has become more sophisticated and so has sales management. In major sales we've entered a new era where, perhaps for the first time, the sales job can now truly be said to be comparable in complexity and skill to more established professions. But, if you think that the last 10 years have seen advances then, as the saying goes, "You ain't seen nothing yet." The changes that will take place during the next 10 years will be even more dramatic. We're already seeing entirely new concepts of buyer/seller relationships emerging in several markets. Take, for example, the idea of partnering, where two organizations work in such close long-term collaboration that the boundaries between selling and buying organizations have become blurred. Customers work on product design teams, service people have permanent offices on the customers' premises. Joint teams handle issues such as intercompany accounting, administration, and installation. What's the role of the sales function in these partnering arrangements? At the moment, because this is still a new idea, the creation and management of these strategic partnerships has generally been in the hands of top executives from the buying and selling organizations. Too often, the sales function has not played an active role. Yet, where better to manage the interface between two partnering organizations than from the sales function? We see a difficult but exciting role emerging here for the sales management of the future. For some organizations more than half their future revenues will come from partnering arrangements. As the trend to partnering continues, so will the need for sales managers who specifically understand the skills of how to enter into partnering arrangements and how to cultivate them successfully. Managing strategic partnerships will, almost certainly, require different skills from those we conventionally think of today as "sales management" skills.

Another change, already visible at the upper end of major account selling, is the use of sales teams. It's increasingly common in accounting and consulting firms, commercial and merchant banks, or sophisticated capital goods companies for the sales task to become too complex for one individual to handle. As a result, there's a need for a strategic sales team that works together closely on the development of a sales strategy and its execution. The skills required to manage these teams are necessarily complex and sophisticated. Simple teamwork skills will be a hopelessly inadequate answer. What's required is altogether more strategic and involves the development of such things as better planning and analysis tools, a common strategic language, and mechanisms for helping the team understand and evaluate its strategic options at different points of the selling cycle.

We believe that the models, concepts, and ideas that are contained in this book are relevant, not only to sales management today, but also to the exciting and challenging sales management world of tomorrow. In the chapters that follow, we'll share with you our experiences from working for many years with some of the world's top sales organizations. We hope that the insights we've gained from our association with these leading-edge companies, will help you face the demands of managing major sales today and some of the challenges in managing major sales in the future.

2

SELLING HARDER OR SELLING SMARTER?

Improving Productivity through Sales Efficiency and Sales Effectiveness

The phone was ringing at seven-thirty in the morning. At the other end was a very disturbed client. "I've got to see you, Neil," he said. "As you may know, I moved jobs recently and I'm now managing a sales force of 150 people selling industrial equipment. When I took over, sales were in a slump, so I've started doing some analysis of what's wrong. The first results came in yesterday and I've been up most of the night worrying. I need to talk about them. When can we meet?" It's hard to challenge the urgency of anything that merits a seven-thirty phone call, so a meeting was hastily arranged for later that day. We assembled four members of our team so that we had a range of experience to cover all the bases. Waiting for the troubled client to arrive, the four of us sat around playing the usual consultants' guessing games. "What's he so worried about?" we asked ourselves. "What did he find from his analysis that's keeping him (and us) awake?" Normally these speculations are over and done with in a matter of minutes but, as it happens, the client's plane was delayed for an hour, so our guessing game went on a little longer than usual. To pass the time, while we waited, one of our colleagues suggested that we should play our game with higher stakes. We should each write our answers to two questions about the client's problem and its solution. The person whose answers turned out to be closest to the truth would win a dinner for two paid for by the rest of us. Our questions were:

- Out of the various salesforce problems he's probably analyzed, which single one is troubling him the most?
- Out of the various answers he's come up with, which one will be hardest to talk him out of?

As it turned out, the winner made these predictions and they were so remarkably accurate that the rest of us cheerfully paid for a very expensive meal:

- The most disturbing single fact for this client is that sales force activity levels (call rates) are lower than he or his management had predicted.
- We will try to talk him out of various attempts to increase call activity levels and we shall almost certainly fail.

A Classic Case Study

In retrospect, this was an easy bet to win. The client's story was typical of what happens to many sales managers faced with an urgent need for increasing the productivity of their sales forces. It was so typical, in fact, that we can take his story—with or without the seven-thirty panic phone call—as a case study of how sales force productivity problems arise, are analyzed, and dealt with in most organizations. Poor sales results had prompted the company to look for a new head of sales, which was how our client got his job. Faced with the urgent issue of how to improve sales performance, he had begun by collecting some facts and figures. Among these were analyses of activity levels of the sales force. Management had fondly assumed that salespeople were making three or four calls on customers a day. The figures showed that the true activity level was less than two calls a day. This was startling news and our client, like many sales managers before him, panicked. However, the problem had an obvious solution. Management must find a way to increase sales activity—to push up the call rate. After all, if the sales force were to make twice as many calls, then sales productivity should increase in proportion. In vain we tried to persuade our client that this was another example of a strategy that might work in small sales but was doomed to failure in large ones. Nothing we said could dissuade him from setting up activity management systems and controls aimed at increasing the activity level of his people. He set call rate targets, instituted call reporting systems, and began monitoring and evaluating both managers and salespeople in terms of their call activity levels. All this effort certainly succeeded in pushing up call rates. Within a few weeks his people were averaging almost three calls a day. However, sales results didn't show the expected improvement. It wasn't until six months later, with sales still sagging, that he came back to us ready to think about an alternative approach.

Put yourself in his shoes. You've been brought in to increase sales. You find your salespeople are making, at most, two customer calls a day. You'd expected twice that. What would you do? Our client, like most sales managers, had never questioned the basic common-sense productivity formula:

$$more\ calls\ =\ more\ sales$$

As his salespeople were now making an average of only nine calls a week, he assumed that if he could just increase their activity level to 18 or 20 calls a week, sales would double. "Well, perhaps not quite double," he told us when we probed more deeply, "but certainly increase significantly." What was wrong with his assumption? Superficially it sounds logical; but to understand the serious flaw in his logic, we must look more closely at the relationship between call rates and sales.

Call Rates and Success in Small Sales

Let's begin with a case study which seems to support the *more calls = more sales* notion. A company, based in Florida, manufactured cleaning equipment, such as mops, brushes, and scourers. Rather than operate through distributors, the company had a sales force that sold directly to restaurants, offices, and small businesses in major cities. In the New York area, the company had 12 salespeople who were managed by a relative of the company's owner. This relative was the proverbial sleeping partner, who paid little attention to managing the business. Unfortunately, most of his sleeping took place in Florida and not in the New York area where his salespeople were based. Eventually, he overslept the patience of the company's board and left the organization. His replacement, a promising and energetic young woman who had been one of the New York salespeople, was appointed in his place. Before she became manager, the New York salespeople were making an average of six new business calls a day in addition to their maintenance calls on existing customers. On average, two and one-half of these six calls resulted in a sale. Feeling that this call rate was too low, the new sales manager set about increasing the new business activity level. She set targets of fifteen new calls a day. Three months later she was able to show some very impressive figures. As figure 2.1 shows, she had doubled call rates, and as a result, new business sales volume from the New York area had

FIGURE 2.1
Increase in activity levels leads to increase in sales

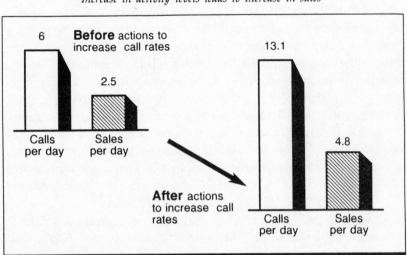

almost doubled. This increase in sales is dramatic, whether we measure it in terms of sales per day or overall dollar value of these sales.

A Dangerous Conclusion

What conclusion can we draw from a case like this? The first thing we should ask is whether this is just an isolated example—a rare but lucky chance. Or do cases like this happen regularly when determined sales managers work hard to increase call rates? The evidence here is fairly clear. There are many well-documented cases that show sales increases resulting directly from increases in call rates. We've seen examples from sales forces selling cosmetics door to door, from nonprofit organizations "selling" the merits of the charities they represent, and from a variety of sales operations like the New York cleaning supplies company. In each of these cases there's evidence that a manager has greatly increased sales by increasing call rates. With cases like this to back up the notion that more calls equals more sales, it's no wonder that so many sales managers have come to believe that the first step to increasing sales productivity is to increase call rates.

If there's evidence linking call rates to sales volume, why were we advising our client *not* to work on an activity management system to increase his call rates? To understand why we were so critical of his focus on more calls, we should look closely at those cases where an increase in call rates has led to an increase in sales. There's an important common factor in these cases. In each one, the sale is very small. Whether we're talking about our cleaning supplies company, cosmetics sales, or charities, the average sale is less than $100. What's more, the sales force is often literally knocking on doors. The rule for success in these small sales seems to be that the more doors you knock on, the more sales you will make. This rule has been well understood by generations of knock-on-doors salespeople. One of us had an uncle who, in the 1950s, managed a sales operation selling vacuum cleaners door to door. When asked by his children what heaven was like, he would tell them, "Heaven is an infinitely long street with doors to knock on both sides." He certainly understood that in his business there was a direct relationship between knocking on doors and making sales. The link between calls and sales isn't found only in sales forces that literally go knocking on doors. In many small sales, where business can be transacted in just one call, there's a measurable link between the number of calls and the number of sales. Increase your call rate in most small sales and business increases as a result.

However, this relationship breaks down as the size of the sale increases. In major sales, the image of the infinitely long street rarely applies. In fact, in major sales we have to search very hard to find examples where attempts to increase call rates have resulted in an increase in sales volume.

Call Rates and Success in the Larger Sale

Why should increases in call activity bring rich rewards in smaller sales but have little or no positive impact in larger ones? Basically, there are two reasons:

- Increasing sales activity is a strategy that works well where success can be achieved by selling *harder*. That's often the case in small sales. However, in those sales where success depends on selling *smarter*, increasing call activity generally has only minimal impact.

- When managers try to increase call activity, their efforts usually create some highly undesirable and unintended side effects. In the small sale, these side effects don't do much damage. However, in large sales, they often cause such damage that sales results actually get worse because of them.

Selling Harder or Selling Smarter?

The first, and most important, question to ask yourself before trying to increase people's activity levels is, "Do my people need to sell harder or to sell smarter?" Most forms of activity management are designed to make people sell harder—to make them increase their call rates. Selling harder is most likely to produce results under these conditions:

- The size of the sale is small.
- Sales are generally completed in a single call or transaction.
- Success depends as much on energy and enthusiasm as it does on skill and strategy.
- The available and unpenetrated market is very large in comparison to the size of the sales force (in other words, there are lots of doors left to knock on).
- There is distinct evidence that salespeople are not putting enough effort into their selling.

It's clear that in most major account sales, the first three of these conditions don't normally exist. Major account sales are large, multicall, and almost invariably more dependent on skill and strategy than on energy and enthusiasm. But the other two conditions *do* exist in some major sales. It's not uncommon to have a sales force that's too small to penetrate a very large potential market, and many major account sales managers fervently believe that their people are putting insufficient effort into their sales. These were exactly the issues behind our client's 7:30 A.M. panic phone call. "I know all national sales managers *think* their people are lazy underperformers," he told us, "but mine *really* are. Some people have been sitting in the sales office so long that there's a layer of dust on them." His other problem, equally severe, was that his company had produced a new and exceptionally innovative product. "It's only a matter of months," he explained, "before the competition will have an equivalent product. I've got to get these people off their backsides and into customers' offices or we'll lose our precious lead time." He presented a very logical and persuasive case for activity management. His activity level was low and lots of doors were waiting for his people to knock. No wonder we couldn't talk him out of it.

Side Effects of Activity Management

Why should we want to talk him out of his plan for activity management if there was evidence it was needed? It wasn't that we completely mistrusted his diagnosis—although we suspected that his people worked harder than he imagined. Our fundamental objection lay in the second reason why activity management fails in major sales. We suspected that his system would result in damaging side effects. In particular, we were afraid that his attempts to increase his people's call levels would lead to four problems, namely:

- A focus on small sales
- A proliferation of paperwork and administration
- Attention to the wrong end of the sales pipeline
- Demotivation of top salespeople

These unintended side effects of activity management are so common, and so deadly, that it's worth examining each in detail.

Focus on Small Sales

When managers attempt to increase activity levels, particularly if their attempts are backed up by formal systems such as targets, call reports, and call tracking, their people tend to focus on quantity rather than quality. As a result, the easy small sale becomes a much more attractive target for salespeople than the complex strategic one. This isn't just a theoretical observation. There are case studies which eloquently illustrate the existence of this small sale focus and how much damage it can do to an organization's sales. Consider the case of a major manufacturing company based in Chicago, illustrated in figure 2.2. As you can see, an activity management system was introduced in July as an attempt to boost sales. It was a relatively conventional system. Call reports were beefed up, a tracking form was introduced which had to be filled out weekly, call targets were set. In other words, the company did exactly what most other organizations have done when introducing activity management systems. But look closely at the results. In the five months after the system was introduced, the number of orders increased by 16 percent, clear evidence that the new activity management system was succeeding in its attempts to increase call activity. Now see what's happened to the average value of each order. There's been an 18 percent decline. In bottom-line terms, the company's sales revenue *fell* by 1.5 percent as a result of the new system.

We're not saying that activity management always brings a fall

FIGURE 2.2
More sales means less revenue

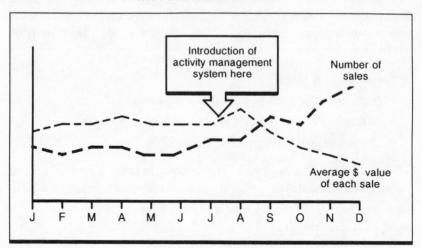

in sales. However, cases like this one should make us very cautious about what may happen if an activity management system predisposes salespeople to go after the quick hits rather than to focus on the larger strategic sale. There are very few studies of the effects of activity management on sales. Most organizations like to keep their sales data confidential, and they discourage research. For example, we've only been allowed to use the case of the Chicago company in figure 2.2 on condition that we don't use the company's name and that we disguise certain aspects of the case. However, you can see the same phenomenon all around you on a smaller scale. Almost every experienced sales manager we've worked with can quote cases like this one, from a corporation that makes packaging machinery.

> When I was younger we had a new boss. He was a real hard driver. "One more call" was his motto. It didn't matter how hard you'd been working—there was always time to fit in one more call. Soon he had us all buzzing around like flies. We worked our tails off, but the funny thing was that it didn't make any difference to our sales results. In fact, as I remember it, they might even have gone down a bit.

Yes, most of us have seen cases like this, where great activity and effort have little or no impact on sales results. Worse still, management pressure for increased activity doesn't just mean that salespeople knock on more doors. It can also mean that they knock on the same door more times. In other words, under pressure to complete more calls, it's easy for salespeople to make real nuisances of themselves by overcalling on existing customers with no clear sales or customer-care objective beyond the necessity to demonstrate to management that they are active. As customers, we were once the victim of overcalling driven by an activity management system. One of our operating companies was served by a bank that had just introduced a new sales activity management system to boost the number of customer visits made by its calling officers. The first visit we received from our friendly neighborhood calling officer, after the system was introduced, was a pleasant enough opportunity to have a two-hour chat. Three weeks later we had another visit. There was no clear purpose for this second visit, and after investing another couple of hours, we were left wondering why we were the chosen recipients of all this free-floating attention. The following month the calling officer phoned us to arrange a third visit. This time we were more reluctant to participate and asked that the meeting should be kept brief. When the meeting began it was clear that the discussion would be no more productive than the others. Acting on a plausible guess, we asked the calling officer, "Have you, by any chance, been set some call targets recently?" That's when he confessed and told us about the new activity management system. In our case, the person who knocked on our door three times in seven weeks didn't have anything to sell. It would have been equally irritating, from a customer's standpoint, if a salesperson with a clear product objective called on us too frequently when we either didn't have a need or were not ready to discuss next steps.

Activity management can generate an impressive amount of additional sales energy. From a distance, that energy looks to be a step towards greater sales productivity. The senior management of our bank, for example, may have been delighted to see how many more visits their calling officers were making now that a new system was in place. But that energy is often misdirected. We've seen how easily it can lead to a focus on small quick-hit sales or to an irritating level of overcalling on existing accounts. Unfortunately, in the "all heat and no light" atmosphere of intense activity, few salespeople give enough attention to those long-term strategic sales that are the key to profitable major account selling.

Proliferation of Paperwork

Most activity management systems depend on some form of call reporting and tracking which, in turn, depends on paperwork. Paperwork is an unmitigated evil in many sales organizations. It's not just that salespeople, especially top performers, seem to have an instinctive hatred of paperwork. It's more fundamental than that. You can almost measure the health of a sales organization by the energy it puts into dealing with its customers compared with the energy spent on its internal demands, of which paperwork is a significant component. Over and over again, our advice to clients has been, "Cut your paperwork in half." Most call reporting systems are dubiously accurate—which is a charitable way of saying that many call reports are rationalizations or even downright lies. Much time is spent in justifications, cover-ups, and explanations of failure. If half the effort that goes into call reporting was put instead into call planning, there would be fewer failures to report about. For this reason there was great rejoicing in the land when IBM recently abolished its mighty call reporting system and focused instead on planning.

Almost every activity management system we've seen has resulted in an increased paperwork demand. In one extreme case we know of, following the introduction of an activity management system, salespeople were spending an additional hour each day on paperwork associated with call reporting. That was more than 10 percent of their selling time, and in terms of sales productivity, it was a disgrace. In less extreme forms, most activity management has a paperwork component that distracts salespeople from their central task of being with their customers. Our advice is this: if you want to increase sales productivity in major sales, focus on planning, strategy, and the customer. Do your best to minimize reporting, paperwork, justifications, and all the assorted nonsense that can cause sales management systems to sink under their own weight.

A word of caution is appropriate here. We've talked with sales managers who assure us that they don't have a paperwork problem any more because they have moved to computerized reporting. "Now that all our reports are entered directly into the system," explained a sales manager from a shipping company, "everything is electronic and we've cut our reporting paperwork down to nothing." Her salespeople were less enthusiastic. "Same old junk under a new name," one of her people told us; "it takes just as much time to type lies onto a screen as it did to write them down."

Wrong End of the Pipeline

There's a curious phenomenon that often goes with activity management or any other managerial attempts to make salespeople work harder. We're not quite sure why it happens, but it happens so often that it demands some attention. Most organizations institute activity management systems because they are disturbed about sales performance. Their focus, crudely, is on closing more sales. As a result, they give most attention to calls nearest to the decision. Managers scan reports to find which sales are nearest to closing, they help their people plan these closing calls, and if the sale is important, they go out with their people to make the vital final call. Because closing calls get so much managerial attention, there's a corresponding neglect of those calls at an earlier point in the selling cycle. What's wrong with that? If a manager's efforts succeed in closing more sales, then surely attention to closing calls is the best contribution a manager can make to sales productivity. That may be true in simple sales where the number and size of sales closed are the only measures of sales productivity; but in larger sales, there's another important factor that managers often neglect—the number of calls required to make the sale. Let's take an example of a case where the number of calls in the selling cycle had a bigger impact on sales productivity than the number of sales. A large multinational computer company approached us several years ago with a problem. "Our new generation of minicomputers," they told us, "can do everything a mainframe could do five years ago but at less than one-tenth of the cost." We didn't see why that should be such a problem. "It's not the price of the machine that's the problem," they explained, "it's the way we're selling it. We're using salespeople who started their career selling mainframes. Now they're using the same methods to sell a machine that, although it has the same capabilities, costs only a small fraction of mainframe price. On average it's taking them about seven calls on a customer to sell a mini. That was fine with a mainframe where we had a fat margin. On a mini, seven calls is eating up our profits." In other words, the productivity issue wasn't the number of sales closed but the resources required to close each sale. We agreed to help and started an investigation of factors that determined the length of their selling cycle. One of these factors is shown in figure 2.3.

We correlated the number of calls needed to make the sale with the point in the sale where the manager participated. Those sales where managers were present in late-cycle calls (what we've been calling "closing calls") had a longer—and therefore less productive—selling cycle than those sales where managers had been present in the early part of the sale. What do results like this mean? Here's how we interpreted them. Manager presence in the call, whether early or late, is a sign of where managers are putting their efforts. Those managers who gave their attention to closing calls late in the cycle had longer

FIGURE 2.3

Effect of managers' presence in the call

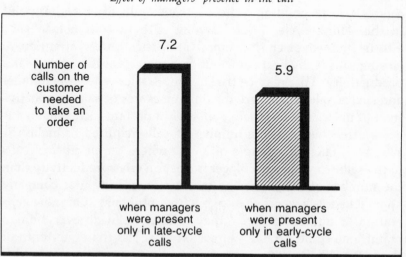

selling cycles than those who put their attention on early calls. Why? The answer is straightforward. However brilliantly a manager operates late in the cycle, after seven calls have been made on this customer the best the manager can do is to get the business on the eighth call. You can't rewrite history. Attention to the eighth call will never close the sale in less than eight calls. In contrast, managers who put their attention on the early part of the selling cycle were able to get the sale off to a better start and, because of that, their people had significantly shorter selling cycles. As a manager, the earlier you put your efforts into the selling cycle, the greater impact you will have on one of the key components of major account sales productivity—the length of your selling cycle.

It's evidence like this that makes us worried about the tendency of many activity management systems to focus efforts on calls late in the selling cycle. Of course, it's unfair for us to lay all the blame on activity management. It's possible to design a system that directs equal or greater focus on calls early in the selling cycle. Unfortunately, that doesn't happen often. When managers take steps to get their people working harder, disproportionate attention usually goes to late-cycle calls.

Demotivation of Top Salespeople

A final unintended side effect of activity management systems is that they can create serious conflict with top salespeople. Top performers usually chafe against restrictions of any kind. They hate to be told, "Your target is to make four calls a day," or "You must fill in these call reports." As far as most top performers are concerned, reporting systems are onerous, restrictive, unproductive and, even worse, a sign that their management doesn't trust them or respect their professionalism. Top performers are scarce, and as demand for skilled major account salespeople continues to grow, they are likely to become scarcer. You can't afford to demotivate them. Being top performers, they can vote with their feet by moving to a competitor who allows them the freedom they need.

The antipathy top performers have for restrictions is nicely illustrated by a study we did for Xerox Corporation to find out why salespeople left the company. We analyzed reports of exit interviews, classifying reasons for leaving under five headings:

- *Compensation*   dissatisfaction with pay
- *Job satisfaction*   unhappiness with present job
- *Relationships*   problems with management or peers
- *Prospects*   opportunities for advancement or growth
- *Restrictions*   unproductive or restrictive management systems and controls

Using these headings, we compared the reasons why top performers and poor performers left. As figure 2.4 shows, the number one reason why top performers left the company was their dissatisfaction with *restrictions*. The most common restriction mentioned by top performers was the activity management and call reporting system. In contrast, poor performers tended to choose reasons such as compensation, prospects, or relationships. They seemed quite happy to live with the restrictions of the activity management system. It was evidence like this that made us advise our client to be very cautious about introducing any system to increase call rates that could appear restrictive to his top performers.

FIGURE 2.4
Why did you leave the company?

Rank	Top performers		Rank	Poor performers
1	**Restrictions**		1	Compensation
2	Job satisfaction		2	Prospects
3	Prospects		3	Job satisfaction
4	Compensation		4 =	Relationships
5	Relationships		4 =	**Restrictions**

A Word of Caution

We've been very critical of activity management as a tool for increasing sales productivity in major sales. We've shown how it can de-motivate good salespeople and how it leads to a focus on small sales at the expense of larger ones. We've also seen how easily activity management surrounds itself with time-consuming reporting and paperwork. For reasons like these, many attempts to increase productivity through tighter activity management have ended in failure. However, we're *not* saying that activity management is intrinsically bad. If it comes to a choice between activity management and no management at all, then our vote is for activity management. Our plea here is for activity management in moderation. We become concerned when the management of sales activity is taken to such an excess that it defeats its own purpose. So, while we challenge the central assumption of activity management that *more calls = more sales,* we aren't in any way suggesting that the opposite is true. Clearly that's not so. If *fewer* calls led to more sales, then—taken to its logical conclusion—salespeople who made no calls would have the best sales records. The reality, in major sales, is that the relationship between calls and sales results is much more complex than in simpler sales. Attempting to improve sales results solely by increasing call rates is a naïve strategy that rarely succeeds.

Working Harder or Working Smarter?

As we've seen, a fundamental question for improving sales performance is whether your people need to work harder or to work smarter. Generally, in major sales, working smarter is the answer—and that's why it's a central theme throughout this book. But, as in the case of our client, sometimes there's reason to focus on working harder. Our client felt he had evidence that his people were not working hard enough. You may have the same feeling about your salespeople. However, before you introduce methods and controls to make people work harder, pause for a while to review your evidence. Don't plunge unthinkingly into activity management just because you find your people are making fewer calls than you expected. As our old friend Doug McNair says of his work in the telecommunications industry, "Prospects are a precious commodity. Activity without purpose uses up your prospect base very quickly." Over the years we've worked with dozens of sales forces who have analyzed their salespeople's activity levels or call rates. In almost every case the analysis has created alarm and despondency among management because they had expected a higher level of call activity than they actually found. In fact, we can't think of a single case where management has discovered their people have been making *more* calls than they had imagined. All too often, when sales management is confronted with lower activity levels than anticipated, they have responded by introducing measures that result in one or more of the undesirable side effects we've discussed. They haven't stopped to question the sacred formula *more calls = more sales.*

Testing the Formula *More Calls = More Sales*

How do you know whether or not the *more calls = more sales* formula applies to your salespeople? As we've seen, in some sales forces there *is* a relationship between call activity and sales results. In other sales forces that link doesn't exist. Is there some way to predict in advance whether your sales force could potentially benefit from activity management? On the face of it, that sounds an unanswerable question. We know of many sales forces who have decided that the only way to tell whether increased activity will mean increased sales is to introduce tighter activity management and to see what happens.

Fortunately, there *is* a way in which you can make a quick and easy test of the *more calls = more sales* formula. The simplest method is this:

- Take your top performers—not more than about 15 percent of your sales force—and analyze the number of calls they have made during the last month.
- Then take the average call rate of the rest of the sales force for the same time period.

- Look at the differences. If your top performers are making *more* calls than the rest of the sales force, then there's a possibility that better activity management will improve results—that more calls will bring more sales. However if you find, as often happens in major sales, that your top performers are making *fewer* calls than average, then it's unlikely that activity management will produce a dramatic improvement in sales results.

This is a quick rule-of-thumb method. If you want to carry out a more precise analysis, you can use the method for comparing call rates and business volume described in the appendix and shown here in figure 2.5. As you can see in this example, taken from a capital goods sales force of thirty people, the top five performers all had new business call rates between seven and fourteen calls a month, compared with the sales force average of twenty-two calls a month. Management had been contemplating tightening their activity management on the assumption that more calls would mean more sales. The evidence here didn't suggest a strong rela-

FIGURE 2.5

Relationship between calls and sales volume in a high-value capital goods sales force

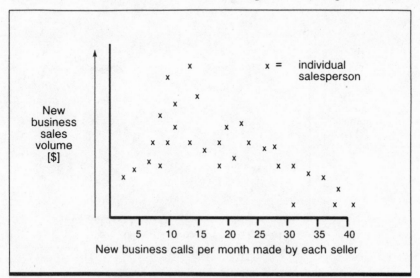

tionship between call rates and success. We were able to persuade the company to put their effort into helping their people sell smarter rather than sell harder.

When More Calls Bring More Sales

In contrast, let's look at some equivalent data from a classic small sale shown in figure 2.6. In this case, the sales force was the eastern region of an office equipment and supplies company. In contrast to the earlier capital goods example, you can see that:

- On the whole, high performers were making *more* calls than the sales force average.
- The top five performers out of a sales force of twenty-eight were averaging seventy calls per month compared with an average of fifty-five calls per month for the rest of the sales force.

FIGURE 2.6

Relationship between calls and sales volume in the eastern region of a low-value office supplies sales force

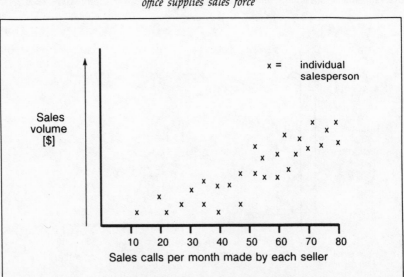

In circumstances like these there's a much stronger case to be made for the value of actions to increase overall sales force activity levels. Here, the *more calls = more sales* equation has the ring of truth.

Analyze the performance of your own people. If you find that your top performers are indeed the ones making the most calls, then you've built a good case for putting energy into activity management. However, even if your analysis shows that you could gain sales by increasing call rates, be careful that you try to minimize the side effects we discussed, such as the focus on small sales or the proliferation of paperwork.

Sales Efficiency and Sales Effectiveness

The cases we've just discussed illustrate a great truth about sales productivity. The methods that bring you productivity and improve your performance in small sales are generally very different from the ones that work best in large sales. Activity management is a good example. As we've seen, in small sales you can often increase performance by increasing call rates. Working harder is a formula for success. In large sales, working smarter is likely to be the name of the game. Actions that aim to increase selling effort, such as activity management, have a poor record of success in major account sales. To get a better understanding of why this is, and what sales management must do to improve performance in major sales, we'd like to introduce two important terms, *sales efficiency* and *sales effectiveness*. As figure 2.7 shows, sales efficiency and sales effectiveness are the two components of sales productivity.

These terms have been around for many years in selling, so they may be familiar to you. However, because they have been used with a variety of meanings, we should start with definitions.

- *Sales efficiency* is about how to get in front of the right customers, for the right amount of time, at a minimum cost.
- *Sales effectiveness* is about how to maximize sales potential once you're there.

FIGURE 2.7
The two components of sales productivity

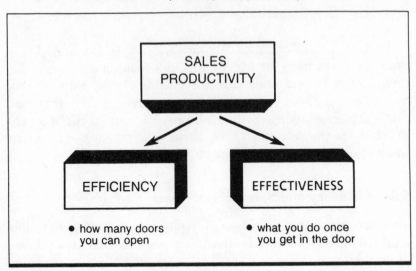

The efficiency/effectiveness distinction has great utility for helping us understand and improve sales productivity. It has been the basis of some elegant work done by McKinsey and Company, which makes this an appropriate point to acknowledge the impact that McKinsey, and in particular John De Vincentis, has had on helping us to clarify our own thinking in this area.

Efficiency, Effectiveness, and Size of Sale

It's generally true that sales forces selling lower-value products make many small sales to a large number of customers. Major account sales forces, in contrast, tend to have comparatively few customers but the average size of a sale is much larger. The number of potential customers in an organization's customer base usually has significant implications for whether a sales force should focus on efficiency or on effectiveness. To take an extreme example, a manufacturer of commercial aircraft, such as Boeing, has only a few hundred customers worldwide. Efficiency doesn't enter much into the equation—Boeing already knows, and is talking to, just about every potential customer in the world. Their

FIGURE 2.8
Sales effectiveness and account characteristics

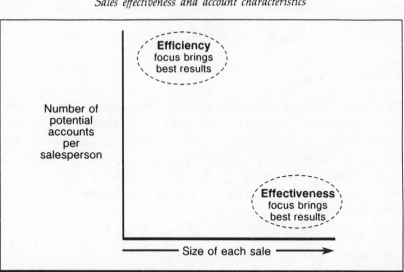

problem is not one of identifying the doors and knocking on them. Success for Boeing depends almost entirely on what they do once they are inside the door—on their *effectiveness.* In contrast, we remember talking to a manufacturer of fax machines in the days when facsimile was a brand new technology. "What's the market for these things?" we innocently asked. "The worldwide fax market could easily exceed a hundred million customers," our client told us; "the limiting factor of our sales force will be our ability to get to even a tiny fraction of the potential." If ever a market could justly be described as an infinitely long street with doors on both sides, this was it. Because of the large customer base, the limiting factor for success was *efficiency.* Tight activity management and improved call rates could well be the secret of success in a market like this. As figure 2.8 shows, a focus on efficiency brings best results in circumstances where each sales-person has many accounts and the size of each sale is small. We've already seen one of the reasons why this should be so. For a salesperson who has many potential accounts to cover, effi-ciency improvement helps open more doors. The other reason why efficiency may be more important than effectiveness in small sales is that small sales demand less skill and strategy from the seller. As a consequence, small sales are easier to make, so improvements in effectiveness, such as better selling skills, have less impact on small sales than they do on large.

It's Not So Simple

This book is about managing major sales so, naturally, our primary attention is on how to improve effectiveness. We're concerned with how to sell smarter rather than how to sell harder. But we must be careful not to oversimplify things. The idea that in small sales only efficiency matters and in large sales it's only effectiveness is just not true. Let's examine a couple of cases that illustrate this.

Case: Increasing Face-To-Face Time with Doctors

We worked with a sales force in the pharmaceutical industry whose business looked, in almost every way, to be the classic small sale. Their salespeople each called on hundreds of doctors in their territory, trying to interest them in their company's drugs. The average salesperson called on seven doctors a day; not a high call rate when you consider that the average face-to-face time with the doctor in each call was a mere three minutes. The drug company was therefore paying their sales force for an alarmingly inefficient use of sales time, getting just twenty minutes a day in front of customers. Even by the luxurious standards of the pharmaceutical industry, this case had all the hallmarks of a serious efficiency problem. There were lots of small sales: only seven customers a day were being visited. Surely, by introducing tighter activity management to push up call rates, the company could do better than its present, pitiful twenty face-to-face minutes a day.

On closer examination, the problem was less straightforward. Doctors are very busy people—and even idle doctors like to *pretend* they are busy. Consequently, salespeople had to wait for an average of almost thirty minutes after arriving on the premises before the doctor was ready to see them. There was nothing salespeople could do to shorten this period. As the seven calls required an unalterable three and a half hours a day of pure waiting, not to mention another three hours of travel time between calls, there was little or no latitude to increase productivity by increasing efficiency.

We decided to take an alternative approach. An analysis of the average three-minute call revealed that its length wasn't the only problem. Conditioned by the general atmosphere of hurry that doctors conveyed, most salespeople spent the three minutes blurting out a list of product features and advantages. Then, leaving a trail of samples behind them, they rushed off to their next call and next half-hour wait. We reasoned that, if we couldn't increase face-to-face time by better efficiency, then we might be able to achieve an improvement by using effectiveness methods. We taught salespeople a different selling approach based on questions rather than on features and advantages. In other words, we tried to increase the effectiveness of the call. Doctors were impressed by the change in selling style. They rated the new style of calls as more informative, more interesting, and better still, they gave more time—an average of eight minutes rather than three. In this way, with a constant efficiency level of seven calls a day, we were able to improve call effectiveness to give more than fifty face-to-face minutes a day rather than twenty.

Case: Efficiency Problem Prevents Effectiveness

In the pharmaceuticals case we can see how, even in small sales, apparent sales efficiency problems can contain significant effectiveness elements. The opposite can also be true. Occasionally, in large sales, you'll encounter an apparent effectiveness problem that has its cure in better efficiency. Take the case of a large multinational computer company. Average size of sale was well into the six figures. The selling cycle was complex. On the face of it, effectiveness was much more important than efficiency. At the time when we were called in, sales had started to sag and competition was eroding market share. Interviews with customers where sales had been lost suggested that the company's products were rated as technically superior and well supported. The most common reason given by customers for lost sales was that the company was outsold by competition. This sounded like an effectiveness problem if ever we saw one.

When we looked more closely, we found a different story.

Historically, the company's salespeople made 80 percent of their calls on data processing managers, who had been the decision makers for their products. However, decision power had been shifting inside many accounts. Functions other than data processing were having a larger say in the acquisition of data processing equipment. Competitors who had realized this early changed their sales strategy. Instead of calling mainly on data processing departments, they called on a wide range of potential influencers in each account. Our client's salespeople, however, were not calling on these important influencers. Why? Not, as it turned out, from lack of willingness or a failure to realize that these influencers were the key to sales success. No, it was purely an efficiency issue. Each salesperson had too many accounts. Management had allocated accounts in the days when the sales job was only to influence the data processing department. There just wasn't the extra time needed to sell to several other functions in each account. The solution didn't lie in typical effectiveness measures such as selling skills or account strategy training. Instead, the company was able to regain sales by reducing the number of accounts each salesperson had to cover. This allowed more time for each account and made it possible for salespeople to call on the new range of influencers. Questions of territory configuration and coverage are typically efficiency issues. In this case, an efficiency solution helped to turn round a situation that, superficially, looked to have all the symptoms of an effectiveness problem.

More Diagnostic Tools

Despite these cautionary cases, it's true that the majority of opportunities for increasing productivity in smaller sales will be through efficiency measures. In larger sales, effectiveness will usually be the key to success. Here, as researchers, we feel obliged to introduce one further complication. What if your sales force is somewhere in the middle? What if you're not really making major sales, yet you have relatively highly priced products and a multicall sales cycle, so you're not making small sales either? In the middle-sized sale, it's hard to tell whether your productivity improvement opportunities come more through effectiveness or through efficiency. We once faced such a case in a business unit of Xerox. This unit sold midrange copying machines to a customer base that varied from individual purchasers to divisions of large corporations. The 40-person sales force was geographically organized. The size of each salesperson's territory had been decided when the unit had been set up, about five years before we came on the scene.

Our entry, predictably, was the result of a severe and sustained underperformance by the unit. Equally predictable was the circumstance that before we arrived the unit had gone through an intensive effort to improve its activity management. This effort had resulted in several of the sins we described earlier. Paperwork had proliferated to a point where it was getting in the way of selling. Three of the five top performers had left. Small sales had increased a little, but the overall sales volume was down. The worse the situation became, the more the unit's management put frenetic energy into collecting call-reporting information. It was one of the nastiest examples of activity management gone wild that we had ever seen. The call data was collected on an infamous green form, known to the sales force as "the green weenie." Stories of sabotage were rife. As one salesperson told us, "We were convinced that management never read beyond the first few pages, so somewhere about page 7 of the green weenie we started making things up. We'd put in imaginary customers and fake calls. One week, on page 8, I reported a call on the President of IBM and none of the high-ups took any notice. Possibly that's because they were too busy reading the report by one of my colleagues who on the same day had been making a cold call on Ghengis Khan."

The only good news for us in all this was that a vast amount of data had been collected by the call-reporting system. Probably, if we watched out for fake calls and cleaned the data up a little, we had some raw material for an initial test of whether the problem was one of efficiency or effectiveness. We took two immediate actions. First, we persuaded management to suspend call reporting for a month so that people could put some of their attention into other tasks such as selling. As you can imagine, this caused great rejoicing among the sales force. Second, we scooped up a truck load of existing call reports and took them back to our offices for analysis. When we arrived home, we took a deep breath and thought about what to do next. "We *must* start by deciding whether we've got an effectiveness problem or an efficiency problem," we argued, "if we don't get that right, then we'll end up with another wrong solution." But how could we decide with no better ammunition than a ton of call statistics? After much gloom, more coffee, and even more cursing, we came up with two simple diagnostic measures that solved the problem. To our discredit as innovators, after all the coffee and curses, these measures weren't even original—we've since seen variations on them used by sales managers all over the world. Our first measure was a way to assess whether an efficiency problem existed. We called it the *suspect/prospect ratio.*

$$\text{Efficiency ratio:} \frac{\textit{Suspects} \text{ (unknocked doors)}}{\textit{Prospects} \text{ (doors where you've entered and found an opportunity)}}$$

The suspect/prospect ratio is a guide to the potential of a territory. The more suspects there are compared with the number of prospects, the more evidence that there's inadequate territory coverage. We defined a *suspect* as a potential customer, who had never been called on, where there *might* be a sales opportunity. Suspects were identified through telephone directories, business directories, and similar sources. By the very nature of the identification process, there was no way to know whether or not a suspect really offered a sales opportunity. We only knew there was a door waiting for a knock; we didn't know what was behind it. A *prospect,* on the other hand, was a known quantity. A seller from Xerox had visited the potential customer so the door had been opened at least to the extent that we could see some sales possibilities behind it. From looking at suspect/prospect ratios we learned:

- In the city center territories, where general business activity had declined in the five years since territories were drawn up, there were very few suspects compared with the number of prospects. Most doors, in other words, had already been knocked on by Xerox salespeople.

- In the suburbs, however, there were three suspects for every prospect. Business growth since the original laying down of territories meant that suburban territories were too large. Salespeople didn't have time to call on all the available opportunities. The suburbs definitely had an efficiency problem.

- By redrawing the territories so that city center territories were enlarged, while suburban territories were reduced, we were able to effect an improvement in efficiency.

In passing, we should note that our method for improving efficiency was territory configuration rather than activity management.

Diagnosing Effectiveness Problems

The suspect/prospect ratio proved a useful tool for looking at efficiency problems such as those created by uneven territory size. However, we also had reason to believe that efficiency would only be part of the productivity answer. In organizations with midrange sales, like this Xerox unit, there are usually effectiveness problems as well.

$$\text{Effectiveness ratio:} \frac{\textit{Calls} \text{ (total number of selling calls made by salesperson)}}{\textit{Orders} \text{ (number of orders resulting from those calls)}}$$

Our diagnostic tool for assessing whether effectiveness problems existed was a *call/order ratio*. From an analysis of call reports, we took the total number of calls made by each salesperson where the objective was to sell, rather than to resolve existing customer problems. We then compared this figure with the total number of orders resulting from these calls. As figure 2.9 shows, we found an alarmingly wide range of ratios. While some salespeople required less than ten calls to take each order, others were requiring over thirty calls.

We also had some data on how similar sales units were performing in terms of call/order ratios. Compared with other units,

FIGURE 2.9

Call/order ratios show an effectiveness problem

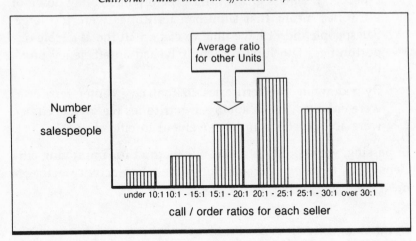

the one we were working with needed an average of 20 percent more sales calls to take each order. It looked as if there were some effectiveness problems to be solved. Our solution was to invest in two of the classic techniques for improving effectiveness—coaching and training. We trained managers to coach those salespeople who had a higher than average call/order ratio, using some of the sales effectiveness models we'll be describing later. Within six months, call/order ratios had fallen from an average of twenty-two calls required to take an order to thirteen calls. What's more, overall unit performance had improved significantly. Unfortunately, we had no way to measure how much of this improvement was due to call/order changes in effectiveness and how much was the result of efficiency improvements and other managerial actions. Establishing the cause of sales productivity changes is a notoriously difficult area, more fully discussed in our book, *SPIN® Selling.*

Limitations of Call/Order Ratios

The call/order ratio is a particularly useful diagnostic for effectiveness problems when the following conditions are present:

- The unit size of sale is small enough for each salesperson to be making a significant number of sales each year. There's no exact number here, but to give you a rough guideline, we probably wouldn't want to use call/order ratios where the average number of sales per salesperson per year is less than about fifteen.

- The value of each sale is within a relatively narrow price band. In our Xerox case, for example, most sales fell within a $15,000–$60,000 range. The average large order, in other words, was about four times the size of the average small order. In general, call/order ratios work well if this range between large and small doesn't exceed 6:1. Above that point, other factors enter into the equation and the call/order ratio has to be replaced by an alternative method reflecting sales volume rather than orders.

Most major account sales fail on one or both of these conditions, which is why the volume-based method shown in figure 2.5 is generally a better approach when you are dealing with high value sales.

Moving from Diagnosis to Action

Our theme is the major sale, so—when we turn from diagnosis to action—we'll look at things that individual managers can do to improve sales effectiveness. Future chapters will cover such tools as training, coaching, and account strategies that can help you develop your people's sales effectiveness. We shall not say much more here about efficiency tools. That's partly because efficiency tools usually have little impact on sales productivity in large sales, but there's also another reason. Efficiency is often an organizational rather than a managerial issue. In our Xerox case, for example, none of the sales managers had individual authority to take the required efficiency actions, such as territory reconfiguration or abolition of the existing activity management system. In contrast, each of them had considerable latitude in the effectiveness area. They could decide how to coach and train their

people, they could influence account strategies, they could counsel and motivate. While efficiency can be tackled by decisions
from the top, effectiveness lies in the hands of salespeople and
their managers. Effectiveness is created at the level where there's
most interaction with the customer.

Let's look more closely at this difference, to see why it can
sometimes have a profound impact on attempts to improve
sales productivity. As figure 2.10 illustrates, most of the actions
that influence sales efficiency can be decided on an organizational level and implemented top-down. What's more, we can
make the decision this afternoon, and by tomorrow morning,
we can put it into action. In our Xerox case, for example, the
decision to suspend the activity management system was made
at a meeting of ourselves, the unit manager and the national
sales manager. At the same meeting we decided on the territory
configuration. Within twenty-four hours, both those decisions

FIGURE 2.10
Who drives efficiency and effectiveness?

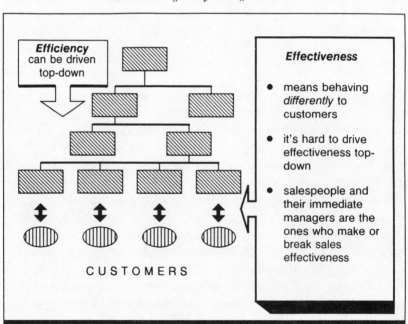

Efficiency can be driven top-down

Effectiveness

- means behaving *differently* to customers

- it's hard to drive effectiveness top-down

- salespeople and their immediate managers are the ones who make or break sales effectiveness

CUSTOMERS

were in full effect. Salespeople had new territories and the call reporting system was gone. In contrast, sales effectiveness decisions can't be made at the top and instantly implemented. To be more effective, salespeople must behave differently to customers. That normally requires new skills which take a long time to learn. In our Xerox case, for example, it took six months of very hard and concerted effort from us, from the sales managers, and—most of all—from their salespeople, before we had positive results to show.

Because efficiency measures can be implemented from the top more quickly and decisively than effectiveness measures, it's natural that efficiency strategies should have a greater appeal to most senior managers. Efficiency has another irresistible attraction. It's easier. Often, to increase efficiency, all you've got to do is to work harder—make more calls, knock on more doors, telephone for more appointments. You're doing more of something you already know how to do. Effectiveness, in contrast, is about doing something *different.* It's about doing better rather than doing more. We used to joke that most national sales managers had a single button on their desk labeled "The More Button." When sales figures slumped, they pressed this More Button to get more calls, more activity, and—hopefully—more sales. "Somebody ought to tell them about the Better Button," we suggested, "just think what it could do for their results." Over the years, we saw so many senior sales managers repeatedly pressing their More Buttons that we began to suspect that their Better Buttons had been disconnected. We were once trapped in New York in a blizzard. The city had closed down, and we were sitting in the executive suite of a Fortune 100 company waiting to see an executive vice president who, because of the weather, had failed to arrive for work. We wandered around the deserted executive suite until we came to the chairman's office. On an irrational impulse we went in, just to see if there was a More Button on his desk. Sure enough, under the desk was a discreet little red button. To be fair, it was probably an unobtrusive way to signal to his secretary to interrupt when a meeting had gone on too long; but we had great delight in telling people that we'd actually seen the fabled More Button. Alas, sales productivity is too often an exercise in pressing the More Button. Sales effectiveness requires the elusive Better Button which, unfortunately, is not located on the chairman's desk.

Last Words on Sales Efficiency

If we seem less enthusiastic about methods for improving sales efficiency than we are about methods for improving effectiveness, it's because we need to correct an imbalance. Over the years, sales effectiveness has received too little attention from senior sales management. In contrast, efficiency has had more than its just share. We've seen the reasons for this. Efficiency is easier, it can be introduced from the top by management decision and—perhaps most important in this short-term age—it can be implemented quickly. No wonder that we so often see inappropriate efficiency measures, like rigid activity management, being introduced as an answer to effectiveness problems. It's our hope that the work of researchers like ourselves will help sales organizations redress this imbalance and find better ways to deal with effectiveness problems. We would like to think that the future of serious selling lies with the Better Button rather than with the More Button. Many sales managers were brought up in the days when pressing the More Button actually worked. Today, pressing the More Button brings disappointing results. In the future, it may become an even less useful sales management tool.

That's not to say that we should judge all efficiency measures as unthinking exercises of the More Button. Clearly they are not. Efficiency tools can have a powerful impact on sales productivity, even in the major sale. We've seen impressive figures from McKinsey, for example, showing the very tangible productivity benefits that can come from taking a thoughtful and systematic approach to sales efficiency. However, as McKinsey would be the first to admit, these results are always more impressive where the sales force is working under the twin conditions of small sales and a large number of potential accounts. In major accounts, effort spent in improving effectiveness almost invariably pays greater dividends.

Summary

In this chapter, we've taken an initial look at the twin components of sales productivity, sales efficiency and sales effectiveness, summarized in figure 2.11. We've argued that

- Sales effectiveness generally has more influence on success in major account selling than sales efficiency does.
- Lack of efficiency can inhibit or prevent attempts to improve sales effectiveness.
- Many efficiency tools, such as activity management, turn out to be counterproductive in the major sale because they have unintended side effects.
- Efficiency can be influenced quickly and decisively by top management actions. Effectiveness, in contrast, must be de-

FIGURE 2.11

Sales efficiency and sales effectiveness—some distinctions

	Sales efficiency	Sales effectiveness
Definition	How to get in front of the right customers, for the right amount of time at minimum cost	Once there, using skills and abilities to maximize your sales potential
Typical mechanisms for improving performance	Working **harder** mechanisms such as • time management • incentive payments • call reporting • activity management systems • territory design	Working **smarter** mechanisms such as • coaching • selling skills training • account strategy and account reviews • effectiveness models, frameworks, & tools
Typical measures	• penetration • call rates • cost per call	• success rates • repeat business • sustainable margins

veloped at the level of the salesperson through longer term mechanisms such as coaching and training.

- Efficiency is usually an organizational issue; effectiveness is invariably a managerial issue. Top management may set strategies that determine efficiency but it's day-to-day sales management down in the trenches that has most influence on sales effectiveness.

In the remainder of this book we'll focus on how to improve sales effectiveness. We'll see the tools and techniques that enable practicing sales managers to increase the productivity of their people in the major sale.

3

SHOULD YOU KEEP A DOG AND BARK YOURSELF?

The Manager's Role as a Salesperson

The national sales manager was giving a speech to a group of newly appointed sales managers in a division of Xerox Corporation. "You've all been very successful salespeople," he told them, "and that success will probably cost some of you your jobs." He paused to let the effect of his words sink in. Waiting until the uneasy murmur subsided, he continued, "About a third of you will not be with us this time next year. You'll fail. And the reason you'll fail is that you can't let go of selling. My advice to you is this: never forget that you're now a *manager*. Selling is for your people, not for you. They sell, you manage. Remember, don't keep a dog and bark yourself."

At the end of his speech, we applauded the loudest and the longest. As researchers, we knew there was ample evidence to show just how right he was. Our own studies in his division had shown, for example:

- Successful managers kept out of sales calls, while the less successful ones still played an active face-to-face selling role with customers.

- Those managers who became actively involved in face-to-face selling created real resentment in their salespeople. In answer to the interview question, "What one change would you most like to see from your manager?" a common response from salespeople was that managers should stop trying to behave like supersalespeople.

After his speech the national sales manager asked us for advice. "How do I keep my managers out of the sale?" he asked. "As you see, I take every opportunity to let them know I expect them to be managers, not salespeople. Yet I'll guarantee you that next time they go out on a call with their people, at least half of them will be jumping in, taking over the call, and acting just like they are still selling." We knew what he meant. A couple of months earlier, as part of our research, we had carried out a study of termination reports to find why salespeople left the company. One of the reports we'd examined had memorably expressed the problem. In the space where the supervisor summed up the performance of the person leaving, the sales manager had written, "His selling skills are poor." Underneath, where the seller himself was invited to add comments, were the words, "My manager has been out with me on six calls. On every call he did the selling and I didn't get a chance to open my mouth in front of a customer. So I don't know how he's able to judge my selling skills because he's never seen me sell. However, I've seen *him* sell and he's unspeakable."

It was this kind of evidence that made us so supportive of the national sales manager. Everything we knew confirmed that the three most important words for any sales manager to remember were, "Manage, don't sell." During the next six months we worked hard to get this message across to the division's sales management. We lectured, we coached, we begged. Our work was successful by most objective measures. Following our efforts, sales were up and relationships between sales managers and salespeople also showed an improvement. In fact, based on our experiences in this division of Xerox, we were ready to persuade the whole world that the three magic words "Manage, don't sell" were the key to successful sales management.

Face-To-Face Selling in the Major Sale

By now, readers familiar with the central message of this book will be asking, "But what kind of sale were you working with in Xerox? Was it a major sale?" That's a good question. As it happens, the division we were working with sold small copiers. Many sales could be made in a single call and most calls were made to sell a single machine to one decision maker. In other words, this was a classic small sale. In retrospect, the advice we gave Xerox was good because it certainly worked in their low-end sales. However, when we began to offer the same advice to clients in major sales, we quickly realized that things were not so simple. As one manager in Honeywell told us, "Telling me to keep out of a multimillion dollar sale that my whole team has been working on for nine months, is exactly like telling a mother not to get actively involved in the birth of her baby."

The fact is, in major sales managers *must* be actively involved in the face-to-face selling effort. There's good evidence to show that manager involvement in small sales is damaging and unproductive. That's not so in major sales. Any manager who stays remote from face-to-face selling is risking disaster. In a major sale, you may keep a dog, but you still do a lot of the barking yourself. However, the way you sell as a manager is very different from the way you sell as a salesperson. The selling role brings with it some new and difficult demands. In this chapter, we shall look closely at the sales manager's active selling role and some of the pitfalls that active selling holds for the unwary.

Some Common Mistakes

Active involvement in face-to-face selling selling is an essential part of successful sales management. However, we've seen some sales managers with an unhappy history of very *un*successful face-to-face experiences with their customers. For too many managers, getting directly involved has hurt their sales instead of helping them. What's gone wrong? Perhaps the most common reason for this situation can be traced back to the habit patterns people developed long before they became managers. Few managers started their sales careers in major accounts. Most started in smaller sales and worked their way into major account selling through success in lower value sales. Unfortunately, face-to-face selling habits learned years ago in small sales can easily intrude into today's major sales. We've seen too many managers unthinkingly adopt selling roles that were successful for them as salespeople in smaller sales but that are now hurting them badly.

Four Selling Roles That Fail

The tendency for small sales thinking to damage major sales manifests itself in a whole multitude of selling sins. These range from the detailed sales behaviors discussed in our book *SPIN®* *Selling* to the more complex issues of overall sales roles. We've observed four telltale sales roles used by managers that show small sale thinking inappropriately applied to major sales. These are

- Firefighter
- Objection Handler
- Exception Maker
- Supercloser

Each of these roles is a sure sign that a manager is letting past habits in small sales get in the way of major sales success. Let's briefly examine these roles to see why each can be so damaging in the major sale.

The Firefighter

The Firefighter is characteristically a high energy individual who likes nothing better than an opportunity to get involved in the sale. So, the moment there's the least trouble in an account, the Firefighter is there on the spot trying to beat out the flames. Terms like *planning* or *account strategy* are often completely absent from the Firefighter's vocabulary. As a result, the Firefighter is reactive, letting problems in the account decide issues of priority or emphasis. In managing small sales, Firefighters can superficially appear very effective. Their high energy and hands-on approach can bring them respect both from their salespeople and their customers. Unfortunately, by the very nature of small sales, there are usually more customers for a manager to cover than a Firefighter role can cope with comfortably. Consequently, because the Firefighter can only be in a few places at once, the utility of this role is limited when there's a large customer base. Where the sale is small and the number of customers is limited— such as in the initial stages of many start-up sales operations— we've seen Firefighters who were very effective sales managers. It's natural that any manager who found the Firefighter role successful working with a limited customer base in small sales, should be tempted to try the same method as a manager of the larger sale. After all, the central objection to Firefighter managers is that they can't be everywhere at once: there are too many fires. Because larger sales normally mean fewer customers, logic would suggest that a Firefighter could be effective in the larger sale.

Unfortunately, in major sales, the Firefighter can be a liability. In one Fortune 500 company we worked with, a Firefighter had been promoted into a senior sales management position. By background, this Firefighter had started selling Bibles in his early teens and progressed through used cars, kitchen equipment, and copying machines into his present position. In other words, he had a typical small sales background. One of his first acts in his new position was to call for weekly reports on the status of sales to the division's ten top customers. When he felt something was wrong, or that the sale wasn't progressing fast enough, he insisted on making a personal visit to the account. Without an adequate understanding of the very complex account relationships involved, he said things to customers that undermined many months of sales effort and, in one case, caused a top salesperson to resign in protest at his interference.

This is an extreme case, but in a milder form, your own organization is likely to have some sales managers who are Firefighters because they never gave up a set of habit patterns that helped them succeed in the small sale. Every major sales organization we've worked with has had its share of Firefighters. And, we suspect, some of these Firefighters were also closet arsonists. Their need for active involvement was so great that they would sometimes manufacture trouble in order to get the visceral satisfaction of sorting it out with the customer. We were once involved with a classic case of a Firefighter turned arsonist. We were running a sales training program for a company that sold very accurate weighing machines and balances for scientific and industrial use. On the second day of the program, two of our participants vanished. When they returned they explained that they had to leave unexpectedly for an emergency damage control visit to their largest customer. Normally, they told us, they kept their Firefighter manager as far from this customer as possible. However, with the two of them away on our training program, the manager had taken the opportunity to telephone the customer to find out how things were going. The customer mentioned that there was a minor calibration problem with a new balance that was being tested in one of the customer's labs. Within minutes, the Firefighter had assembled a couple of technicians and rushed off to visit the customer. Once there, the manager decided that the problem equipment should be removed and replaced with an older model which had less sensitive calibration requirements. "What he *didn't* know," one of our participants explained, "was that the new model was being evaluated in this lab as a pilot project. If successful, the customer was going to install another fifteen throughout the research complex. By taking out our test model he undermined the whole sale. When we talked to the customer, she told us, 'I don't know why he took it out. It was only a small problem and—by the time he got here—we'd fixed it.' "

The Objection Handler

Managers caught in this role treat the sale as if the customer was erecting a series of barriers that have to be overcome by anticipating and defeating objections. In preparing for a presentation their first question is often, "What objections are they likely to raise?" Face-to-face they specialize in giving customers clever answers to tough questions and seem at their happiest with a customer who raises difficulties that they can overcome through their selling skills. Again, in the small sale, this role can appear effective, but it's inappropriate in the larger sale. As part of our research, we've interviewed customers to find the reasons why major sales have been lost. Often the customer will initially give us an answer like, "The product was fine but the chemistry was wrong." On closer analysis, we would discover that wrong chemistry often meant that the customer was treated almost as an antagonist. As one of these customers put it, "Their whole sales effort seemed to be point scoring, as if they were competing against us in some kind of verbal battle. They were very clever and their answers were good, but we couldn't help getting the impression that we were the enemy."

Just as the Firefighter will light fires in order to put them out, the Objection Handler will often raise objections in order to overcome them. We've watched and inwardly groaned through many a customer meeting where an Objection Handler has created unnecessary objections in order to show off skills in overcoming them. A manager we worked with in a medical equipment company was particularly proud of his ability to overcome objections. "Our new machine," he told us, "is a great piece of technology but the software does have a few bugs in it—and that means we get objections about reliability. I'm good at handling these reliability issues but my people seem to have difficulty. Whenever I'm with them on calls I have to answer reliability objections for them." His people told a different story. "I was with him visiting a customer who didn't have the slightest concern over reliability. He said things like, 'I guess you must be worried that the software has bugs,' then he answered his own objections and showed that the bugs were no big deal. It sounded impressive but I couldn't help feeling that, at the end of all this, the customer felt much more uncomfortable about reliability than if we'd not brought it up."

The Exception Maker

Another unsuccessful selling role in the larger sale is what we call the Exception Maker. This is the manager who, during customer visits, will make concessions that the seller doesn't have authority to give. The Exception Maker will be the one to offer discounted terms, to make exceptions, or to promise something special for the customer. What's wrong with that? It's a classic sales manager role in the small sale. It's almost standard practice, for example, in car sales for the sales manager to be an Exception Maker. "Let me talk with my manager," says the salesperson and disappears into a back room. A few minutes later the manager appears and says, "We don't usually do this, but in your case, I'll make an exception and include the steering wheel in the basic price." The role of the manager as Exception Maker is well accepted in smaller sales, particularly those that involve some degree of negotiation over price or specification. Why doesn't it work in the major sale? The fundamental reason lies in the effect the Exception Maker has on seller credibility. If the customer gets concessions from the manager, not from the seller, then how will the seller be perceived? In all probability, the customer will see the seller as less accommodating, less helpful, and less sympathetic than the manager. What effect does that have on the seller's relationship with the customer? At the very least, it undermines the seller's credibility. As we'll see later, an important principle of manager involvement in the major sale is to build seller credibility, not to reduce it. An effective manager will always contrive to let the salesperson be the one to offer the customer any concession or good news.

In our experience, one of the sure signs that managers are falling into the Exception Maker role is when we hear them complain that they can't disengage themselves from accounts because the customer insists on talking only with them. Clearly, if previous conversations with the manager have resulted in concessions, special terms, or other positive outcomes for the customer, it's just human nature that the customer will prefer talking with the manager.

The Supercloser

The final role where we often see behavior from small sales leaking inappropriately into larger sales is the Supercloser. Here the manager can't resist being in at the kill and, as a result, gives disproportionate attention to calls where business might be closed. This isn't a very effective managerial role even in smaller sales. In larger sales this closing emphasis leads to a number of serious problems. For example, in most complex sales, less than one call in twenty results directly in an order. So a manager whose attention is on the 5 percent of calls that close the business may be neglecting the other 95 percent. That would be fine if, as many managers have been brought up to believe, the closing calls are the only ones that matter, but that's just not true. On the contrary, extensive research studies, including those quoted later in the chapter, suggest that sales success may depend much more on the early calls in the selling cycle than on the closing calls.

It's bad enough to give disproportionate managerial attention to closing calls, but it's even worse when managers insist on having an active face-to-face role in closing the business. We recall how much resentment this created in our sales management studies in Xerox. Salespeople complained bitterly about managers who insisted on being in on the close. What's more, it seemed that managers just couldn't win. If they were very successful at closing the sale, their people would make comments like, "My manager comes in at the last minute and takes the credit for closing a sale that I've worked on for months." If the manager failed, on the other hand, salespeople would make comments like, "My manager's lack of selling skills lost me a major sale." So, the role of Supercloser is a perilous one. Even if you succeed, you lose.

It's easy to criticize the Supercloser. In fact, given all the disadvantages of adopting a Supercloser role, it's hard to understand why any smart major sales manager would ever behave in that way. Yet there are a lot of Superclosers out there managing large sales. Many of these managers aren't playing the closing roles through choice. They are often forced into it by intense pressure from their own management. We once worked on a coaching skills project with a sales manager in a computer company. We were in his office warning him about the dangers of becoming too involved in closing calls. During our meeting the phone rang. The sales manager picked it up, listened, said a few words, then gloomily put down the handset. "It's my manager," he told us. "One of my people has a final meeting with a customer and he wants me in there to close. I don't think today's a good day to talk to me about getting out of closing calls." He had our sympathy. Yet, to be a successful manager in major sales, it's important to fight the pressures that can push you into the Supercloser role.

There's a common factor in these unsuccessful sales roles. In each case the manager unintentionally takes something away from the salesperson's authority or stature in the account. Later, we'll examine some roles that succeed because they achieve the opposite effect; they add to the salesperson's impact on the account. First, let's examine some overall principles for how a manager can become productively and successfully involved in face-to-face selling.

Principles for Involvement in Face-To-Face Selling

We believe that there are five fundamental principles to guide any sales manager's face-to-face involvement in a major sale.

Principle #1: Only become involved in face-to-face selling when your presence makes a unique difference.

Principle #2: Don't make sales calls on a customer unless your salesperson is with you.

Principle #3: Before any joint call, agree on specific and clear selling roles with your salesperson.

Principle #4: Be an active *internal* seller for your salespeople.

Principle #5: Always have a withdrawal strategy that prevents any customer from becoming dependent on you personally.

In the rest of this chapter, we'll examine these principles in more depth to understand the rationale behind them and their implications for managers' successful face-to-face involvement in the sale.

Principle #1: Make a Unique Difference.

Most sales managers are promoted into management because they were outstandingly successful as salespeople. Consequently, most managers are able to sell at least as well as their best salespeople. (Cynics might add that even those sales managers who can't sell better than their people usually *believe* they can.) As a result, it's tempting for managers to become overinvolved in face-to-face selling because they feel their personal presence will increase the chance of getting the business. When the stakes are high—as they invariably are in major sales—it's difficult for managers to take the risk of leaving key sales calls or important presentations to their salespeople. We've no hard research to back our opinions here, but years of watching major account selling convinces us that most managers would be twice as effective if they were involved in face-to-face selling half as often. That would unquestionably be true if their involvement was based on one of the unsuccessful roles we've just discussed.

A simple test to help managers decide whether to become directly involved in the sale is to use the concept of the *unique difference*. It's legitimate for managers to take a selling role if their contribution

- *Is unique:* in other words, if a manager brings something that salespeople can't provide, such as negotiating authority.
- *Makes the difference:* in other words, if the success of the sale is likely to be made or broken as a result of the manager's direct face-to-face involvement at this point in the selling cycle.

A common example of a unique difference is when a salesperson can't get access to higher level decision makers in an account. By involving the sales manager, the customer may agree to a meeting at a higher level. In such a case, the manager's contribution would be *unique* because the manager had done something the seller couldn't do. Similarly, if a manager made the final presentation in a very competitive sale, it might be that the manager's extra experience would *make the difference* and win a sale that would otherwise be lost. In cases like these the manager's involvement could be said to bring a unique difference that influences the success of the sale. This unique difference needn't be limited to the call itself. Sometimes a manager's presence in the call may be justified by something that will happen afterwards. For example, by being present in the call, a manager might gain an understanding of special customer requirements that, afterwards, will enable the manager to go back to influence other internal functions that the salesperson has little contact with, such as manufacturing or service. In this way, the manager's unique contribution is to act after the call as a bridge to other parts of the company that have an impact on the sale. On the other hand, many managers become involved in sales just because they can do something a little better or a little faster than their salespeople. In these cases, where the manager doesn't make a unique difference, our experience suggests that it would be smarter for the manager to stay out of the sale.

We recently carried out a small experiment in the paper processing industry, asking a group of major account sales managers to describe their last ten face-to-face sales contacts with customers. We then asked them to make an honest assessment of each contact to judge whether their involvement did, in fact, make a unique difference. By their own admission, less than 40 percent of their sales calls passed the unique difference test. The rest were made on the basis that their involvement was somehow *helpful* but not a unique use of their skills. We invite you to try the same exercise. List your last ten visits to customers where you played an active selling role. Then, for each sales call, ask yourself these two key questions:

- *Could the seller have done it without me?*—If so, your contribution was not unique.

- *Did my presence significantly alter the outcome of the meeting positively?*—If not, then your involvement didn't make the difference.

If less than 50 percent of your calls pass the test of unique difference, then there's a high probability that you are becoming too closely involved in face-to-face selling.

Why are we so emphatic that you should only become involved in the sale if you make a unique difference? There are several reasons. For example:

- Most of the major account managers we know are overworked and, as a result, they neglect important aspects of their jobs, such as planning, strategy, or coaching. If you are spending selling effort on unessential calls, then it's poor leveraging of your time.

- As we've seen, it's fatally easy to unintentionally undermine the salesperson handling the account. Salespeople's credibility can quickly become eroded if customers see managers involved in routine calls. Too much manager involvement signals to customers that you don't trust your salespeople or that they lack competence.

- The more you become involved in an account, the more difficult it will be for your salesperson to leverage your seniority to advantage. It can be hard, for example, to persuade a customer to set up a meeting with senior management unless the salesperson can offer to bring you along as his or her sales manager. If you are already easily available to customers at a lower level in the account, there's no incentive to agree to a meeting higher up in the customer's organization.

- The more involved you become in the sale, the harder it will be to withdraw at a later stage. When customers get used to talking with you, they will not want to talk to your people instead. As some buyers have expressed it, "Why talk to the monkey when you can talk to the organ grinder?" Many managers come to regret ever getting involved in the sale when, afterwards, they become the conduit for every little complaint and request from the customer. A senior VP in a West Coast shipping company told us of a Midwest retailer who had been his customer some years ago. Despite the VP's three promotions since then, and despite having no direct connection with sales in his present position, he still gets calls from this retailer. "You can run, but you can't hide," he told us; "once you're sucked in, you're there for life."

In summary, then, our first principle is to work ruthlessly to keep yourself out of unessential selling. Remember that your salespeople will often try to involve you in noncrucial sales calls because your presence makes their selling task easier. By involving you, it's not their fault if the call fails, and if it succeeds, it helps them in the account. Bringing you into the sale is a no-lose strategy for them. Your involvement in noncrucial calls makes your salesperson more successful by diminishing your own effectiveness. Communicate firmly and clearly to your salespeople that you will only become involved in a face-to-face sales call if they can show that you will make the unique difference. In that way you'll reduce the unessential selling load that plagues most major account sales managers.

Principle #2: Don't Make Calls Alone.

Most managers subscribe—at least in theory—to the simple principle of always having someone with them when making sales calls. There are obvious reasons for not making calls without having your salesperson present. For example:

- The salesperson should be the focus of account activity and it's hard for sellers to maintain this role with credibility if their boss is holding meetings where they aren't present.

- If the salesperson isn't present, you'll have to spend additional valuable time explaining to the seller afterwards what went on during the meeting. Even if you can afford the time, there's a risk that you'll leave out something vital or unintentionally distort what happened.

- When sales managers meet alone, there's always the possibility that the customer can play "divide and rule." We've often heard customers say things like, "Your sales rep promised special terms . . ." or "When I met with your manager last week, she told me that I would get expedited delivery." The best protection against this is not to meet alone.

- By definition, if you make a call as a manager, it should be an important one. Consequently there may be complex issues discussed during the call that have a bearing on the outcome of the sale. It will be hard for you to sell and also to take adequate notes. It's risky to make a call alone without another person present to take notes and help you to remember the details of what was discussed.

Despite these reasons, many sales managers continue to "fly solo" by calling on customers alone. Their salesperson may have a scheduling conflict or be on vacation. They may be calling on a personal contact from years past. Whatever the justification, a dangerous number of solo calls are made by managers. Our advice is to avoid solo calls by whatever means possible. If your salesperson can't make the meeting, reschedule the call. If you can't reschedule the call take *somebody* with you. As we'll see in the next section, even a very junior person can play a useful role in the joint call.

Principle #3: Agree on Specific and Clear Selling Roles.

We've sat in on hundreds of precall meetings between managers and sellers. Generally, in the hands of a competent manager, these meetings help the participants to do a fairly good job of laying out a broad sales strategy. They discuss questions like "What are our objectives in this call?" "Where are our vulnerabilities?" "What should we do if they raise issues about implementation?" Then the discussion turns to roles that each will play during the meeting. There's considerable discussion of who introduces whom at the start of the call. Then, just when we're expecting people to begin serious discussion of selling roles, it becomes horribly clear that nothing is going to be decided. "I'll start and then let's play it by ear" seems to be the most common conclusion when people discuss their respective selling roles.

No other area of the joint call is so neglected, or so misunderstood, as the setting of workable selling roles. Yet having two people on the same call, each unclear about who should be leading where, is obviously risky. Perhaps one reason why managers seem so reluctant to define selling roles is that they have a history of unhappy experiences setting roles that didn't work. If so, we sympathize and we have a few words of warning. Some writers have suggested that you should set *behavioral* roles. So, for example, one of you should play *nice-guy* and one play *tough-guy*. Or one play *expert* while the other plays *generalist*. In our experience, this sort of role setting only works if that role is your normal and natural way to behave. Our advice is to set roles but never indulge in role-playing. Pretending to be something that you're not can work in the simple one-call transaction. In selling used cars, for example, there's plenty of anecdotal evidence to show that it can often prove very successful for seller and manager to play *nice-guy* and *tough-guy* roles. But that kind of thinking is dangerous in the major sale where you have an ongoing relationship with the customer. Anything that introduces tricks or pretense into the relationship will almost invariably hurt you in the long term. So avoid any division of roles that leads you to pretend or play games.

If role playing doesn't work, what does? One answer is to use roles that define the degree and type of participation each person will play in the meeting without defining the type of behavior that people should adopt. In this way, setting appropriate roles for a joint call can be done simply and effectively without indulging in unproductive game playing. Let's take three examples of roles that specify participation levels but that don't involve any role playing.

The Coach: Suppose you are making a joint call with one of your most experienced salespeople. Let's assume that this person can handle the selling role well enough so that your active involvement in face-to-face selling would not constitute the unique difference that our first principle suggests should determine manager involvement. In this case, you should have no selling role at all. Then why are you there? Your most valid role is to be present in the sales call as part of your overall responsibility for coaching the salesperson. Coaching is a vitally important management tool in the major sale and we are not in any way suggesting that the coaching role should be used only with experienced and able salespeople. As a manager you can and should coach people who are at every level of experience and proficiency. However, coaching is singled out as a role here because it's the coaching role that justifies a manager accompanying a seller but not playing an active face-to-face part in the call. By agreeing to this role in advance, you make it clear that your salesperson will be the active leader in the discussion and that your role is primarily that of an observer. You each know the degree of participation the other will play in the discussion and you can then both plan the call with the knowledge that the seller will take full face-to-face responsibility for the call's content, structure, and continuity.

The Scribe: At the other extreme, suppose you are making an important call on a key account where you *do* make the unique difference that justifies an active selling role. You might choose to take a very junior person with you in accordance with the principle that it's better not to make important calls alone. What role should this junior person have? Clearly, in a call of this importance you don't want them to do any selling. Instead, you may decide to give them the role of *scribe.* In this role division you will be the active participant and you will do all the selling. The role of the junior person is exclusively to take notes—to act as a scribe.

The Topic Leader: The Coach and Scribe roles are at extremes. In one case the seller is experienced enough to handle the call alone; in the other case the seller is too inexperienced to participate at all. What should you do when you are making a joint call with a seller who is experienced enough to handle some parts of the call but not others? It's in these cases that most people just play it by ear with both manager and seller participating randomly in the call. We've so often seen disaster result from this casual division of participation that we've come to advise people strongly against it. Instead, we recommend a division of participation based on topic areas. As a manager, you should plan the call on the basis of our first principle of unique difference. Out of the topic areas that may come up with the customer, which are the ones where your contribution will make a unique difference? Working with your salesperson, agree that you will cover these unique difference areas and the seller will be responsible for other topic areas. Of course, have a plan about who will lead if a totally unexpected topic comes up. You might, for example, suggest that if an unanticipated area arises, the seller will normally take it but, if uncomfortable, will give you a signal and you will step in.

Is this elaborate planning of topics worthwhile, or is it overkill? Many managers argue that they work well enough with their salespeople to make this kind of role planning unnecessary. We wish that our experience supported people's glib confidence in their ability to work well together in a sales call without role planning. Yes, when you've been working with someone closely for years, it's possible to make joint calls without any topic division at all. However, it *does* take years. Many people believe that they can improvise their way through a joint call with one of their salespeople so that both contribute to the discussion and each supports the efforts of the other. From time to time we've seen this work with spectacular success. Alas, we've more often seen such attempts fail as each seller gets in the other's way, the conversation never reaching the penetrating depth that marks a first-class sales call. Unless you have a considerable rapport and experience selling together, our contention is that it's not good to have two people selling simultaneously. So agree in advance which topics each of you will take during the call.

In summary, then, our third principle is to plan joint roles carefully and systematically; to avoid game-playing roles but to focus on the kind of role definition that lets you both know who will lead the discussion at any point in the call.

Principle #4: Be an Active Internal Seller for Your Salespeople.

Most books and programs on how to sell, treat selling as if it's an activity that only happens face-to-face with customers. In recent years it has become plain to those of us who study selling that the more complex the sale, the more important it becomes to do a good *internal* selling job within your own company. In a simple sale it's possible to be very successful without doing any internal selling. So, for example, a manager in a typical "knock-on-doors" small sale may be able to achieve all that's necessary to get things done internally by making a couple of phone calls a week to the warehouse and filling in some company paperwork. In contrast, major account sales managers may spend the majority of their time trying to influence internal decisions. They may, for example, need to expedite deliveries, argue for special exceptions, or fight for technical resources. None of these things can be accomplished without active sales manager involvement.

In chapter 1 we talked about our research in a telecommunications giant that showed three successful types of sales manager. One of these, the *Coalition Builder*, specialized in building and using a network of contacts. These managers, you'll recall, were less active in face-to-face selling. Instead, they worked behind the scenes, using their network of contacts to help them and their salespeople surmount any obstacles in the selling cycle. In particular, these successful managers were able to use their internal networks to get things done. At the time we were conducting this research, we thought that their success might just be because the telecommunications company was a mighty bureaucracy. We felt that, in a *normal* organization, these skills of oiling the internal machinery might be less essential to success. Perhaps we've become more cynical with age and experience, but almost every sales organization we've worked with seems to have an intricate array of barriers and obstacles that stand in the way of delivering what the customer wants when the customer wants it. Your role as an effective major account sales manager must be to sell long, hard, and skillfully internally to get things done for your people and their accounts.

If this sounds startlingly obvious, pause for a moment. We've seen many sales managers who have excellent selling skills with customers but who *never* use those skills internally to help them get resources and cooperation inside their own companies. We recall running a training program for major account sales managers during which one of the topics was the importance of "selling" internally. During the break, as is a ritual in sales management training, everybody rushed to the telephones. Walking past, we couldn't help overhearing one manager on the line to the factory cursing them over a late delivery while another was engaged in an equally abusive interchange with technical services. Ten minutes earlier, this pair had nodded impatiently while we talked about the *obvious* idea of using selling skills rather than authority or abuse to achieve cooperation inside the corporation. As is always the case, obvious ideas are often the hardest for people to put into practice. It's amazing how many managers switch off their selling skills when they aren't with customers. Ask yourself whether you treat your own organization with the same level of selling skills you would employ with a major account customer. If you are going to help your people and their customers, you should use every ounce of your selling ability internally. As one very successful salesperson in IBM once told us, "I get things done here because I treat IBM as my biggest major account customer."

The role of internal seller becomes particularly important when you're in the apparently happy position of having greater demand from customers than you can supply. We say *apparently* because, as any manager who has faced excess demand will know, it can lead to some very difficult problems with unsatisfied customers. One information processing company we worked with launched a dynamic new product that was years ahead of any competition. Within weeks of the launch, the first year's sales targets had been exceeded. The problem sales managers faced was no longer one of getting new business, it was the equally difficult challenge of keeping a growing list of impatient customers happy while they waited for installations. The most successful sales managers during this period were those skilled in internal selling. They were the ones who came out ahead during internal meetings on machine allocation, and it was their skills that persuaded overworked and tired installation technicians to put in the special effort needed to keep installation promises.

Principle #5: Prevent Customer Dependence by a Withdrawal Strategy.

As the fat fees of divorce lawyers testify, relationships are generally much easier to get into than to get out of. The more active you become in major account selling, the harder you'll find it to disentangle yourself from customer involvement once the sale is complete. We've seen many major account managers who spend more than half their time fulfilling minor customer requests that should have been handled by the salesperson but that came directly to the manager because of the manager's prior involvement with the account. Sometimes, when we're running programs for major account managers, we include a session where we invite managers to bring up the toughest problem they face. It's surprising how often the number one problem turns out to be demands on their time made by customers who refuse to deal with anyone else in the organization. "I'm going crazy," one partner from an international accounting firm told us. "I get calls from clients who I haven't managed for ten years asking me for tiny things they could find in a desk reference book. I can't refuse to take the calls. So what can I do?" Our advice to managers with problems like this sounds curiously parental. You should have thought about that, we tell them, before you even got into the relationship. Unhelpful though this advice may be, it's true. The time to prevent a customer from becoming dependent on you personally is before the relationship gets established.

Let's look at some of the ways you can set up relationships that allow you to withdraw gracefully at the appropriate point and turn the relationship over to others. Managers with track records of successfully withdrawing from relationships and leaving happy customers behind, seem to do three things:

They never visit the customer alone: As we saw in our second selling principle, it's generally smart selling for a manager to take along another person on all calls. The additional benefit in terms of a withdrawal strategy is that the other person can start to build an independent relationship with the customer, thus freeing the manager. That process can be accelerated if the accompanying person takes on follow-up responsibilities that involve further contact with the customer, and include such duties as writing follow-up letters, sending samples, arranging further meetings, and the like.

They build the stature of their people: The basis of a successful withdrawal strategy is to provide the customer with a contact who is even more valuable than you are. Consequently, managers who are successful in disentangling themselves from accounts will go to great lengths to first build up their salesperson in terms of credibility and in terms of value to the customer. We shall discuss some of the most effective ways to do this in the final section of this chapter, which deals with effective selling roles for managers.

They are never seen to make things happen: You won't find it easy to withdraw successfully from an account if the customer believes that you can make things happen that the salesperson can't. We recently had an illustration of this—and a nice little case study of how *not* to behave—with one of our printers. We wanted a book reprinted in a hurry, so we needed the printer to make a special exception and let us have reprints within three weeks rather than the usual seven. Our sales rep didn't have the authority to change delivery dates and it seemed as if we were doomed to miss our reprint deadline. Another meeting with the sales rep, during which we stressed the urgency of our needs, and several more telephone calls with her, only succeeded in moving the date up one week. That wasn't enough. In desperation we called her manager. "Sure," he said, "if you want it in three weeks, I'll personally make sure it's done." From the manager's point of view he probably felt he'd handled things well. After all, he'd kept a customer satisfied. From our point of view he'd made a fatal mistake. In the future, whenever we want something, we'll bypass the sales rep and go directly to her manager. He made the dangerous error of showing us he was the person who could make things happen. We'll never leave him alone as a result.

What *should* the manager have done? If he'd been smart, he would have told us that our sales rep was working hard on our behalf to get a better delivery date and that she would be back to us within an hour. He would then have called her, authorized a three-week delivery and told her to contact us. He would have emphasized to her that she must make it very clear to us that it was her work that led to the three-week delivery and nothing to do with our call to her manager. In that way we would have believed that she was the one who could make things happen and she would have been our preferred contact in the future. The moral of this tale is that the ability to make things happen can be a millstone around a manager's neck. As one experienced manager in Honeywell once told us, "By making sure my customers think my salespeople have more clout than I do, I've saved myself at least two hours a day."

Sales Roles That Work

Finally, now that we've looked at some principles for determining the nature of your involvement in face-to-face selling, let's consider some active selling roles that are successful. Notice that in each of the roles we cover, there is a common thread. In every case, the manager's face-to-face involvement succeeds in building up the stature and the credibility of the manager's salespeople. This is the exact reverse of the unsuccessful roles we discussed earlier. The Firefighter, the Objection Handler, the Supercloser, and the Exception Maker all undermine the salesperson in the account.

There's another common factor in these successful roles. They each make use of that all-important first principle of involvement, the unique difference. In every case, the manager adopts a role that allows something to happen in the account that could not happen easily without the manager's face-to-face involvement. The five successful face-to-face roles are

- The Foundation Builder
- The Access Creator
- The Team Coordinator
- The Coach
- The Negotiator

Let's examine each of these roles to see how it contributes to leveraging the manager's unique differences and to building the salesperson's position in the account.

The Foundation Builder

In the last chapter, we described a sales productivity study we carried out for a large multinational computer company. We were looking for factors that correlated with the length of the selling cycle. In a nutshell, the company found that the selling cycle took too long and cost too much to be justified at a time when hardware costs were falling fast and profit margins were under pressure. Our job was to discover why some sales cycles were shorter than others and to see whether we could learn some principles for what made a quicker, and therefore a more cost-effective, sale. We investigated dozens of variables, most of which aren't relevant here. However, one of the things we looked at that has a bearing on the manager's selling role was the point in the sale where managers became involved. The data took us by surprise. We had been expecting that those managers who achieved the shortest sales cycles might be those who put a strong emphasis on closing calls and therefore restricted their sales involvement to those calls that were nearest to the point of closing the sale. But the results were just the opposite. We found that selling cycles were shorter when sales managers were present in the early calls of the selling cycle. In retrospect, we suppose that this result could have been predicted. After all, as we said earlier, if a manager doesn't become involved until the seventh call in a selling cycle, then even the world's most effective sales manager can't achieve a selling cycle less than seven calls long. On the other hand, by becoming involved in calls very early in the selling cycle, the manager can help build a solid foundation for the sale that allows the overall cycle to progress faster. It was this research that first alerted us to the role of Foundation Builder. Since then, we've observed that many of the most successful major account sales managers we've worked with put a disproportionate amount of their sales effort into ensuring that selling cycles start well. In particular, successful managers focus on two vitally important selling elements which, if handled well in the early part of the sale, will make the whole selling cycle proceed more smoothly:

- They help their people uncover and develop strong needs, positioning their products and services as the best solution to the needs they have uncovered.
- They help their people build value in the areas that most differentiate them from competitors. In this way they avoid the common early cycle trap of selling the concept but doing so in a way that lets competitors come in to take the business.

Naturally, this effort isn't just in terms of face-to-face selling. Much or even most of it lies in helping people plan, review, and form strategies during the early parts of the selling cycle. The underlying point here is that no selling effort is better than the foundation it's built on. If, by going with one of your people on a call, you can help a selling cycle to start on a solid footing, you're probably contributing more to their sales productivity than by giving attention to their late cycle closing calls.

The Access Creator

One of the unique ways to leverage your managerial position is to use it as a means of creating access to a different level of customer in the account. Your salesperson may find it much easier to set up a meeting with a more senior person in the account if they are in a position to promise that you will attend. We should here add the caution that while you should use your position to gain access, you should *not* use your position during the meeting itself in a way that undermines your seller. So, for example, it's not very effective, having set the meeting up, for you to do all the talking or to behave in a way that forces your salesperson into a secondary position. You're walking a difficult tightrope here. If the meeting has been set up around your presence then it's natural for the customer to expect you to have a central and active role. You can't realistically stay quiet. On the other hand, your presence must build your salespeople up and not undermine them. So, before the meeting, plan a number of areas where the seller can take the lead. It's a good idea, for example, for the seller to be responsible for introducing the key items you'd like to discuss. Also, if you have some special offers or concessions to make, it's important that these come from the seller, not from you, the manager.

The Team Coordinator

Sometimes the problem isn't one of getting access to people in the customer account, it's one of assembling resources from your own organization and making sure that they act appropriately. Most managers have faced challenges in getting cooperation from support staff groups such as technical support, marketing, service, or finance. In complex sales your internal functions will almost invariably interface with the customer. Often, these functions act in a way that's counterproductive or damaging to the sales effort. That's not surprising. After all, very few finance people, for example, are measured against their contribution to the sales effort or to customer satisfaction. It's only natural that people from other functions will, in their customer dealings, reflect the general objectives and measures of their own functions, not the needs of the sales organization.

As a manager, you may be able to handle these interfunctional issues much better than your salespeople. For example, while technical support may not be willing to attend a customer meeting with one of your salespeople, you may be able to use your position—and your own presence at the meeting—to persuade a representative from technical support to attend. At the meeting, if you are playing the role of Team Coordinator, it's important that you see yourself as representing your *company*, not the sales function. That should be the role of your salesperson. By acting as the company's representative you achieve two things. First, you don't undermine your seller by taking over the sales role. Second, by acting from a broader perspective, you will find it easier to get the cooperation you'll need from other functions who may not have much sympathy with a purely selling perspective.

To some extent, the increasing preoccupation with quality in major organizations has brought a new degree of common focus on the importance of customers and their needs, but, even here, lack of training in customer handling skills may mean that other functions seem to hurt the sales effort more than they help. As the Team Coordinator, you may be in a unique position to help the customer see the value that other parts of your organization contribute to helping solve customer problems.

One of the most spectacular changes in business philosophy in recent years has been the emergence of partnering arrangements between customers and their suppliers. Here, the issue is not the individual sale but the relationship. Partnering teams, with representatives from both customer and supplier organizations, meet on a regular basis to monitor the relationship and make sure it's proceeding smoothly and in the interests of both parties. Some organizations estimate that more than half their future sales volume will be generated from partnering arrangements. Curiously, sales functions have been slow to take ownership of partnering teams. We've seen the supplying company represented by such diverse functions as marketing, finance, corporate planning, and manufacturing. Yet there's no more logical function than sales to coordinate the supplier team. We expect that many major account sales managers will spend much more time in the future acting as Team Coordinators in partnering teams.

The Skills Coach

The role of Skills Coach is so central and so essential to success in major account sales management that we have allocated a whole chapter to it. Skills coaching, although a face-to-face role, isn't strictly speaking a selling role at all. In chapter 6, we'll see how good skills coaching requires that the coach stay out of direct involvement in selling during the call. Coaching, as we'll see, is much more than the old "curbside conference" where manager and salesperson discuss what happened in the call. In major account selling, coaching covers strategy as well as skills. It's a complex series of activities which, when performed well, can bring dramatic improvements to sales effectiveness. When clients ask us to help them decide what skills to look for in selecting managers of major account salespeople, coaching comes right at the top of our list. A good coach can do more for the performance of a major account sales team than the best sales efficiency systems. The reason, as we saw in the last chapter, is that major account selling is about *effectiveness,* rather than efficiency. Effectiveness doesn't happen by management edict. It has to be patiently developed and that's where coaching comes in.

We'll say a lot more about coaching later, when we discuss the results of our coaching research studies. For now, let's focus on just one aspect of coaching, the role of the Coach in developing face-to-face selling skills. There's a reason why we cover only skills coaching in this chapter. We've seen excellent *strategy* coaches who have helped their people develop effective account strategies without ever leaving their offices or ever meeting the customer. Skills coaching, on the other hand, always involves a face-to-face element. That's not only true of sales coaches. Any skills coaching, whether we're talking about coaching in golf, in singing, or in flying aircraft *must* involve the coach in observing and analyzing the performance of the person being coached. To coach in a skill you must be there watching the skill as it's performed. There's no such thing as a skills coach who sits in the office. To coach selling skills you've got to be present in calls with your salespeople—and that's why we include skills coaching as a key face-to-face role for major account sales managers.

One of our studies, carried out in Xerox Corporation, provided us with an interesting conclusion about skills coaching. We worked with managers who had an outstanding record of success in developing their people through coaching during joint calls. We compared their coaching strategy with a group of managers who were making a similar number of joint calls with their people but were not doing such a good job helping to develop selling skills. We wanted to know whether the more effective managers coached in a different way. We found two differences:

- Less effective coaches put nearly all their attention into post-call discussion. They played very little part in the call planning process and saw coaching mainly as a way to review a call after it had happened. In contrast, effective coaches spent as much time with their salespeople in call planning as in call reviewing.

- Less effective coaches frequently tried to combine a coaching role with a selling role. So they would actively intervene in the face-to-face discussions with the customer. Effective coaches, on the other hand, would either take a selling or a coaching role. They would not try to combine both roles in a single call. If they became involved in the discussion, they would not afterwards try to coach the seller.

What lessons does this study have for taking an effective skills-coaching role with your salespeople? We think it underscores the point we've been making that roles need to be clear and specific. A role that combines two purposes, such as coaching and selling, will usually fail to achieve either purpose well. In deciding whether you should take the role of Coach, you should recognize that, in doing so, you will not play an active part in the selling. Incidentally, many managers have argued with us over this point, protesting that they have the ability to make some small but important intervention at a critical point in the call. Then, so they claim, they withdraw from the call and continue with the coaching role. Our experience suggests that although this is an attractive idea, it's usually a delusion in reality. If the manager joins in the selling and makes an important point, the customer usually recognizes that the manager has something useful to say and starts to talk with the manager and not with the seller. In this way, the manager gets dragged into the discussion and can't easily withdraw into the coaching role. What's more, in the process of becoming involved in selling, the manager may have unintentionally succeeded in undermining the seller's credibility. On the other hand, if the manager makes a point inconsequential enough for it to be easy to withdraw from the conversation, then the point is probably not worth making and would have been better unsaid or left to the salesperson. Trying to combine two different roles sounds easy, but in real life, it rarely works well.

The Negotiator

The final role that uses the manager's ability to make a unique difference is the Negotiator. For many managers, the role of Negotiator is one of using their greater level of authority to make concessions that salespeople are not authorized to give. This is a very limited, and very dangerous, view of negotiation. As we've seen, if you are the one making concessions, then you risk both undermining your salesperson and dragging yourself into perpetual customer involvement. We've suggested, and we'll emphasize it again here, that you should *always* strive to make it appear to the customer that concessions come from your salespeople and not from you.

So, what's your negotiating role if it's not concession giving? We believe there are several useful ways for a sales manager to make a unique difference as a Negotiator. For example:

Listening: One of the most frequent complaints from customers is that they are not listened to by their suppliers. As a result, they become frustrated and feel an unnecessary antagonism. Much of this antagonism can be diffused simply by listening. Most people have attended enough listening skills training to know that listening is not a passive process. This isn't the place to review listening skills, but there are a couple of specific points worth making about listening as a Negotiator. First, try to listen as a representative of the company, not of the sales organization. And make that perfectly clear to the customer by saying things like, "My colleague, Ms. Seller, is here to deal with sales issues but, as a representative of my corporation's management, I'm here to make sure we have a full understanding of what's concerning you on a business level." In this way you don't raise expectations that you will be taking over the sale or making sales concessions.

The second piece of advice on listening is to be quite certain in your own mind about the precise difference between *agreeing* and *expressing understanding.* As a Negotiator you must inevitably be very cautious about *agreeing* with positions the customer puts forward. We've seen many managers who, because they know it's dangerous to agree, just ask questions or sit passively. Remember that the point of listening is for customers to feel they have been heard. The best way to do this is to *express understanding* of their position without expressing agreement. For example, if the customer voices a concern over delivery, and you don't think you can negotiate the faster delivery for which the customer is asking, then, instead of just inquiring why delivery is so important, *express understanding* of the customer's position by saying something like, "I'm not sure that we will be able to give you the faster delivery you're asking for. However, I understand why faster delivery would be useful in terms of both your workflow and the new stock system you've explained to us." In this way, without committing yourself to agreement with the customer's position, you demonstrate that you have heard and understood.

Supporting the Seller: Your presence in the meeting can give your seller confidence and support, particularly if there are signs that the meeting could be difficult. It's not just the moral support of your presence that helps the seller. More than anything, sales negotiation is about creative problem solving. Sometimes, having another person in the negotiation allows a fresh look at a problem and generates creative solutions that are acceptable to the customer. We recall being present in one negotiation where the customer was insisting that, to get the contract, a component supplier had to guarantee twelve-hour delivery. The negotiation had come to an impasse because the supplier was unable to make that guarantee. The sales manager, realizing that if this problem remained unsolved the sale would be lost, offered the creative suggestion of setting up a buffer store on the customer's site, which they would keep supplied with all components. This fresh look at the problem won the business.

However, as we've said before, creative problem solving—like any other intervention in the sale—has to be done in a way that doesn't undermine the seller's credibility. Listening to the customer's problems and working behind the scenes to help the seller come up with a solution is much more effective in the long run than rushing in yourself with creative options. Again, a fundamental principle of being a good Negotiator, like all other sales roles, is to support your salespeople, not undermine them.

Bringing the bad news: This is a tough role but an important one. It's the reverse of the Exception Maker role that we were so nasty about earlier in the chapter. The Exception Maker is ever anxious to be the one to make the concessions or to take the credit and, in doing so, diminishes the salesperson's importance to the customer. Sometimes, as a Negotiator, there will be bad news to bring. A showstopper may have arisen, there's a need you just can't meet or a concession you're unable to make. Unpleasant though it may be for you to bring this bad news to the customer, it's often better for you to do it than your salesperson. For one thing, by announcing the bad news through a manager, your company demonstrates that the issue has been considered at management level and not just dismissed out of hand. What's more, by bringing the bad news yourself you may be able to preserve the warm and positive relationship that your seller has built with the customer. Alas, the advice we must give here is that the more unpalatable the news will be to the customer, the more important it is for you to be the one who brings it. Who said major account management was easy?

Changing the players: A final Negotiator role is for you to help the sale out of an impasse by changing the players. On the customer side, your entry as a manager may succeed in moving the customer contact level up so that new players come into the negotiation. On your own side, you may sometimes need to temporarily introduce a new player if the relationship has reached a point where the salesperson can't make progress.

The Selling Role in Summary

As we've seen, unlike the smaller sale, managers *must* have an active face-to-face selling role in the major sale. The two overriding considerations in making that selling role work are

- To ensure that, as a manager, you are only involved in face-to-face selling when your presence makes a unique difference.

- To sell in a way that builds and supports your salespeople, while allowing you to withdraw from the account leaving behind a satisfied customer.

It's not an easy balance to achieve. Many managers never make it because their own ego needs force them to play the hero and to undermine their people rather than build them up. Don't let your own need for taking the credit stand in the way of your success as a manager.

4

PUTTING SUCCESS UNDER THE MICROSCOPE

Defining Sales Effectiveness

At the risk of slightly simplifying the conclusions we drew in chapter 2, we can say that

- Sales productivity has two components: efficiency and effectiveness.
- Effectiveness, or what happens during the sales call, generally has a greater impact on productivity in major sales than efficiency.
- Effectiveness, however, is much harder to improve than efficiency.
- While efficiency can be improved by top management policies and systems, effectiveness is best improved by immediate sales managers.

What do these conclusions mean in practice for sales managers? The implication of chapter 2 is that the single most important function of a manager in major sales is to improve the effectiveness of salespeople. And everything we've seen in our research and consulting work confirms this. Nothing else a sales manager does, whether it's brilliant selling, superlative administration, canny politics, or outstanding negotiation, has one-half the potential impact that comes from doing a good job of building sales effectiveness. As John De Vincentis of McKinsey put it, "The pivotal job in a sales organization is the immediate sales manager and the most important role of that sales manager is to improve sales effectiveness."

Defining the Atoms of Effectiveness

Sales effectiveness isn't the easiest concept to grasp, although there are rich rewards for those who can do so. On the surface, effectiveness can be defined simply as those things a salesperson does during the sales cycle which cause the customer to decide in the salesperson's favor. Unfortunately, such a broad definition doesn't help managers grapple with the practical issues of how to improve effectiveness. You can't help salespeople to be more effective unless you have a clear idea of what effectiveness looks like. Over the years we've worked with thousands of sales managers. Some were able to recognize effective selling when they saw it, but only a small fraction of them were able to describe the component behaviors. It's not easy to identify those specific behaviors, but it *is* important. By having a clear and detailed picture of what effective sales behaviors look like, you can diagnose effectiveness problems in your people, and through coaching, you can significantly improve their skills. Your understanding of effective behavior translates directly into sales productivity. This isn't an empty claim. In one experiment we measured the productivity improvement of 1,000 salespeople whose managers coached them using effectiveness models based on specific behaviors. The average increase in sales revenue of these 1,000 coached people was 17 percent compared with a control group. That's a worthwhile enough improvement to make us excited about the tremendous potential for improved productivity if you can combine the three things that were present in our experiment. These were:

- *An effectiveness model:* In other words, we had a clear idea of what salespeople should be doing in order to be more effective.

- *Specific behaviors:* Our model described specific behaviors like "asks questions to uncover customer's problems," not broad concepts like "empathy."

- *coaching:* Managers used the behaviors in the model to systematically coach and develop improved skills in their salespeople.

Can you get increases in sales revenue in the range of 15 to 20 percent just from using an effectiveness model? We're naturally cautious about generalizing from a specific set of research studies, but our 1,000 cases convinced us that the productivity gains are there to be had. The improvements in our experiment resulted from the efforts of a wide cross section of over 300 managers from more than 30 industries. There's no reason why you shouldn't achieve some very worthwhile results, provided you're prepared to put in an equivalent amount of effort. That effort starts with thinking long and hard about behavior—what it is, and how it relates to sales effectiveness.

Effective Behavior

Ask yourself, "What *exactly* is it a salesperson does to be successful during the call? What are the individual behaviors that have most impact on the customer's decision?" Unless you can answer questions like these, you can't begin to isolate the key components of sales effectiveness. But these are challenging questions to address. Years ago, when we were starting our sales research, we recorded some typical sales calls, hoping that we could analyze them and answer those very questions. As it turned out, we found that there were literally hundreds of different ways to classify the component behaviors of each call; it proved extremely difficult to show which individual behaviors were linked with call success. You might ask, what's so important about *component behaviors?* Why are we apparently moving away from more general concepts of sales effectiveness and concentrating instead on these detailed and seemingly less significant individual behaviors? Think of it this way. A component behavior is one of the atoms out of which the structure of the sales call is built. For example, explaining a product feature is a component behavior, as is asking a leading question, or using a closing technique. These atoms of sales performance are just as important to selling as physical atoms are to chemistry or physics. Just as the science of chemistry emerged from magic and alchemy through understanding how atoms combine together to make compounds, so, by understanding component behaviors—the atoms of sales performance—we can begin to treat sales effectiveness as a true and teachable science rather than as a magical ability that some people are born with. In short, the only way to understand sales effectiveness is to get away from broad general concepts of what makes a salesperson effective. We must think instead at the level of behavioral atoms. So, instead of describing the effective salesperson in such broad terms as *a good listener, has empathy, is credible,* or *develops customer needs,* we must break each of these broad headings down into behavioral components—the more specific the better. We must, for example, specify what the credible salesperson actually *does* to create credibility. Is it by using product knowledge? By showing familiarity with the customer's operation? Through asking intelligent questions or demonstrating a street-smart knowledge of business? Or is it just having a few gray hairs? Then some of these smaller headings may have to be broken down still further. What, for instance, do we mean by *intelligent questions?*

Learning from Specifics

This may sound like an elaborate and difficult way to set about understanding sales effectiveness. We recommend it because it works. If there was an easier way to improve effectiveness, based on broader, more general concepts, we would be the first to use it; but, as a practical reality, you can't improve sales effectiveness using broad concepts. Take *listening,* for example. Few managers would dispute that effective listening is important to sales success. Most sales managers we know have at least one member of their team who, in the manager's opinion, could become more effective thorugh better listening skills. We've seen managers counsel and coach these individuals, saying things like, "Try to listen better" or "You've got to work on hearing what the customer is saying." The trouble with this kind of broad advice is that the salesperson doesn't know how to put it into action. Saying *listen better* is like saying *sell more*. It does nothing to help a person's performance unless you can help with the details of *how* to listen better or *how* to sell more. That's why the idea of component behaviors is so important to sales effectiveness. If you can break a broad concept like *good listening* down into its component behaviors you can communicate the *hows* of sales effectiveness. So, for example, a good listener frequently paraphrases and summarizes what the customer is saying. Paraphrasing and summarizing are two observable behaviors that are components of listening skill. They are examples of the behavioral atoms out of which effective listening is built. It's relatively easy to teach people how to summarize, because the idea is concrete, easy to communicate, and relatively easy for the learner to understand and to put into practice. In contrast, *good listening* is abstract, hard to communicate, and very difficult for people to understand and implement.

The most important single principle for improving sales effectiveness is to work at the level of the behavioral atoms. By breaking effectiveness down into small, measurable, observable, and communicable components you can define sales effectiveness in useful and actionable terms.

Defining *Behavior*

How do you discover these behavioral atoms that are so important to success? Technically, the best way is to use what researchers call *behavior-based* methods. We use the term *behavior-based* to distinguish these methods from *opinion-based* methods such as questionnaires and interviews. As we'll see, opinions on sales effectiveness, whether gathered from top performers by interview or questionnaire, can give you a misleading picture of what's really effective. Behavior-based methods, while providing much more reliable information, can be difficult even for professional researchers to work with. To the average person, they are often a total mystery. All of our readers must have filled in a questionnaire or participated in an interview. Consequently you probably have a fairly good idea of how opinion-based techniques work. But how about behavior-based methods? How would you go about finding which behaviors are associated with sales success? Your first step, in the methods we've outlined here, would be to select some behaviors to observe. That raises the question, "What do we mean by a *behavior?*" We define a behavior as an observable unit of performance. Jumping out of a window is a behavior. Asking questions, walking, eating, or cleaning your spectacles are all behaviors—an observer can see them happen, they are all visible pieces of human performance, they all involve *doing* something. Internal states, on the other hand, are not behaviors. Feeling happy is not, in itself, a behavior. You can feel perfectly happy without any sign being detectable by an observer. However, the things you may *do* when you are happy—laughing, smiling, and so forth—are behaviors; they are observable units of performance. This distinction may seem like playing word games but, as we shall see, it's crucially important to investigating and developing sales success. Ask people what behaviors a successful salesperson uses and, like the top performers we interviewed, they will probably list such things as "sincerity" or "confidence." By our definition neither of these is a behavior—but does that matter? Surely sincerity or confidence are so important to success that we shouldn't worry about whether or not they fit into our definition of a behavior. Let's take both of these qualities in turn and illustrate some of the reasons why, as they stand, they aren't much help in explaining what makes effective selling.

Sincerity?

One large computer organization we worked with used a team approach to selling so that most sales calls were carried out in pairs by a seller and a systems analyst. In one team the seller, David W., had a very clear philosophy. "I joined this corporation because it pays me best," he confided; "I don't believe in its products—they are overpriced and have no better features than the competition. I'm not interested in customers. As far as I'm concerned, I'm in this job for two years. I'm going to make a killing and move on. When I look at a customer I don't see a face, I just see my commission paycheck. I'm prepared to do or say anything which will get some fool to sign money into my pocket." His colleague Alan J., the systems analyst, had a different approach to selling. "I really believe in this company and its products," he said, "and I think we try to achieve the best for our customers. In the eight years I've been in this job, the client has always come first, and I believe that sales success depends on a real and genuine desire to help each customer."

So which of these two has the all-important quality *sincerity?* Clearly it's Alan who has been in the job eight years and earns 30 percent less than the blatantly insincere David. But when we conjecture how far sincerity has advanced Alan's career, the story takes on a curious twist. We asked customers to judge salespeople they knew, including Alan and David, on a series of items, one of which was a rating of *sincerity.* We found that the self-seeking David was judged by his customers to be much more sincere than his caring colleague Alan. Why was this? For the very reason that makes us so emphatic about the importance of behavior: customer's can't actually see sincerity—it's not a behavior. In our case study customers were judging David and Alan by their behavior, by what they could see. David was a master of the firm handshake, steady eye contact, a relaxed open posture, the concerned smile, and reassuring words. All of these things were behaviors—the customer could see them and be influenced by them. Alan, on the other hand, tended to avoid eye contact. He would sit hunched up, he would be jerky in his speech, and he would say things like, "I can't really answer that for you." In short, his behaviors gave the impression that he was concealing something—so customers judged him as insincere. The conclusions are simple. Customers judge by what they can see. They can't see sincerity, so they can only guess whether it's there by drawing conclusions from observable behaviors. Consequently a really sincere person like Alan can seem insincere, while David, by using behaviors normally associated with sincerity, can conceal his true feelings. Because customers only act on what they can see—on behaviors, in other words—the insincere David is more successful.

Confidence?

Let's apply the same thinking to another quality that is often thought of as a key to success—confidence. One of the top computer engineers in Europe was employed as a trouble-shooting specialist on a certain model. The man was a genius. He knew more about that series of computers than anybody else alive. Just by sniffing the air in a computer room he seemed able to detect when something was wrong. Other engineers in his organization greatly admired his skill and confidence. We were working with one of his customers, a major airline, and we were amazed when their data processing manager told us he thought very little of the expert engineer. "He doesn't seem to know what he's doing," he complained; "he's always saying, 'It could be this, or it could be that,' and he changes his mind a lot. He's got no confidence in his own judgment and I haven't much confidence in him." The customer was assessing confidence (and competence) from features of the engineer's behavior such as the tendency to offer alternative hypotheses to the customer. He interpreted these behaviors as a lack of confidence.

In complete contrast, one of the weakest engineers in the corporation had an outstanding reputation with customers. We had met the engineer in question. He was technically incompetent and knew it. His survival, and his success, depended on displaying a confidence to his customers that he certainly didn't feel. He would go into an installation and, from the customer's description of the fault, would say, "OK, I know exactly what's wrong," even when, as often happened, he didn't have the faintest clue. (Notice how this behavior contrasts with the expert's, when he would tend to say, "It could be x or it could be y.") He would then stride confidently to the machine and remove a panel— sometimes at random. When the fault baffled him he would go to the customer and say, "I've tracked the problem down, but so that I can get the machine operating quickly, I'll just call our specialists to see whether I can use a shortcut I've thought of."

He would then desperately call friends for advice. Returning to the computer he would nonchalantly say, "While the specialists are sorting things out I might as well do a little extra maintenance work for you." At this point the true diagnosis of the problem would often begin while the customer, believing that the engineer was just looking for extra things to do, was undismayed by the unsystematic searching and testing.

Back to Behavior

Once again we see the importance of behavior. The second engineer was judged by customers as much more confident that the first. He was trusted more and generally seen as a better engineer than one of the top experts. So when we say *confidence* is important to selling, what do we mean? We are really saying that what's important is not confidence in itself, it's the behaviors that confident people tend to show. Confidence and sincerity can't be seen—they are not behaviors. We don't suggest they are unimportant, or that you succeed better through insincerity and lack of confidence. We are saying that being sincere or being confident isn't going to help your selling unless it's translated into activities—into those observable units of performance that we call behaviors. Specific and detailed behaviors, because they can be communicated, practiced, and learned are the indispensable atoms of effective sales performance.

Component Behaviors

How do you set about defining these component behaviors, these behavioral atoms of performance? It's not easy. At one extreme, there is a very precise and scientific approach called behavior-interaction analysis. We've used this behavior analysis technique to measure effectiveness in studies of over 35,000 sales calls. Unfortunately, behavior analysis isn't the best tool for practicing sales managers. It needs large and costly observation samples and it requires specialist training and statistical interpretation. At the other extreme from the scientific measurement approach of behavior analysis, there's inspired guesswork. You can use your own experience and intuition to take a guess at what behaviors are most likely to be effective. The value of guesswork based on experience and intuition shouldn't be dismissed out of hand. Researchers like ourselves are often inclined to pour scorn on "gut feel" conclusions about sales effectiveness because they are subjective and can't be backed up with hard statistical evidence; but what's wrong with gut feel if it's based on a lifetime of successful sales experience? Surely, a sales manager who has an outstanding record of success in real world selling is likely to have a better practical understanding of sales effectiveness than any number of statistical studies.

Alas, that's just not so. Most sales managers have an alarmingly inaccurate picture of the behaviors that make up effective selling. Successful salespeople are no better. We've learned the hard way not to trust experienced people when they tell us what effective performance looks like. Before you conclude that we're just a pair of prejudiced researchers trying to bolster our own wisdom by putting down the practical experience of others, let's offer some evidence. Early in our research we were much less cynical about the insights of successful salespeople. In fact, we started our own investigations by asking dozens of top salespeople to describe what it was they did that made them so successful. We found:

- Many successful salespeople didn't have any idea at all about what was making them succeed.

- When we pressed them, they tended to describe the conventional wisdom about successful selling.

- Very little relation between what top salespeople *said* was effective and what they actually *did* when we sent researchers into the field to watch them during actual sales calls.

Top Performers Don't Know How They Do It

This lack of accurate insight isn't unique to salespeople. Very few top performers in any field can describe what it is that makes them so successful. Among the many top performers from other fields that we've questioned have been an olympic skier, an internationally famous violinist, a top football coach, and a leading actor. None of them could give us an accurate description of the specific behaviors that made them so successful in their respective professions. "Luck, I suppose," said the actor. "The right attitude," was the response from the football coach. The skier and the violinist were more helpful. They each described several specific behaviors that they had worked on over the years. The violinist, for example, told us that one of the most important component behaviors that made him effective was standing still while playing. He explained that when he was younger he "swayed from side to side like a yo-yo." It took years of self-control for him to learn to play with feeling while standing still. On the surface this sounds like a good example of a specific behavior that might be linked to effectiveness, but let's look more closely. We questioned other leading violinists and violin teachers. Their general opinion was that standing still has negligible impact on a violinist's ability. Our violinist had described a small behavior that probably has very little true relevance to effective violin playing. However, because it was a behavior he had to work on, the violinist remembered it and therefore emphasized it when describing effective performance to us. Over and over again we've seen similar cases. Good performers pick out the little extras that they have worked on. The real skills, many of which come naturally and are unnoticed by the top performers, are rarely described.

Let's apply this to sales effectiveness. We've found that when top salespeople struggle to tell us what it is that makes them succeed, they too will often pick out the things they have worked on rather than the things that are important. So, for example, we had a top performer from IBM tell us that the secret of his sales effectiveness was learning not to cough during sales calls. This outstanding salesperson, early in his career, had a little nervous cough which, he told us, irritated customers. If the customer showed signs of irritation or impatience, it made the seller even more nervous and the cough got worse. Once it became so bad that a customer offered to call a doctor. By careful practice, and through taking lessons in voice control, the salesperson learned to control the nervous cough and sales improved. Since then, he's firmly believed that developing voice control, which helped him to suppress his cough, has been the main contributor to his sales effectiveness. We were able to go with him on a number of customer calls. It's true that he didn't cough once during the time we were with him. However, we would be more inclined to ascribe his success to the superb questioning skills he showed. In this area he was one of the most outstanding salespeople we had ever observed. His use of questions was natural, smooth, and extraordinarily effective. Curiously, he didn't pick out questioning skills when we interviewed him to find his own view of what made him so effective. Once again, it was an example of how top performers pick out the things they have worked on rather than the things that they do naturally.

In our experience top salespeople rarely have accurate insight into which component behaviors are linked to sales effectiveness. How about sales managers? Do they have a more accurate or more objective picture than their best salespeople? Again, the answer is no. Most sales managers were themselves good sales performers and they suffer from all the problems we've described. What's more, managers naturally judge sales effectiveness in terms of the things they believe made them successful. If markets change, it's notoriously easy for a manager's picture of effectiveness to get dangerously out-of-date. We meet examples of this with depressing frequency in some high technology markets. Many high tech managers sold in the good old days when the task was to sell boxes and the competition was always a deadly enemy. For some of these people it's a difficult transition now that they have to manage systems selling. In today's complex systems world, for example, the competition is *not* always the enemy. You may compete against them in one account but, in another, you must work in close cooperation to interface with their equipment. We often see managers who haven't understood this change and who damagingly coach their people to sell with an "our-box-versus-theirs" mentality.

As a manager, especially if you work in a fast moving and rapidly changing industry, it's important to question the relevance of your own experience. Exactly the things that made you successful may make your people fail.

. . . And Now the Good News

This chapter is starting to sound depressing. We've said that improving sales effectiveness is the single most important task of any manager in major sales. We've also said that you can't rely on your own experience to tell you what's effective. The only alternative we've mentioned is behavior analysis research. This costs millions, takes years, and needs top level professional researchers. Hardly a practical proposition for the average manager. Aren't there some other options between these extremes? Some methods that are more objective than relying on your own experience but more practical and simpler than research? Fortunately there are.

Three Ways to Define Sales Effectiveness

We've used three different methods, or tools, for helping us to get a better understanding of sales effectiveness. Each of these tools, summarized in figure 4.1, recognizes the dangers of using personal experience and, instead, introduces a more objective way to look at effective selling. The three techniques of *Performer Analysis, Contrast Analysis,* and *Call Analysis* are ways to help you define those all-important behaviors. Let's examine each technique in more depth.

FIGURE 4.1

Tools for analyzing sales effectiveness

Tool	What it is	Especially useful when:
Performer analysis	Identifying and specifying the dimensions that differentiate **high performers** from **average performers**.	Clear performance criteria and master performers exist in a relatively stable market.
Contrast analysis	Identifying and specifying the dimensions that differentiate **present performance** from desired **future performance**.	Radical change in products, markets, or strategies dictate substantial alterations in the performance of salespeople.
Call analysis	Identifying and specifying the dimensions that differentiate **successful calls** from **unsuccessful calls.**	Success in a relatively stable market is influenced by intervening variables such as territory configuration or large but infrequent sales. Useful where performance criteria are unclear or no master performers exist.

Performer Analysis

Performer Analysis is probably the simplest of these tools for most managers to use. In common with the other two methods, Performer Analysis rests on making comparisons between the effective and the less effective. In this case, effectiveness is defined as the behaviors used by top performers. To carry out Performer Analysis, you simply watch your top performers in action and compare them with average performers. One caution here: it's generally less useful to compare top performers with low performers. That way you usually end up learning a lot more about bad performance than good. Performer Analysis depends for its success on figuring out what makes top performers different from the average.

Performer Analysis is the most useful method for defining sales effectiveness where these conditions exist:

- You can identify top performers. It's surprising how often that isn't possible. For example, you may be managing salespeople whose performance levels are all very similar, so that nobody stands out as a master performer. In this case, you can still use Performer Analysis if you have individual peo-

FIGURE 4.2
Performer Analysis

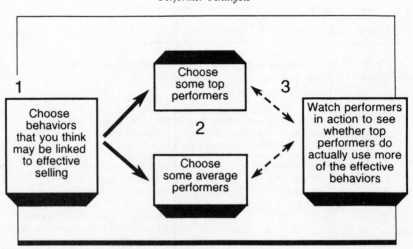

ple who are good at different parts of the sales process. If, for example, Jane makes outstanding presentations while Fred has impressive questioning skills, you can watch Jane as the master performer to help you understand effective presentations and Fred as your master performer for probing skills.

- Your future market is not facing radical change. Top performers are successful on the basis of their past performance in your existing markets. If your market is undergoing very significant change, then it can be dangerous to rely on past performance history to predict what will work in the future. In this case you would do better to use Contrast Analysis.

Preconditions for Performer Analysis

Performer Analysis compares top performers with average performers. It's the easiest of the three techniques to use. Performer Analysis works best when you have three preconditions:

- *Clear performance criteria:* Make sure you have an objective way to identify your master performers. That's not always as easy as it sounds. Sometimes, for example, salespeople can succeed more because they have good territories than because they have effective selling skills. Consequently, sales volume alone may not be enough to help you pick your top performers.
- *Master performers:* Performer Analysis is easiest if you have some individuals who stand out head and shoulders above your average salespeople. However, because outstanding salespeople are rare, you may have to choose different people for different effectiveness areas. One person, for example, may be average in terms of selling skills but can write superb proposals. Another might be very effective at using technical support. Your master performer may be a composite of several actual performers.
- *Stable markets:* Top performers are successful because they have performed effectively in your existing market. If your market is changing rapidly, so that what worked in the past isn't likely to be equally effective in the future, you may find

that Contrast Analysis is a better technique. Performer Analysis assumes that those things that make you successful right now will continue to be successful in the future.

Here are the steps for carrying out a Performer Analysis:

1. *Pick some top performers:* If possible find one or more people who are outstanding master performers. As we've noted, be particularly careful that the people you choose are successful because of their skills and not just because of good territories. Look for evidence that individuals have sold effectively in a number of different territories or have, in their present job, achieved a greater sales volume than the previous job holder.

2. *Pick some average performers:* Whatever you do, avoid comparing top performers with *poor* performers. We've seen many studies that compare high performers with low performers. Almost without exception, these studies tell you far more about bad performance than good. It's fatally easy, if you are looking at what's different between high and low performers, to end up with conclusions that tell you about what *not* to do in order to avoid poor performance. While these results can be interesting, they don't help you define the detailed behaviors that make up sales effectiveness. For example, comparisons of high and low performers usually show that high performers follow up after the call while low performers don't. What should we conclude from this? That follow-up is a characteristic of high performers? Not quite. Average performers are just as likely to follow up on their calls as are high performers. Follow-up, of itself, isn't a characteristic of high performance—but lack of follow-up *is* a characteristic of poor performance. Let's continue the example a little further. We've said that average and high performers both follow up their calls. So what's the high performer doing in follow-up that's different? By comparing *how* high performers follow up calls, we find that the high performer is more likely to follow up with *actions that advance the sale.* The average performer, for example, might telephone to thank the customer or write a letter confirming points covered during the call. In contrast, a top performer is more likely to follow up with *actions* such as arranging for a technical specialist to visit the customer, sending the customer some new information, or suggesting a date for another meeting. By comparing

top performers with average performers we discover that an action orientation is a characteristic of effective follow-up. We would have entirely missed that important point if we had compared our top performers with poor performers. We can't emphasize this point too strongly. You will always learn more by comparing your top performers with average performers.

3. *Produce a* first approximation *of the key skills:* Once you've decided on who your top performers and your average performers are, you should make a first guess at what makes the top performers different. The purpose of this first approximation is to alert you to what to look for when you actually watch your people sell. Think of your top performers. Make a list of everything they do that's different. Figure 4.3 shows an example of a typical *first approximation* list.

FIGURE 4.3
Performer Analysis—the first approximation

TOP PERFORMERS	AVERAGE PERFORMERS
• plan *questions*	• plan *presentations*
• focus on large strategic sales	• go for the quick hits
• use different strategies for different competitors	• use one strategy to cover all
• get quickly to business	• spend a lot of time in preliminary chatter
• ask questions with impact	• ask questions that have less focus and often seem to go nowhere
• hold back from giving product details early in the sale	• jump in early in the sale with product presentations / descriptions
• don't talk about our capabilities unless they are important to the customer	• 'dump' product features and capabilities on the customer
• end the call by agreeing on 'next steps' and joint action plans	• often end calls with no actions agreed

First approximations, by their nature, are broad brush descriptions. They provide a rough outline of what effective selling might look like. As the example in figure 4.3 shows, this description isn't detailed enough to use for improving sales effectiveness. So, for instance, an item such as, *questions have impact,* must be defined in much more detail to be useful. What do we mean by *impact?* What kinds of questions? In the next step of Performer Analysis we must provide the details necessary for answering questions like these.

4. *Carry Out Initial Observations:* The next step is to go out with your average and top performers to watch how they each sell in terms of the broad categories of your first approximation. While you can produce your first approximation sitting at your desk, you can only carry out this next step in the customer's office. You've got to watch your people in action. That means, among other things, keeping quiet yourself during the call—which, as we'll see in the next chapter, can prove a taxing task for some sales managers. Watch several calls with each person. You should try to answer three questions from your initial observations:

- *Do the differences in my first approximation hold up in real calls?* In our example, for instance, we said that top performers get down to business quickly while average performers spend a lot of time in preliminary chatter. Is this *really* true? By watching a few calls you may quickly decide, even though the idea of getting quickly down to business sounds plausible enough in theory, it doesn't happen that way in practice. If so, delete the item from your list. Most people who try performer analysis find that up to a third of the items from their first approximation don't hold up in real calls.

- *Are there any areas I've missed?* As you watch actual calls, you'll often find something important is going on that you hadn't even thought about when you made your first approximation. For example, you might notice that your top people are handling objections differently or that they are spending less time on technical issues. From watching calls, you may be able to add some new items to your list.

- *What behaviors are top performers using?* The most important reason for watching real calls is to help define the detailed behaviors that top performers are using. In our example, we said that top performers asked questions that had *impact.* By listening to top performers' questions, you should get a clearer idea of what *impact* means. You might find, for example, that average performers tend to ask questions about technical details while top performers ask questions about business problems. In this case, you would have an actionable behavioral definition of *impact.*

5. *Express your list in the form of specific behaviors:* From your observation of actual calls, you should now have a more precise idea of what your top performers are doing differently. "Asking questions with impact," for example, has now been reexpressed more precisely as "asking questions about customer's business problems." This behavioral list is, in effect, your definition of what sales effectiveness means. In preparing it, bear in mind that the more specific you can be, the better. It's worth noting that it isn't easy to come up with a really good list. Your first attempts will probably need to be rewritten several times and gradually improved as you become more experienced. However, the important thing is to make your first attempt. Even if you feel that the result is crude, it will almost certainly give you a more precise and accurate idea of sales effectiveness than you could get by relying solely on your own experience.

6. *Use your list to diagnose performance gaps:* Now that you have a detailed list of behaviors that define sales effectiveness, you can begin to use your list as a practical management tool. Watch your people. Ask yourself, "Which of these effective behaviors are they using? Which ones do they need to practice? Which ones should I focus on when I'm coaching them?" You'll find that the more you use a systematic procedure of this kind to define effective performance and to diagnose performance gaps, the clearer you will become about what sales effectiveness really means and how you can help your people to improve.

Contrast Analysis

Our second technique, Contrast Analysis, is a tool to use when your products, competition, customer base, or strategies are changing so much that what worked in the past is unlikely to

FIGURE 4.4
Contrast Analysis

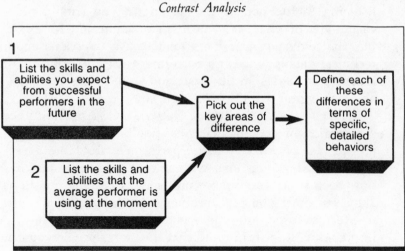

work well in the future. It compares how people have been selling up to now with how they must sell in order to succeed under the new changed conditions. For example, we found Contrast Analysis is a very useful tool in helping us understand effectiveness in a medical sales force. In the past this sales force had been selling to end-user hospital technicians. Massive changes in the health care industry meant that future decisions were likely to be made by hospital administrators not by the technicians with whom the sales force had such a comfortable relationship. Contrast Analysis let us compare the existing sale, which was technically based, with a future sale that was likely to be financially based. This difference had implications for every part of the sales cycle. For example, the financially based sale required different questions to develop needs, raised a different set of objections, and had different customer benefits.

Because Contrast Analysis is about a change which may not yet have happened, it is often hypothetical. Unlike Performer Analysis, where you are drawing conclusions from watching real people, Contrast Analysis uses a "best guess" approach. Its purpose, as we'll see later in the examples, is to focus your thinking around a change and what it means in terms of effectiveness.

When to Use Contrast Analysis

Contrast Analysis is most useful when

Master performers can't be identified: In other words, sometimes you aren't sure who your most skilled performers are. It might sound extraordinary for a sales organization not to know the ability of its own people. Yet it can happen and it's a problem we meet fairly often. Sometimes accidents of territory or history are more important than effective selling in determining sales volume. In banking and insurance, for example, it's sometimes very difficult to identify skilled performers. That's also likely to be true in organizations that are expanding fast. Years ago, we were working in Xerox during the time when it was the fastest growing major company in the world. The demand for Xerox machines was so great that the limiting factor on sales success seemed to be how quickly people could write out order forms. We had no idea of who the most skilled performers were and neither did Xerox's sales management. If you can't identify skilled performers, then you can't use Performer Analysis, so a modified form of Contrast Analysis becomes the best tool for defining effectiveness.

Markets or products are radically changing: Contrast Analysis is the best technique for defining sales effectiveness in organizations where the sales force of the future will need to behave very differently from the sales force of today. Typical examples are where the customer base is changing or where new products demand very different selling skills.

Here are the steps for carrying out a typical Contrast Analysis:

1. *List skills and abilities required in future:* The first, and probably the hardest, step in Contrast Analysis is to specify the skills that future performance will demand. It's hard partly because the details of future performance are usually unknown. For example, suppose your company is introducing a radically different product which you will be selling to a new type of customer. Although there's no way that you can know in advance *exactly* what skills will be needed to sell the new product effectively, you can make an intelligent guess—and that's what Contrast Analysis is about. We have found that Contrast Analysis is easiest to use if you define your future skills in three stages:

- Start with your best guess about how customers make the decision to acquire your future products or services.
- Next, specify the broad selling tasks that you expect salespeople to perform in order to sell the future product or service.
- Finally, take each of these selling tasks and specify the behaviors needed for a future performer to be effective in carrying out this task.

Figure 4.5 illustrates these steps in action. The product is a blood analyzer. At present, the sales force is selling lower cost items and has little experience with products of this size and complexity. In order to specify future skills, the company sales managers worked through the stages we've described:

- *Describe customer decision steps:* First, sales managers outlined the buying steps that they believed doctors would go through in acquiring a blood analyzer. Notice that these steps are specific to the medical procurement process. They mention things like AHA meetings and DRG qualifications. For Contrast Analysis to be useful, it must be specific. Avoid generic steps like *identify vendors, choose vendors,* or *make decision.* Instead, try to describe the decision process specific to your market.
- *Describe selling tasks:* Next, in this example, sales managers specified the broad selling tasks that they expected salespeople to perform in order to influence each customer decision step successfully. So, for instance, a customer decision step was, "Doctor prepares request to Hospital Capital Expenditure committee." The selling task for this step was, "Help doctor prepare initial cost justification." By describing the selling tasks in this way, managers provided a first broad description of what it would take to sell the new product, although this description was still too broad to provide workable effectiveness behaviors. Another step was needed to break the selling tasks down still further.
- *Identify effective behaviors:* In this final step, for each of these selling tasks managers specified the behaviors needed for a future performer to be effective. In this case, for example, a selling task is, "Make conference presentations. Give

FIGURE 4.5

Contrast Analysis—steps for defining future skills and abilities

Customer step in making the decision	Selling task at each step	How effective future performers will behave
doctor sees / hears about blood analyzer at AHA or AMA conference	make conference presentations, give mini-demonstrations at "vendor fairs" and medical trade shows	• make lively presentations and demos using showmanship and humor • focus on how analyzer helps doctors, not on features
doctor evaluates whether analyzer meets needs	develop needs, uncover problems analyzer can solve	• ask about problems with existing equipment • develop needs before talking about analyzer
doctor prepares request to Hospital Capital Expenditure committee or equivalent	help doctor prepare initial cost justification	• rehearse doctor in how to present justification for analyzer
committee sends out RFP to DRG qualified vendors	influence spec through hospital administrator	• visit administrator's office and influence spec *before* RFP goes out
committee interviews approved vendors meeting screening spec	present to committee showing ability to meet spec	• give presentation which specifically shows how analyzer meets or exceeds RFP criteria
committee gives approval of (usually) two vendors	differentiate our analyzer from competitors' products	• show importance of unique features which differentiate analyzer and justify its higher cost
doctor may have concerns [e.g. liability] to resolve before final purchase	reassure doctor	• draw out doctor's concerns, help doctor resolve them, take doctor to other hospitals to see analyzer in action, arrange for satisfied user to call doctor
training of technical staff	train hospital technicians	• give good technical training but also use training as an opportunity to "sell" to hospital technicians

minidemonstrations at 'vendor fairs' and medical trade shows." To turn this selling task into behavior, our managers had to ask themselves the question, *"How* will an effective salesperson give a demonstration or make a trade show presentation?" After discussion, they agreed that an effective presentation or demonstration needed, above all, to catch doctors' attention. It therefore needed to

Be *lively* or doctors would become bored and leave.

Use *showmanship* and *humor* to keep attention and stand out from competitors' presentations.

This led them to a description of effective behavior as, "make lively presentations and demos using showmanship and humor."

2. *Assess present performers in terms of these skills and abilities:* The next step in Contrast Analysis is to compare the behavior of effective future performers with the behavior of present performers. Once again, it's helpful if present performance is described by thinking of how *average* performers behave, not poor performers. Sometimes, if the existing sales force has no experience of selling in the new market, you've no way to know how the average performer would behave. In such a case you have to imagine your hypothetical average performer selling in the new marketplace. How will this person behave compared with the effective future performer? In the example in figure 4.6, we have an in-between case. The sales force hasn't yet sold the blood analyzer, so we don't know exactly how an average performer would behave selling the new product. However, we *do* know how the sales force behaves selling simpler products in a similar medical market. We can extrapolate from our knowledge of present performance to make a fair guess at how average performers will handle the new product.

3. *Identify key areas of difference between present and future performers:* As you can see from figure 4.6, present performers are behaving very differently from effective future performers. With the exception of giving good technical training to customers, which existing performers do well, there are clear performance gaps. In our example, most of these gaps are serious. Each one may be enough to damage or prevent potential sales. It's crucial for the success of the new blood analyzer for sales managers to help their people narrow these performance gaps. Let's take a particularly serious gap as an illustration. Present performers sell well only when the company has a price advantage. However, the new analyzer will be at a price premium and effective future performers must be able to justify its higher cost. This will be difficult for most of the present sales force. To increase their people's effectiveness in this area, managers must first be able to specify how effective performers justify cost.

FIGURE 4.6

Contrast Analysis—comparing present and future performance

Selling task	How effective future performers will behave	How present performers behave
give presentations & demonstrations at "vendor fairs" and medical trade shows	• make lively presentations and demos using showmanship and humor. • focus on how analyzer helps doctors, not on features	• presentations and demos give technical information • lots of features
develop needs, uncover problems analyzer can solve	• ask about problems with existing equipment. • develop needs before talking about analyzer	• pitch the product range • can't wait to "give answers" and talk about about products
help doctor prepare initial cost justification	• rehearse doctor in how to present justification for analyzer	• offer brochures and "canned" boilerplate to justify any cost issues
influence spec through hospital administrator	• visit administrator's office and influence spec *before* RFP goes out	• wait for end-user customers to make requests
present to committee showing ability to meet spec	• give presentation which specifically shows how analyzer meets or exceeds RFP criteria	• inexperienced at presenting, presentations are usually general and "canned"
differentiate our analyzer from competitors' products	• show importance of unique features which differentiate analyzer and justify its higher cost	• sell well only when we have a price advantage • unable to differentiate us from lower cost alternatives
reassure doctor	• draw out doctor's concerns, help doctor resolve them, take doctor to other hospitals to see analyzer in action, arrange for satisfied user to call doctor	• ignore difficult concerns or pretend they don't exist • say "trust me" if doctor has doubts
train hospital technicians	• give good technical training but also use training as an opportunity to "sell" to hospital technicians	• give good technical training

4. *Define each difference in terms of specific, detailed behaviors:* That brings us to the final step of Contrast Analysis. In the steps so far, we have identified broad performance gaps. Now, in order to narrow each of these gaps, we must once again get down to the level of specific behaviors. Taking the cost justification example further, we need to understand the specific behaviors that our effective future performers will use to justify the higher cost of the blood analyzer. That's not an easy task. If we had been using Performer

Analysis we could discover the behaviors of top performers by going out with them on calls. With the blood analyzer, there are not yet any performers—effective or otherwise—to observe in action. So how can the managers in this case establish the specific behaviors needed to justify the analyzer's price premium? In theory, there are several possible methods:

- They could observe people selling other products that are at a price premium and, from their own observations, identify behaviors that their people should use.

- They could rely on the work of researchers like ourselves who have studied the skills involved in selling price premium products.

- They could get together and pool their own experiences of how to justify costs of higher priced and premium priced products.

In this case, the managers chose a combination of each of these options. Another division of the company sold price premium capital goods, so they were able to watch some top salespeople in action and to talk to sales managers who had experience in cost justification. They also read books on selling which described a number of sales effectiveness models that were relevant to value-added and price premium sales. Finally, they met as a group, compared experiences, and agreed on a list of effective behaviors for justifying a price premium. Among the behaviors they chose were:

- *Postponing price discussion:* They believed that effective performers wouldn't enter into price discussions early in the sale but, instead, would deflect price issues with assurances that the price was competitive until they had built strong needs for the blood analyzer.

- *Developing needs for added value elements:* They felt that successful future performers would selectively develop needs for the special and unique capabilities of the analyzer that differentiated it from competition and justified its premium price.

- *Defining total cost:* They thought that effective performers would justify the cost by putting it in the context of total cost of carrying out tests—which included such additional elements as labor costs, repeat testing costs, and costs of doctor involvement in test interpretation. In this context, because the blood analyzer saved on labor costs, reduced repeat testing, and cut doctor involvement in interpretation, its overall cost to the hospital or doctor would be less than competing alternatives.

In this way, the managers in our case study were able to define sales effectiveness for a new product. They now had specific behaviors which let them identify performance gaps, coach their people, and begin to develop the new skills that their future market would demand.

The case we've described required considerable effort on the part of a group of managers. For them, it was worth the effort because millions of sales dollars were at stake, but can individual readers, as practical sales managers, realistically use Contrast Analysis? On the surface it sounds too elaborate and complex. Is it worth the trouble? Our answer, for both Contrast Analysis and Performer Analysis is a resounding "yes." You don't necessarily have to work at the level of detail we've described here. Suppose, for example, that you've just heard that your company will be introducing a new product that involves a different market or a different kind of customer. In less than an hour you can carry out your own first shot at a Contrast Analysis.

1. *List skills and abilities required in future:* You can draw up your own simple version of figure 4.5. Start with the steps the customer is likely to go through in making a decision to buy your new product. Next list the selling steps and how you imagine an effective future performer will handle each step. In thirty minutes you should have a first rough cut at what sales effectiveness will mean in the future.

2. *Assess present performers in terms of these skills and abilities:* Next, think of your existing salespeople. Imagine them selling the new product and describe how you think they would act. This step, shown in figure 4.6, is relatively easy and ten minute's work should give you an initial picture of how

your existing people will be likely to behave when selling the new product.

3. *Identify key areas of difference between present and future performers:* Spend a few minutes looking at the gaps between existing performance and desired future performance. It's quite possible that the gaps you'll uncover will be few and small. If so, then good. You already have salespeople who are likely to be successful with the new product. However, if you come up with some serious gaps, then Contrast Analysis will have given you advance warning of what you must do in order to sell the new product.

4. *Define each difference in terms of specific, detailed behaviors:* Whenever you have a serious performance gap, it's worth spending time thinking more deeply about exactly which new behaviors your people must learn in order to narrow the gap. We are cheating a little here. You probably won't come up with answers within our time budget of an hour; but if, through doing Contrast Analysis, you've been able to pinpoint an area that could make or break your people's success with the new product, then it's certainly going to be worth your while to invest the time needed to define effective behavior more precisely.

Contrast Analysis is most valuable if it's used *before* you get into trouble. We've often worked with sales managers who have introduced a new product or entered a new market and are not making the sales that they, or their senior management, had hoped for. It's clear that they face significant sales effectiveness problems. When we've used either Contrast Analysis or Performer Analysis to help define these problems more closely, we invariably have managers tell us, "If only we'd done this six months ago." They are right. The time to analyze effective performance is before you enter the market. Once you've introduced your product and lack of performance is hurting your results or eroding your competitive advantage, you've a lot of catching up to do. Sales effectiveness can't be built overnight. The sooner you start, the better your chances of preparing your people for the challenges of new products or new markets.

Call Analysis

We've discussed Performer Analysis and Contrast Analysis in depth because, in our experience, they have proved to be practical methods for sales managers to use to get a better and more objective definition of what sales effectiveness means in their marketplace. Our final method, Call Analysis, is more specialized. It's the chosen method of researchers like ourselves. The steps of Call Analysis are described in figure 4.7.

- First, you list some behaviors whose link to sales effectiveness you want to understand better. Suppose, for example, you want to investigate effective probing skills. You might start by listing probing behaviors such as *asking open questions, asking closed questions,* or *asking leading questions.*

- Next, you go with a variety of salespeople to customer calls. Unlike Performer Analysis, in Call Analysis it doesn't matter whether the performers you watch are good, bad, or indifferent. In general, you try to watch people with a wide range

FIGURE 4.7
Call Analysis

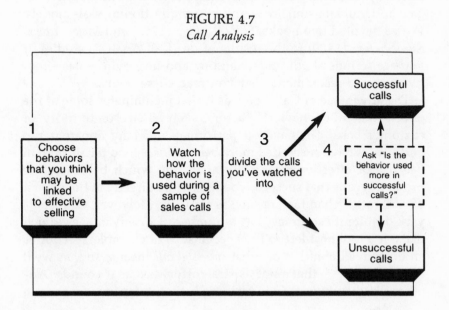

of performance and experience levels. During the calls, you count how often each of your chosen behaviors was used. You might find, for example, that in one call a seller asked seven *open questions,* fourteen *closed questions,* five *leading questions* and so on.

- At the end of the call, you decide whether the call has been successful, using some carefully designed, objective criteria for measuring call success (we discuss some call outcomes criteria in chapter 7).

- Next comes the tricky bit, which is why Call Analysis is generally best left to the researchers. You carry out statistical analysis of the call data you've collected, correlating the frequency of your chosen behaviors with the outcome of the call. That's an elaborate way of saying that you find whether successful calls show more or less of your chosen behaviors.

Using Call Analysis, researchers like ourselves have been able to challenge much of the conventional wisdom about effective selling. In one of our studies, for example, we found that contrary to popular belief, open questions were no more effective than closed questions. By using Call Analysis, we were able to investigate and validate some new and better questioning skill models. We've devoted two books, *SPIN® Selling* (1988) and *Major Account Sales Strategy* (1989) to the results of our Call Analysis studies. If you are serious about understanding and improving sales effectiveness, we recommend that you read these books.

The advantage of Call Analysis is that it eliminates some of the effects that nonbehavioral factors, such as size of territory or customer base, can have on performance. Many apparent top performers have succeeded more because of a good territory than because of effective selling. By analyzing which behaviors are present in calls that succeed, you look more directly at the impact of skill rather than factors such as territory. However, Call Analysis, despite its accuracy, has a number of disadvantages which make it a tool best left to the specialists. For example, it requires an objective definition of what *successful call* means, and, as we'll see in chapter 7, that's not as straightforward as it sounds. Another disadvantage of Call Analysis is that it depends on the use of some fairly sophisticated statistical techniques. The most serious disadvantage of all is that you may have to watch several hundred calls before you get really useful results.

Is Effectiveness Analysis Worth It?

Call Analysis requires more resources than most organizations can reasonably afford. By comparison, Performer Analysis and Contrast Analysis are simpler, but each still needs a lot of effort and thought. Is all this effort *really* worth it? Many managers we've worked with have expressed initial doubts. As one of them put it, "I can't believe that by going through this I'm going to learn something that twenty-five years of experience in major account selling hasn't taught me already. Either this Performer Analysis is some kind of magic or else I've wasted twenty-five years in the field." We've already discussed one answer to doubts like these. We've said that many top performers haven't a clue about what it is they do that's so successful. We've shown that there's a tendency for performers to emphasize little extra things where they've had to exert conscious effort rather than central mainstream skills that they may be using without even knowing. Reasons like these have led us to mistrust experience and "gut feel" as guides to sales effectiveness. The most dangerous, and the most misleading, consequence of relying on your own experience is something we've not yet mentioned. It's a rather complex phenomenon which psychologists sometimes call the "reward recency reinforcement effect." Put simply, this means that people—or even laboratory rats—will tend to use behaviors that are rewarded. If a performance requires a sequence of behaviors before the reward—for example, the laboratory rat has first to climb a ladder, turn around three times, and finally press a lever to get the reward of food—then the behavior nearest to the reward is most associated with it. The rat, for example, is much more likely to see the connection between pressing the lever and getting the reward than to see that turning around or climbing the ladder are also part of the rewarded performance.

The Reward Recency Reinforcement Effect

What on earth has this obscure discovery about laboratory rats to do with effective selling? Much more than you might think. We're not suggesting that salespeople behave exactly like laboratory rats, although many we've worked with fervently believe that they are treated like rats in a maze by their own sales organizations. What we *are* suggesting is that salespeople, like people in general, put too much value on behaviors that are nearest to the reward. In fact, we can quote one dramatic case of this "reward recency reinforcement effect" that has led to the waste of hundreds of millions of dollars in sales training and has seriously damaged the effectiveness of hundreds of thousands of salespeople.

Rewarded Behaviors Are Overvalued

Our case involves an area near and dear to the heart of most sales managers—closing. In the opinion of many managers, closing behaviors have a strong claim to being the most important of all sales effectiveness components. Survey after survey of sales training needs show managers reporting that the single most important training need of their people is to improve their closing skills. The importance given to closing can be seen from the space it takes up in books and articles about sales techniques and the millions of dollars sales organizations spend each year teaching their people how to close. Contrary to this emphasis, research shows convincingly that, in larger sales at least, the use of closing techniques is negatively related to success. That's another way to say that the more salespeople use closing techniques, the less likely they will be to make the sale. In our book *SPIN® Selling,* we describe a dozen detailed research studies that show this is so beyond a reasonable doubt. In one study, for example, people's orders *fell* after they had been trained in closing. In another, an analysis of the most successful people in a sales force found that they used fewer closing techniques than their less successful colleagues. Yet another study showed that calls where a lot of closing behaviors were used had a lower success rate than calls where fewer closes were used. During the last five years almost every research study on closing has concluded that classic closing techniques such as the assumptive close, alternative close, or last chance close only work, if at all, in small one-off sales. If you have doubts, please read the research and review the evidence for yourself.

We wouldn't blame you for doubting our claim that closing behaviors are ineffective. After all, can 10,000 sales training programs be wrong? It doesn't seem likely that the majority of sales organizations today are spending good money on expensive closing training if all it's doing is making their people less effective. Unfortunately, that's the reality. Most classic advice on closing doesn't work and actually damages the effectiveness of people who try to follow it. The reason why so many organizations and individuals stubbornly waste millions clinging to these ineffective behaviors is the "reward recency reinforcement effect" that we described earlier.

Let's explain how this effect is relevant to closing by quoting a personal example of how the effectiveness of behavior nearest the reward can become overemphasized.

I had an appointment with a potential client with whom I'd been talking for several months in an attempt to sell a research project. I decided to try an Alternative Close. I'll never forget the result. "Would you prefer the project to begin in September or in November?" I asked, a little nervously. "Let's start in September," my client answered—and I got my first big sale. I said the magic words and was rewarded with an order. For more than a year after my first success, I closed the hell out of everyone. Like so many other salespeople before me, because my close was rewarded with an order, I'd somehow assumed that using the close had caused the order. Of course, from what I now know, it was the way I'd developed my client's needs that brought me the business. It had nothing to do with my close.*

This is a typical example of the "reward recency reinforcement effect." Most effective sales behaviors are not directly rewarded

*Neil Rackham, *Making Major Sales* (Aldershot: Gower Publishing Co. Ltd., 1987).

by the customer. Good questions early in the selling cycle, for instance, lay the essential groundwork that leads ultimately to an order. Even though penetrating questions may be important component behaviors of sales effectiveness, customers don't usually reward them by signing an order. It may be months before the value of those questions is translated into any tangible reward. However, because closing behaviors are sometimes immediately followed by an order, as in this case, the salesperson easily assumes that the close has been effective in causing the order.

What does this mean when it comes to defining sales effectiveness? Once again, it shows that we can't rely totally on our experience. We tend to put undue emphasis on those behaviors that happen nearest the order. That doesn't only apply to closing techniques. The area of negotiation would provide another good example. Many sales managers have told us that negotiating skills are crucial to sales effectiveness in the major sale, and they firmly believe that the ability to negotiate well is the most important single skill for getting the business. When we have researched their salespeople in action, we have found that the outcomes of most sales negotiations are determined long before negotiation begins. A salesperson who, for example, has done an outstanding job of developing customer needs will usually have to make fewer concessions during final negotiation. In contrast, even brilliant sales negotiators rarely succeed if they have done a poor job during the earlier selling stages of the cycle. There are strong arguments to suggest that, in most major sales, negotiating skills are much less important to success than selling skills. Why do so many sales managers believe the opposite? Because negotiation is often rewarded with a signed contract. Consequently, as we tend to put more emphasis on rewarded behaviors, we give negotiating skills more importance than they deserve. Effective selling early in the cycle, that has made a successful negotiation possible, has no such reward and is therefore easily undervalued. We are constantly reminded of this when we design and run sales training programs. Usually, in our programs, we put heavy emphasis on those bedrock skills from early in the sale that include effective questioning. Frequently, we'll design role plays where the objective is just to ask good questions. It's surprising how often salespeople—even sophisticated ones—feel cheated when the role play focuses on using questions to uncover and develop customer needs and doesn't include either pitching products or closing. "When are you going to let us *sell?*" is a frequent complaint.

Putting Sales Effectiveness into Action

We started this chapter with the premise that your most important single function as a sales manager in major sales is to improve sales effectiveness. In order to do this, you must begin by defining what you mean by sales effectiveness. We showed that it's often dangerous and misleading to rely on your own experience. Instead we suggested some more precise, and more objective, methods for defining sales effectiveness. Performer Analysis involves comparing top performers with average performers. It's particularly useful where you have clearly identifiable top performers and a stable market. The other technique, Contrast Analysis, is most useful when your objective is to define what sales effectiveness means in a new market or with a new product. Either of these techniques can be used by individual sales managers, or by groups of managers, to help them define sales effectiveness.

The next question is, once you've defined sales effectiveness, what do you do with your definition? How do you turn your picture of effective selling into positive sales results? That's where coaching comes in. And that's what the next two chapters are all about.

5

BUILDING EFFECTIVE SALES PERFORMANCE

The Manager as a Strategy Coach

We were working with the sales management of a large food and beverage conglomerate, helping them design a new performance appraisal system for sales supervisors. The discussion turned to whether the appraisal system should encourage coaching efforts. We had expected an easy consensus on the importance of coaching. The only issue, we thought, would be how best to reward it. We were in for a surprise. "Wait a minute," said our sponsor; "I'm not sure we should be putting all this effort into coaching." There was a murmur of agreement from around the table. "Coaching's fine in theory," explained one manager, "but I've never seen it work well in practice." "I used to be with Citicorp," another told us, "and every couple of years we rediscovered coaching and we retrained all our managers. I had people working for me who had been through four different coaching programs. I'm not sure it did any good to them or to their people." Another manager added, "I don't think that coaching is something you can learn. Some of our supervisors will never be able to coach. If they try they'll just do damage. I don't want an appraisal system that forces people to put energy into an area where they'll fail." Needless to say, comments like these were bad news. Try as we might, we couldn't convince these practical and experienced sales managers to put real effort into encouraging coaching. In the end our attempts were defeated by a compelling argument advanced by one of the group. "The purpose of coaching is to make people sell better, isn't it?" he asked. "Yes," we conceded. "Then," he continued, "why don't we forget about the supervisors and go straight to the salespeople? We can bring in some experts to give them sales training. It would be quicker, cheaper, and more effective than expecting our supervisors to coach." The others agreed. It was a simple solution. We couldn't convince them it was wrong.

Training Versus Coaching

In one form or another, similar discussions take place periodically in most major sales organizations. Managers argue about whether coaching is a practical reality. Typically, they decide that:

- Coaching is difficult for us to implement.
- Our managers don't want to coach.
- We tried coaching once before and it didn't work.
- Sales training is a simpler way to improve our sales effectiveness.

Unfortunately, these are all valid points. Coaching *is* hard to implement. Managers are usually reluctant to adopt coaching on a systematic basis, pleading lack of time or alternative priorities. Attempts to introduce coaching in most organizations have met with failure or, at best, only with partial and patchy success. And, finally, sales training *is* unquestionably easier and simpler. So why, in the face of all these practical difficulties, do we persist in our firm belief that coaching is the single most important management tool for improving sales effectiveness?

The Pivotal Job

There's probably no single group on earth that knows quite so much about what makes organizations tick than the management consultants McKinsey & Company. Among the useful frameworks they have developed for thinking about what it takes to get improved performance from an organization is the concept of the "pivotal job." In any major function that's organized as a classic management hierarchy, such as the average sales function, McKinsey argues that there is usually one particular level—or one particular job—that has greater influence on performance than any other. They call this the pivotal job. By influencing how the pivotal job is performed, it's possible to have a real impact on the performance of the whole function. Conversely, if you don't influence the performance of pivotal jobholders, then your chances of improving overall organizational performance are slight. In most sales organizations concerned with larger sales, the pivotal jobholders are the first line sales managers. No other level of management has so direct or so profound an influence on sales effectiveness. As we argued in chapter 2, senior management can easily influence sales *efficiency* through policy decisions and systems; but sales effectiveness can't be so easily influenced by senior levels remote from the day-to-day interaction with the customer. To improve sales effectiveness, the pivotal job is the immediate sales manager and the key management tool is coaching. In our experience, sales organizations too often ignore this pivotal job. At the bottom of the hierarchy, they put resources into training their salespeople. At the top, they send senior management off to executive programs or business schools. However, all too commonly, pivotal jobholders receive very little training or help. In most of the sales organizations we've worked with, by far the greatest return on investment has come from working at the pivotal job level of the immediate sales manager or supervisor. By improving managers' coaching skills, we've been able to bring about consistent increases in sales volume that can't be achieved through sales training alone. That's a practical reason why we encourage our clients to focus on their managers rather than on their salespeople.

Why Sales Training Fails

There's another equally practical reason for our focus on sales managers rather than salespeople. In the late 1970s we carried out an evaluation study of sales training in Xerox Corporation. We wanted to answer a question that had been troubling us for some time. We had developed techniques for measuring how much improvement in skill was brought about by sales training. What we *didn't* know was what would happen after the training was over and salespeople went back into the field. Would skills improve even further once salespeople had an opportunity to practice in real calls? If that was the case, skill improvement on the job should be even greater than the levels we recorded during training. But what if the improvements we were getting from training didn't carry over to the job completely? Was it possible that salespeople learned new skills in the classroom but that these skills didn't transfer back into the real world? This was a vital question for training designers like ourselves and equally important to Xerox Corporation, which at the time, was spending upwards of $15 million a year on sales training without very much evidence of the results training was bringing them. By establishing the degree of carryover from classroom to the job, we hoped to get a better handle on the effectiveness of sales training in Xerox. The results, illustrated in figure 5.1 stunned us. Our study showed that, on average, training suffered an 87 percent loss of skill within one month. We reasoned that if a corporation such as Xerox, which was generally recognized during the seventies for the excellence of its sales training, was losing 87 percent of selling skills, then other corporations might well be losing even more. It was the thought of wasting 87 cents of every skills training dollar that convinced us that selling skills training might not be an adequate answer to sales effectiveness problems. However, closer investigation showed an interesting exception in our Xerox data. Although their was an *average* loss of 87 percent, some salespeople showed a much smaller loss and some even showed a skill *gain*. We investigated these exceptions and found that in most cases where skills actually improved, managers had been involved in systematically coaching the skills immediately following the training. With moderate manager involvement in coaching, the skill loss could be greatly reduced. Once again, the evidence pointed to the importance of coaching in improving sales effectiveness.

FIGURE 5.1
Sales training without systematic coaching wastes 87 cents in the dollar

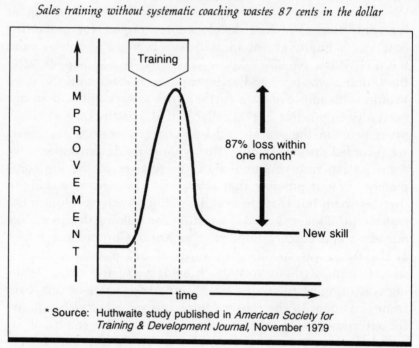

* Source: Huthwaite study published in *American Society for Training & Development Journal*, November 1979

Barriers to Coaching

If coaching really is the vital sales effectiveness tool that we're claiming, then why have so many companies had such difficulty making coaching work in practice? Usually sales organizations are hungry for tools that will make them more effective. Coaching seems a natural candidate for easy acceptance and implementation. It seems strange that so few organizations have successfully put sales coaching into practice. We've found that a number of reasons for the lack of effective and systematic coaching crop up again and again in the sales organizations where we've worked. Among the most common are

- Competing pressures
- Inadequate models
- Fear of coaching
- Lack of reward or reinforcement

These barriers exist in most sales organizations. They are probably there in yours too, so it's worth spending a little time looking at each barrier and how to overcome it.

Competing Pressures

Coaching receives great lip service in many sales organizations. Even motherhood and applie pie don't get better press. We remember one national sales manager we worked with who had a standard speech in praise of coaching that said things like, "Coaching is the mortar that holds us together. Without good coaching the sales function would fall apart. There's nothing I value in my sales managers more than coaching skill." It's not that this speech was insincere. On the contrary, the national sales manager believed every single word of it; but when we worked with his managers, we found that little or no coaching was actually taking place. The reason wasn't hard to find. "Coaching doesn't have to be done by Friday," one manager told us, "so I just put it off until next week. On the other hand, I've a pile of reports here that *must* be done before I leave tonight. If I don't complete this one, my people won't get paid. The one here has to be done before we can bill the customer. If I don't finish this one, then an installation will fall behind schedule. There are things on my desk that I could be fired for if I don't finish them this week. I'll get around to coaching next week when things are a little quieter." Of course, when next week comes, it never turns out to be any quieter. As a result, because coaching doesn't have to be done by Friday, it will be put off for ever.

The sad truth, in most sales functions, is that short-term competing pressures—the things that have to be done by Friday—invariably squeeze out coaching. However much lip service coaching receives, it's unlikely to become a practical reality if business pressures daily demonstrate that coaching is low on the list of real priorities. How can the barrier of competing pressures be overcome? Certainly not by pious words and exhortations. Top sales management has to demonstrate that coaching is important. That means building a coaching responsibility into sales managers' objectives and making coaching activity part of the appraisal and reward system. In the last few years a number of significant sales organizations have begun to do this. IBM, for example, now sets a target for Marketing Managers (IBM's term for first-line sales managers) to spend 70 percent of their time in the field traveling with their people and coaching them.

But target setting alone isn't enough. For coaching to rise above competing pressures it needs to become part of the management reward system. Few organizations reward their managers for coaching. That's in part because it's hard to measure effective coaching. However, unless a sales organization cares enough about coaching to find a way to reward managers for it, then it's unlikely that coaching will ever have enough priority to withstand all the competing things that have to be done by Friday.

One way to help coaching survive competing pressures is to build a systematic and structured coaching process. When we are helping organizations to improve sales performance, an early step in our work is to introduce systematic coaching. However, it doesn't require outside consultants like ourselves to build an effective coaching process. The typical basic steps for setting up a workable coaching process are:

- Bring sales managers together, teach them coaching skills, and obtain their commitment to putting the coaching into practice.

- Ask each manager to choose a limited number of salespeople to coach. As the intention of the coaching process is to help counter competing priorities, it's better that a manager realistically finds the time to coach two or three people well than to have an unrealistic intention of finding enough time to coach the whole team.

- Help managers to set coaching goals in terms of the number of coaching calls or strategy coaching discussions they will make with each salesperson and what sorts of skills they will be trying to develop in each call.

- Meet with the managers monthly to review progress, discuss difficult cases, and reinforce the coaching process.

These methods for countering competing pressures are all at an organizational level. What can an individual sales manager do to drain the swamp when the alligators of alternative priorities are snapping away at every exposed portion of the managerial anatomy? Many sales managers feel totally powerless to resist the competing pressures of all the things that must be done by Friday. It's more comfortable to let coaching remain just a good intention. Although it's admittedly easier to tackle the issues of competing priorities on an organizational level, it is nevertheless possible for a determined sales manager to control competing priorities and to make effective coaching happen. Let's take a case study. The sales manager in question works for a large bank.

One of the problems in our bank—and I suppose in other banks too—is that there really are a lot of very urgent things for a manager to see to. You've got loan applications, for example, where the customer's whole business may depend on whether you can steer the paperwork through the loan committee in time. There's always a crisis or a rush. As a result, I'd been in the job for a year and never got around to coaching. When I thought about this it was crazy. My people, like most bankers, weren't great at selling. I didn't get time to coach them, so they didn't get any better. As a result I was doing most of the important selling—and that made the time crunch even worse. I knew I ought to be coaching but I was working 60 hours a week and there just wasn't time. Anyway, I went to my boss to ask for an assistant so that I could make some time for coaching my people. She didn't buy the idea. We're very conscious of overhead and she felt she couldn't sell it to the Head of Division. So I decided to try a different approach. I took one of my younger people who was an average performer but who was very anxious to learn. Even though it required a lot of extra effort, I worked with him for three months. I coached him, I helped him with strategy, and I did everything I knew how to help him improve. At first results were slow, but after about three months, he began to do better and soon became my top performer. Then I went back to my boss with the figures. She was impressed. "If only I had time to do the same with my other people," I said. Within a week, she'd found a way to take some of my routine load away. I didn't get the assistant but I *did* get enough time to work on coaching two other people. As people's selling got better, it took away some of the pressure on me to sell, so that gave me additional time. I guess I now spend 25 to 30 percent of my time in coaching.

This little case study illustrates three important principles for how an individual manager can fight against competing pressure. In many other cases where we've seen individual managers implement coaching successfully, the same three principles are present:

- *Don't spread yourself too thin as a coach:* If you have limited time, it's invariably more effective to coach one person well than to half coach two people.
- *Build a success story:* If you hope to win more time, you and your management need to be sure that the coaching effort will bring results. There's nothing that persuades better than a success story. It helps convince management to control competing pressures, it strengthens your own conviction that coaching brings results, and last but not least, a success story makes your other salespeople receptive to coaching.
- *Sell your story:* If you have a coaching success, use it. Figures, of course, are powerful tools for selling the results of coaching, but anecdotes and testimonials from people you've coached can be powerful too. If you have a success story, don't keep it quiet. Use it to help you get you the resources you need to create the right conditions for further coaching successes.

Inadequate Models

Although competing pressures may be the most common barrier that prevents coaching, there's no guarantee that coaching will succeed just because competing pressures are controlled or removed. We recall working with one national sales manager who was so determined to make coaching succeed that he split the sales manager job into two. One of the new jobs, administrative sales manager, was responsible for all paperwork, order processing, progress chasing, and the like. The second job, called field sales manager, was *solely* responsible for coaching and developing salespeople. To underline the point that field sales managers were supposed to spend 90 percent of their time traveling with sales-people, none of the field sales managers had offices of their own. It was the most determined attempt to control competing pressures that we'd ever seen. Despite all this, field sales managers spent little time actually coaching. True, they *did* travel with their people, but they spent their time selling, not coaching. Thinking that they might lack coaching skills, the national sales manager sent them on coaching programs. Even after training, they seemed reluctant to coach. It was at this point that we were called in. Interviews with the field sales managers soon revealed a significant problem. The managers didn't have a clear idea of what it took to make a successful sales call. "What am I supposed to say when I coach?" one of them complained. "I watch a sale and often I don't know why it succeeded or failed. Was it the way the rep handled objections? Was it product knowledge? Or just chemistry? I don't know." Other field sales managers had similar problems. As we said in the last chapter, you can't improve sales effectiveness unless you know what a successful sales call looks like. Put more technically, these managers didn't have an adequate performance model. They didn't know what to look for and they didn't know which behaviors to develop. No wonder they felt more comfortable using calls to sell rather than to coach.

In the last chapter we described some methods for developing models of effective performance—frameworks for understanding what skilled performance looks like in terms of detailed sales behavior. Contrast Analysis and Performer Analysis are the easiest of these methods to use. There's also an increasing amount of published material from researchers like ourselves that you can tap into. However you do it, it's important to build an accurate and detailed picture of how your people must behave in order to sell effectively. Without such a picture, coaching becomes almost impossible. Why is an effectiveness model so important to coaching? Because a good model provides:

- *Common language:* A good model gives the basis of a common language that lets manager and seller communicate quickly and meaningfully about effective selling. Most world class sales organizations have developed a common language that everybody in sales understands and uses to describe what goes on during sales calls. This shared sales jargon provides a shorthand that makes it much easier for people to discuss experiences. Without a common language, coaching can be an uphill struggle.

- *Diagnosis:* If a manager has a clear picture of effective behavior it becomes much easier to diagnose the strengths and weaknesses of individual salespeople. A good model alerts a manager to those behaviors that are most important for sales effectiveness. In the last chapter, we said that an effectiveness model must describe the specific and detailed behaviors that successful people use. It's this specificity that makes a model so useful for diagnosis. A good effectiveness model lets the coach pinpoint which skills and behaviors need to be developed through coaching. Conversely, without a success model, it's hard to diagnose which behaviors salespeople need to improve.

How can you ensure that you are working from an adequate model? The last few years have seen some extraordinary advances in the development of better effectiveness models. Older models that have been part of selling since the 1920s—using concepts like open and closed questions or classic closing and objection handling techniques—have given way to more sophisticated models of effective behavior. If you don't have the resources or the inclination to produce your own models using Contrast or Performer Analysis, then be sure to read a wide selection of recently published books on selling. Above all, use your eyes and ears when you travel with your salespeople. Watch for things that work—and for things that fail. A simple definition of an effectiveness model is that it's a list of behaviors that work. Use your powers of observation to find what works for your people and in your markets. That's the first step to becoming a good sales coach.

Fear of Coaching

Strange as it may sound, one of the most common barriers to coaching is fear. Many managers are afraid to coach. It's not the kind of fear that causes sleepless nights and sweaty palms. No, it's something more insidious. It's a kind of uncertainty that can creep up unnoticed behind even the most self-confident sales manager. In one major bank we interviewed managers to find why they were not coaching their people. Typical *fear* replies included, "I was reluctant to try it in case I couldn't think of anything useful to say," "I didn't want to look like an idiot to my experienced people," and "It wasn't worth trying because I knew it would create more resistance than I could handle."

If coaching hasn't been part of a manager's activities from day one, it can be difficult to make a start. Salespeople won't know what to expect, and while coaching is usually welcomed once it gets underway, it's true that there may be some initial resistance. What's more, skills coaching involves watching salespeople actually sell, and that has to take place in front of customers—which can be unsettling for both manager and seller. It's easy to see how reluctance can slowly turn to fear.

Fortunately, this fear is one of the easier coaching barriers to overcome. Coaching training can help, but here we must put in a special plea. When we train coaches we always try to use training designs where a manager's salespeople attend the training program and, during it, are intensively coached by the manager. As a result, by the end of the program, a coaching relationship has been started and both parties know what to expect from coaching. This makes it far easier for coaching to carry over to the real world. Why, oh why, do so many coaching programs train managers alone and in isolation from their salespeople? Coaching is an interaction between two people. It shouldn't require an Einstein of the training world to figure out that the interaction will be more effective, and learning will be better, if both parties are trained together. It's a mistake to give managers coaching training in one room, give their people sales training in another, and then hope that somehow the two will magically combine their respective training into an effective performance out in the real world. We've had great success with program designs that combine sales and coaching training. Although these programs are more difficult to design than conventional training, their superior results unquestionably justify the effort involved.

If, as a manager, you feel nervous or reluctant about handling your role as a coach, there are several simple and effective things you can do to make coaching easier.

- Start coaching with just one person—and choose someone who you know will be receptive.
- Before you go out to coach on real calls, get some practice by coaching in role plays during team meetings.
- Don't see yourself as an evaluator or a judge when you coach. Instead, think of yourself as someone who is there to help. Help plan the call as well as helping to review and critique it.

Simple measures like these can help individual managers overcome the potentially awkward barrier of reluctance to coach.

Lack of Reward or Reinforcement

The final barrier that we see in many organizations is one that the individual manager can't do much about. One of the reasons why coaching doesn't happen is that, in most organizations, managers get little or no encouragement to coach from their own senior management. The message that coaching deserves nothing beyond lip service comes in a variety of ways. One that we've already discussed is the problem of competing pressures. Another is the organization's reward system. It's unusual to find a company that actively recognizes coaching by payment or job advancement. Failure to reward coaching doesn't necessarily mean that an organization has decided coaching is unimportant. Often, the lack of financial or career reward for coaching reflects senior management's uncertainty about how to measure the quality of any coaching that is taking place. As the national sales manager of a telecommunications company once explained to us, "I'd certainly like my managers to do a better job of coaching and I recognize that the obvious thing to do is to compensate them for their coaching efforts. But that's harder than it sounds. How can I tell whether a manager is doing a good coaching job? One way is through the performance of salespeople—but I reward my managers for that already. I don't want to pay just for quantity of coaching because that wouldn't work here. Suppose, for example, I gave a bonus of $50 for every time a manager coached a sales rep. You know what would happen? There would be a whole lot of coaching reported. At least three quarters of it would be fake and I'd have no way of knowing how well the other quarter was carried out." We've heard similar concerns from many top managers when they think about whether to offer financial rewards for coaching efforts.

If it's difficult for management to financially reward coaching, there are alternative ways for an organization to make coaching happen. It's possible to *reinforce* coaching even if it's hard to reward it directly. For example:

- *Make coaching part of performance appraisal:* By including coaching as part of the performance appraisal system, management can make a statement about its importance and ensure that it gets discussed during performance reviews. Frankly, we'd like more than just discussion. When it comes to coaching, we like to see performance appraisals with teeth. Consequently, we approve of those organizations that put a notional percentage of salary review on each performance area so that, for example, 20 percent of a manager's salary increase is determined by how well the manager has coached. Even though it's hard to determine the quality of coaching objectively, it's worth having a less than perfect assessment if it encourages managers to coach.

- *Use peer groups and coaching projects:* We have been able to reinforce coaching by bringing managers together in groups and creating coaching projects. Typically, we work with a group of managers, helping them set coaching objectives and targets. We then meet periodically with the managers to review progress. At these meetings we encourage managers to share their success stories as well as their problems. There's nothing magic about this and most organizations could set up coaching projects without the help of outsiders like ourselves. Incidentally, another plus of setting up a coaching project is that the managers can play a part in building effectiveness models by working together to carry out Performer or Contrast Analysis. In this way, the organization develops better models of sales effectiveness and managers take real ownership for implementing the models they have helped develop.

- *Encourage coaching efforts:* There are many other ways in which management can actively and creatively encourage more and better coaching. For example, we once worked with an airline that set up a "Coach of the Month" competition. To select the Coach of the Month, salespeople were asked to submit examples of how a manager had helped them learn to sell better. A jury of salespeople, chaired by a regional sales manager, reviewed the entries and decided on the winner. Every three months there was a cash prize for the Coach of the Quarter and at the end of the year there was a Coach of the Year award where both the winning manager and the manager's salespeople were given a substantial prize.

The organizational barriers to coaching that we've described here help explain why coaching so often fails to be implemented successfully. However, it's also clear that a determined sales management—or even a determined individual manager—can overcome most of these barriers and create conditions where coaching can potentially make a significant contribution to sales effectiveness. We say "potentially" because, even with all organizational barriers removed, there are still some other issues that must be faced before effective coaching can become a practical reality.

Once Again—Small Sales Versus Large

One of these issues brings us right back to a central theme of this book. Large sales are different from small. Not surprisingly, coaching in large sales reflects that difference in several important respects. We've seen many managers who, working in small sales, were excellent at improving their people's effectiveness through coaching. Some of these same managers met problems coaching in larger sales because they continued to use the methods that had worked well for them in smaller sales. The first time that we realized what a trap this could be came as a result of a research study of effective coaching we carried out for Honeywell. One sales manager we worked with had previously managed a team in a division that sold relatively low value residential control systems—a fairly typical small sale. He came to our attention because his management had picked him out as an outstandingly successful coach. Talking to his people confirmed his reputation. "An outstanding coach," one of them told us; "I've learned more from him in the three months he's been here than I learned in two years under my last manager." There were also objective sales figures to confirm his success. In the three months he'd worked with his team, they had risen from below average sales volume to become the second highest performers in the whole division. Because of this, we were surprised two years later when the manager called us. "I moved last year to another division," he told us, "and now I'm selling large industrial control systems. I thought I'd have an easy time because I remember you saying that coaching skills were the key to being a successful manager in large sales. And, as you know, I seemed to be a good coach. But things have gone wrong. My coaching doesn't seem to have the impact it did before." At the time, we didn't have an answer for him, but his difficulty set us thinking. In the months that followed we came across several similar cases. Each time, a successful coach in small sales was finding that his or her coaching skills didn't work as well in larger sales.

Why was this? What was so different about coaching in major sales? Could it be that coaching was less important to success in larger sales? We didn't think so. Everything we knew about larger sales suggested that coaching was *more* important. So why were these coaches failing? The reason, we concluded, was that larger sales required a different sort of coaching. The obvious difference, which we've already discussed in earlier chapters, is that different behaviors are effective in larger sales. A manager who, for example, coaches people in closing and objection handling techniques, may be much more successful in small sales because it's in small sales that these techniques work best. Conversely, coaching in sophisticated probing skills might be very successful in large sales but might be overkill in small sales where these skills are less important. At first we were entirely satisfied with this explanation. We told clients that the only real difference between coaching in small and large sales was that the coach in large sales had to emphasize different and more complex selling skills. However, through working closely with coaching in major sales for many years, we've come to see that there are other equally significant differences. Three of these are particularly important.

- *Experience or coaching?* In small sales, it's relatively easy for salespeople to improve their performance through selling experience alone without the help of coaching. In larger sales, it's much more difficult for people to learn from experience alone. Coaching therefore plays a more crucial role in learning to be successful in larger sales.
- *Reviewing or planning?* In small sales, the most important task of the coach is *reviewing*—critiquing the skills used by the seller during the call. In larger sales, the most important task is *planning*—helping the seller prepare for the call.
- *Skills or strategy?* In small sales, coaching succeeds by developing *skills*. In large sales, coaching must develop *skills* and *strategy*.

Let's examine each of these differences in more depth.

Experience or Coaching?

We've said that it's easier to learn from experience in small sales than in large. The evidence shows that in small sales it's possible to learn from experience alone without coaching. We carried out a study of sales performance in a division of Xerox Corporation that sold small copiers. We found a strong positive correlation between tenure and sales results. That's another way to say that as people got more experienced, they learned to sell better, whether or not they were coached. That's not to suggest that coaching didn't help learning. In these small Xerox sales, we found that there was also a correlation between people's results and whether they had been coached. However, the correlation between coaching and results was much lower than the correlation between experience and results. We could conclude that experience was the better teacher. In a similar study in a division of Xerox that sold large copier systems, the correlations were the other way around. We found a much lower correlation between length of sales experience and success. A better predictor of success was whether salespeople had been systematically coached. Why should experience be a better predictor of success in smaller sales and coaching be better in larger sales? Because in small sales it's much easier to learn from experience. Take an extreme case of a very small sale where the average seller may be making twenty sales calls each day. That gives twenty opportunities to learn from experience—ten times the opportunities that typically exist in the large sale where few salespeople average above two sales calls per day. Even more important is the fact that in the smaller sale there's minimal time lag between behavior and results. I change my selling style this morning, and by lunchtime, I may have ten customers who have given me feedback in the form of orders to let me know whether my new behavior works. In contrast, it may be a year or more before I see a link between behavior and results in a larger sale. These two factors—number of opportunities and immediacy of feedback—explain why it's so much harder to learn from experience in larger sales. Unfortunately, in large sales, experience is a very confusing and inadequate guide to success. That's why coaching is so important. Good coaching helps salespeople make sense out of their experience. It provides feedback to substitute for the daily results of the small sale. While we emphasize to managers that coaching is an important tool for building sales effectiveness even in small sales, we stress that it is vital in large ones.

Reviewing or Planning?

In small sales, the classic form of skills coaching is the "curbside conference"—a discussion between manager and seller after the call, to review it, decide what went well, what went badly, and what needs to be worked on by the seller in future calls.

This kind of skills coaching is a two-step process, illustrated in figure 5.2. The steps are:

- *Doing:* where the coach observes the seller's performance during the call

FIGURE 5.2

The "curbside conference"

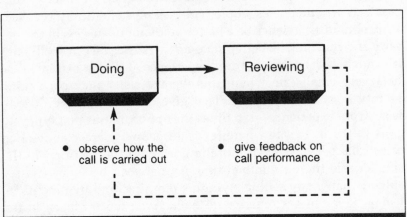

- *Reviewing:* where the coach gives feedback to the seller, discusses how the call was executed, and agrees to any improvements the seller needs to make

The principal emphasis of this simple model is on *reviewing.* In fact, many organizations prefer to use terms like *call reviews* or *call evaluations* rather than using the term *coaching.* The typical coaching sequence in the small sale is a serious of Doing → Reviewing → Doing → Reviewing steps as the coach accompanies the seller on a series of calls. Planning rarely comes into the picture. We recall one coach who insisted that he spent time in planning. "What points do you cover when you plan?" we asked. "We discuss how the rep will explain to the customer what I'm doing there," the coach replied. "What else?" we asked. The coach thought for a moment. Then he said, "Well, I sometimes have an anxiety attack in the elevator as we go up to a customer's office—I suppose you could call that planning."

Moments of anxiety may be viable substitutes for planning in small sales but certainly not in large. This is an important difference. In large sales the coaching emphasis moves away from reviewing and towards planning. Coaching looks more like the model illustrated in figure 5.3.

The good coach, in major sales, puts a very heavy emphasis on

FIGURE 5.3
Skills coaching in major sales

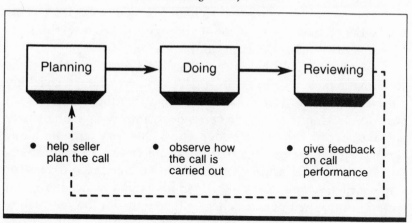

the planning process. In place of the Doing → Reviewing cycle so characteristic of small sale coaching, the effective large sale coach uses the full cycle of PLANNING → Doing → Reviewing. The planning component not only directly makes for a better call, it also leads to a greater clarity of purpose in the call which makes both doing and reviewing easier. When we're working with managers to improve coaching skills, we invariably find that in larger sales an increased emphasis on the planning aspects of coaching results in a much improved coaching performance.

Skills or Strategy?

The final difference between coaching in small and large sales is an important issue of emphasis. In small one-call sales, there's little need for strategy beyond the tactical issue of how an individual call will be handled. In large sales, however, each call must be seen in the larger context of an account strategy. Coaching has to reflect this difference. In small sales it's possible to be an excellent coach with little or no attention to strategy. Our manager from Honeywell was a good example. When he was selling lower value products in the residential market, his coaching focused on helping his people handle individual calls more skillfully. As the sales figures showed, this was a very effective approach. When he became a manager responsible for selling multi-million dollar industrial control systems, the individual call was no longer enough. He needed to help his people see their skills in a wider framework of account strategy. As he correctly diagnosed, skills coaching was no longer enough.

However, it would be an oversimplification to say that skills coaching is most important in small sales and strategy coaching most important in large ones. Like many partial truths it's an attractively simple idea. We've seen organizations make costly mistakes because they have adopted it. One very large multinational corporation, who we are sure would prefer to remain anonymous, came to us asking for an advanced strategy program for some of their people. They explained how this advanced program would fit into their overall scheme. "We train our low-end salespeople and their managers in skills," they told us, "but our national accounts people are too advanced for skills training, so we've been training them in strategy. It's our view that in the low end of our business it's skills that make the difference but, at national account level, skills don't enter into it—it's all strategy." "What do you want from this advanced program?" we asked. "We're not happy with our existing strategy program," they confided; "it doesn't seem to be helping sales as much as we'd hoped. So we've decided that it may be too basic. We think that the next step is to look for something that's really *advanced.*" Superficially, that sounded a very plausible approach. Their national account managers did control multimillion dollar accounts. There was no doubt that account strategy was crucial to their success. And, because the sale was complex, there was an excellent case for the sort of advanced programs they were asking us for. So, if their approach was this well thought out, why have we taken pains to keep the corporation anonymous? It's because of a fatal and costly assumption they made. When we had a chance to watch some of their national account managers in action, we were shocked. These supposedly high-level executives, who were candidates for the most advanced of strategy programs, didn't have the first clue about basic selling skills. They didn't ask questions, they did all the talking, they used simple formula selling techniques that we thought had gone out of fashion for good in the 1950s. Even worse, they had come to think of themselves as much too important to worry about such low-level issues as selling skills. "We are very sophisticated," they told us, "and what we need is the latest and most advanced thinking in high-level selling strategy." Alas, what they really needed was simple fundamental selling skills. Some of the national account managers we saw didn't have the skills to execute even the most basic strategies. Our anonymous client had made a serious mistake and, in all honesty, we had to suggest that an advanced strategy program would be a waste of money.

We can draw some practical conclusions from this case and others like it. For example:

- It's a mistake to see strategy as independent of skills. Selling skills are the means of executing strategies. Even the best strategy will fail unless it's backed by skillful selling. The reason why our client's basic strategy program was ineffective wasn't because people needed something more advanced. It was because national account managers didn't have the basic skills needed to execute *any* strategy.

- It's tempting to focus exclusively on strategy for major account salespeople and to assume that fundamental selling skills are already in place. This was a dangerous assumption in our client's case. It was made worse because the national sales managers had come to believe the myth that they didn't need skills, making them very resistant to training and coaching in the skills area.

- As a general principle, it's usually smarter—whether in coaching or in training—to focus on selling skills first and strategies second. Selling skills take longer to build. Start on them early so that they are firmly in place, ready to help you to implement your new and better sales strategies.

What Makes Strategy Coaching Different?

Despite our caution that it's dangerous to think of strategy coaching independently of skills coaching, it's nevertheless true that a difference between small and large sales is that larger sales demand a greater coaching emphasis on strategy. What does that mean? What is *strategy coaching?* How is it different from skills coaching? How should a manager coach people in strategy? That's what the rest of the chapter is about. Let's begin by looking at some of the ways in which strategy coaching is different from skills coaching.

Strategy Coaching in the Office

In order to coach people effectively in skills you *must* watch them use the skills in action. We don't know of any exceptions to this rule. Whether we're talking about an athletic coach, a sales coach, or a drama coach, watching the performer in action is right at the center of skills coaching. Consequently, you can't coach your people's selling skills unless you go out on calls to watch them sell. An important component of skills coaching therefore takes place on the customer's premises. Strategy coaching is different. Although it's always desirable to see people in action, it *is* possible to be an effective strategy coach without ever leaving your own office and without ever watching the strategy being executed. This makes strategy coaching a very attractive proposition. Because you can coach without going out to customers, you can

- Save the travel and waiting time that can make skills coaching so burdensome.
- Choose coaching time to fit your schedule, rather than plan around customer availability.

What's more, a useful piece of strategy coaching can often be completed in fifteen minutes or less, while the average major sales call takes upwards of an hour excluding travel, planning, and coaching time. No wonder many managers, hard pressed for time, find strategy coaching a much more realistic proposition than skills coaching. A word of warning here: strategy coaching is certainly more time efficient than skills coaching. However, as we saw earlier, even a good strategy will fail unless salespeople have the fundamental selling skills required to turn the strategy into action. It can be dangerous if apparent time advantages cause a manager to focus exclusively on strategy coaching to the neglect of skills.

Reviewing Strategy Coaching

We said earlier that the coaching cycle consists of the three steps of Planning, Doing, and Reviewing. Because strategy coaching focuses on the Planning step, we've seen that in strategy—unlike skills—it's possible to be an effective coach without being present during the Doing step. But what about the third step, Reviewing? This is where many strategy coaches fail. A skills coach goes out on calls to watch people sell. Having watched the call, it's almost automatic that coach and seller review the call immediately afterwards. In skills coaching, Doing leads naturally into Reviewing. But the link between Doing and Reviewing isn't so immediate or so clear in strategy coaching. We've seen many managers who go through the Planning step with their people, sitting down with them to coach them in some element of account strategy. They then capitalize on the great advantage of strategy coaching—they send their people out to execute the strategy but they don't go with them on the call. So far, so good. We have the Planning and Doing steps, but where does the Reviewing step of coaching fit in? Often it doesn't. Because Doing doesn't automatically lead to Reviewing in strategy coaching, it's often neglected entirely. Needless to say, this is a grave mistake.

When we're working with managers to improve their coaching, we find that one of the quickest ways to make strategy coaching more effective is to increase managers' efforts in the neglected area of Reviewing. This makes an interesting contrast with skills coaching, where Planning is more likely to be the neglected area.

Account Focus in Strategy Coaching

We earlier said that a common coaching trap for managers is to spread their coaching too thinly. In skills coaching, the best way to avoid this trap is to work with fewer salespeople and to coach each one in depth rather than partially coach the whole team. Is the same true for strategy coaching? Should a manager focus on fewer salespeople in order to coach each one in more depth? The answer is no, which reflects an important difference between skills and strategy coaching. In skills coaching the best way to use limited coaching resources is to limit the number of people. In strategy coaching it's better to limit the number of *accounts.* There's a straightforward reason for this difference. It's difficult to be an effective strategy coach unless you have a detailed grasp of what's happening in the account. Because of this, a coach must invest a significant amount of learning time in order to understand an account well enough to contribute to in-depth strategy. A strategy coach spread thinly across too many accounts can be a liability. True there are exceptions. We've seen managers who, with no knowledge of an account, have made significant contributions to an account strategy by asking a few penetrating questions. These *are* exceptions. For every time we've seen a superficial involvement succeed, there must be a dozen times when we've seen it fail. Strategy coaching without adequate account knowledge is high risk. That's why we claim it's better for managers who are pressed for time to concentrate their coaching attention on relatively few accounts.

Criteria for Selecting Strategy Coaching Accounts

If managers should be selective about the accounts they choose for strategy coaching, are there any helpful guidelines for deciding which accounts to select? We believe that there are three guidelines for the coach to bear in mind when deciding which accounts to work on:

- *Account potential:* Most managers have a small number of key accounts that provide upwards of half their overall business. These accounts are prime candidates for strategy coaching. For one thing, they are important enough to justify real effort; for another, managers usually already know these key accounts fairly well. This reduces the learning time we were discussing earlier. Notice that there's another contrast here with skills coaching. We advise skills coaches to *avoid* using key accounts for coaching skills. In strategy coaching it's the other way around—the more potential in the account, the better it is as a strategy coaching candidate. As we'll see in the next chapter, in skills coaching you select accounts that are *safe,* while in strategy coaching you select accounts because they are *important.*

- *Unique contribution:* Another useful guideline for helping to select strategy coaching accounts is to ask yourself whether you can make a unique contribution to the account strategy. Do you, for example, have relevant business knowledge that your salesperson lacks? Do you understand the customer's market better? Have you dealt with this kind of buying process before? It's possible, of course, to make valuable contributions to account strategy even if you don't bring something unique. However, if you are making a decision about which account to select for coaching, then your capacity to add something unique should certainly tip the balance in terms of which account you ultimately select.

- *Learning opportunity:* Finally, it's important to ask yourself whether the account provides a learning opportunity for your salesperson. As a result of your coaching involvement, can you teach the seller something new? Can you help develop a capability that will be useful in the seller's other accounts?

Use these criteria to help you pick accounts for strategy coaching. Above all, remember that it's better to coach a few accounts in depth than to superficially coach every account you manage. Now let's turn to the coaching itself and look at some techniques for making strategy coaching effective.

Objectives and Frameworks

At its simplest, strategy coaching requires two things:

- *Clear account objectives:* a shared understanding by coach and salesperson of what the sales effort is aiming to achieve. Without these shared objectives, coaching is unlikely to be effective. Good account objectives, as we'll see later, are not a set of static aims cast in stone at the beginning of a sales strategy. They are fluid, dynamic, and continuously evolving as the sales cycle progresses.

- *An action framework:* a means of putting objectives into action, checking on the success of actions, and revising account strategy accordingly. Later we'll discuss some examples of action frameworks.

Let's begin by looking at account objectives.

Setting Account Objectives

The obvious starting point for a sales strategy is a set of objectives that specify exactly what you want to achieve in an account. Alas, it's never quite that simple in practice. For one thing, there's more than one kind of account objective. Objectives exist at different levels. Consider, for instance, these examples of account objectives:

> *"To increase our share of business in the account this year from its present level of 14 percent to a level of 30 percent."*
>
> *"To build a relationship with the new Head of Purchasing."*
>
> *"To sell a model 2754 to the Accounting Department."*

The first thing that strikes you about these examples is that some objectives are much broader than others. Increasing overall share in the account, for example, is a wider objective than selling a particular machine or building a relationship with one individual in the account. There's been an enormous amount written about objective setting in fields like education and project management. Much of what's been written emphasizes the importance of recognizing and using these differences in breadth of objectives. Some writers have suggested that there are two levels of objectives:

- *Strategic Objectives:* which are overall goals, such as increasing account share
- *Tactical Objectives:* which are day-to-day sales actions needed to meet these goals, such as selling a particular machine or influencing a specific part of the account.

We feel that this division of objectives into the strategic and the tactical can sometimes prove dangerously misleading. Too often we've seen managers who feel that account strategy must— as the name suggests—be about strategic objectives. They see themselves as big-picture people who focus only on overall strategic issues and leave all the day-to-day tactical issues to their people. One such manager, in a division of a large chemical company, told us, "My job is strategy—that's *what* we should achieve in the account. I set the overall strategic objectives like targets, overall volume, or profitability. My salespeople, on the other hand, work on tactical objectives—they decide *how* to put my strategic objectives into action. I never interfere with their tactics and I don't expect them to interfere with my strategy. I'm paid to be the strategist—they are paid to be tacticians." There's an attractively simple logic to this position. The strategy/tactics split has served well in military organizations for several thousand years. However, it's a disastrous way to think about sales strategy. As it happens, we met the manager during a study of *unsuccessful* sales managers we were doing for his company. It was surprising how many of these unsuccessful managers held a similar view of strategy as an overall goal-setting exercise with minimal links to the day-to-day detail. Don't be misled by the words. Sales strategy doesn't just involve managers in setting strategic objectives. Successful sales managers take a much more detailed hands-on approach to every element of strategy, including every level of objective setting.

Levels of Sales Objectives

A more sophisticated way to divide sales objectives into different levels is to use the three categories of *Goals, Objectives,* and *Activities.* We've seen these categories used in a number of Fortune 500 companies.

- *Goals* are overall objectives for the account expressed in global terms, like the Strategic Objectives we discussed earlier.
- *Objectives* are the subgoals that, added together, make up an overall goal. So, for example, "to sell a model 2754 to the Accounting Department" would be an *Objective* as part of the overall goal to achieve a 30 percent share of the business.
- *Activities* are the most basic level, being the actions or steps required in order to achieve an objective.

Figure 5.4 illustrates a typical Goals-Objectives-Activities hierarchy.

It's sometimes very useful to draw a diagram like the one in figure 5.4 to help you and your salespeople see visually how the various objectives in the account fit together into a whole. We've found that a picture of this kind is certainly worth the proverbial thousand words, particularly when a number of people are involved in the same account. We once worked with a team in the computer industry where, in order to make a sale to a large multinational, a total of twenty-six different people each had to play a significant part in the sales effort. The national account

FIGURE 5.4

Expressing account objectives in terms of Goals, Objectives, and Activities

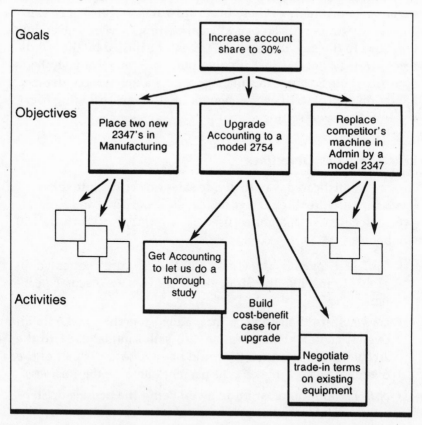

manager, who coordinated the efforts of geographical salespeople, systems analysts, software and technical specialists, built a giant wall chart like the one illustrated in figure 5.4 to show his team how the efforts of each person added up to achieving the overall goal. "My problem," he explained to us, "was to get twenty-six people to all pull in the same direction. By laying out all the objectives on one giant chart I was able to let each person see how they contributed to our overall goals. Even more important, I could show them how others fitted in. This reduced the natural hostility that I've often found between sales and technical people—and it helped us work as a team."

A Word of Warning

There's no single right way to set strategic sales objectives. When managers ask us which type of objective setting works best, we invariably reply, "Whichever one you are most comfortable with." Having said that, we usually add these words of warning:

Keep Objective Setting Simple

The most common reason why objective setting fails is that it gets too complex. We've seen some very elaborate systems for setting sales objectives. Often these systems are associated with considerable paperwork or its electronic equivalent. More than once we've been called in to help pick up the pieces after one of these complicated sales objectives systems has failed. Our report to management, reduced to its simplest, says

- Your salespeople resented it.
- Your sales managers didn't see how it would help them manage.
- The data it produced were unrealistic.
- Nobody felt enough commitment to go through the tedious business of updating and revising objectives as circumstances changed.
- You've bought a complicated failure: replace it with something cheap and simple.

Simplicity is a magic word when it comes to objective setting. Don't be like the manager we knew who spent two hours out of a three-hour objective setting meeting arguing about the precise differences between goals and objectives. However you approach your objective setting, what matters is that you and your salespeople end up with a simple and clear shared picture of what you intend to achieve from your accounts.

Revise Objectives Frequently

The first time you set objectives for an account, they are unlikely to be accurate or realistic. For one thing, you rarely have enough information to set precise objectives. Early in the sales cycle with a new account, or with a new area of an existing account, you may be operating on nothing more substantial than a hunch that some business potential *may* exist. As the selling cycle progresses, so does your knowledge of the account and your ability to set realistic objectives. Too often, we've seen managers and their salespeople invest too much time and effort in detailed objective setting early in the sales process. A couple of weeks later, as a result of new information or developments in the account, all these carefully worded objectives have become an out-of-date fantasy. Objective setting is not a onetime activity. It's a process of constant revision.

That's another reason for keeping objective setting simple. Complex objectives are harder to revise. Bill Allen, one of the great consultants of the 1960s—when the word "consultant" still meant something special—once taught one of his subordinates this lesson in an indelible way. Bill had asked the subordinate, one of the present authors, to prepare a set of objectives for a consulting project that the subordinate was about to start in a chemical company. The subordinate, anxious to impress, spent hours writing goals, objectives, aims, measures of performance, and the like in a five-page document. The next day he proudly presented his work to Bill, whose only comment was, "My problem with these objectives is that your handwriting's too good." The subordinate didn't know what to make of this cryptic response. A week later, Bill asked him for an updated set of objectives. With all the fresh information emerging from the new project, the revision was substantial—more so because each elaborate objective, subobjective, and standard of performance needed detailed revision. Next morning, after a late night updating session, the subordinate presented his revisions. "Your handwriting's still too good" was Bill's only comment. A week later, Bill demanded another update. His thoroughly frustrated subordinate saw no point in another elaborate revision, so he hastily scribbled some quick notes covering only the key project objectives. Bill was delighted, "This is excellent," he said, "your handwriting's so bad I can hardly read it. Now I'm ready to talk about your objectives because you've handed me a working document and not a tablet of stone." That was a powerful lesson. Beware the onetime tablet-of-stone approach to objective setting. Strategic sales objectives need constant revision if they are to be useful guides to practical action.

Link Objectives to Actions to Advance the Sale

The final piece of objective-setting advice that we offer people is that an objective is no more than a pious statement of good intention until something happens to translate it into *action*. We once watched an objective-setting session where manager and seller argued energetically about whether their goal was to sell $150,000 of business or $250,000 to an account. It was a remarkably futile discussion because neither of them seemed to have a clue about the exact steps and actions they would need to take to sell even the first $100 of this new business. Unless you can specify the *actions* that will advance you towards your business goal, your objectives will have little meaning. We'll have more to say about this later, but for now we'd like to make a fundamental point that too many managers overlook in their objective setting. Logic would suggest that the process of objective setting starts with a broad goal, such as "we aim to sell $250,000 of business to this account this year." Then, from the broad goal, comes a series of more and more detailed subobjectives and actions that tell you exactly how the goal will be achieved.

This process, illustrated in figure 5.5, may sound logically compelling, but in practical terms, life doesn't work that way. In reality, you can't set an overall goal unless you know what's

FIGURE 5.5

Traditional top-down approach to setting objectives

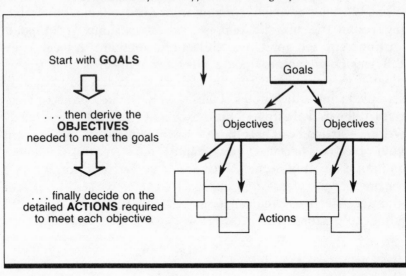

practically achievable in the account. A target of $250,000 may be impossibly high or it may represent only one-tenth of the account's potential. The only way you can know what's practically achievable is to have a detailed picture of the selling actions that would be required to meet your overall objective. Without this detail, objective setting is an exercise in wishful thinking. In reality, objective setting is more like figure 5.6, where goals, objectives, and actions are used to refine and revise each other in a circular, rather than a linear, process.

Unlike traditional objective-setting models, where the big picture comes first, in this circular model the detail interacts with the big picture. In our experience it's been a much more useful way to think about objective setting. Don't try to finalize overall account objectives until you've worked through the specifics. This is one of the reasons why we were so critical of the manager who told us that he set strategy and left tactics to his people. In our view you *can't* set realistic strategic goals unless you have a detailed grasp of the tactics that put the goals into practice. We recognize that many managers may feel unable to influence overall goal setting because their sales goals and targets are set for

FIGURE 5.6

Setting objectives in the real world—a circular process

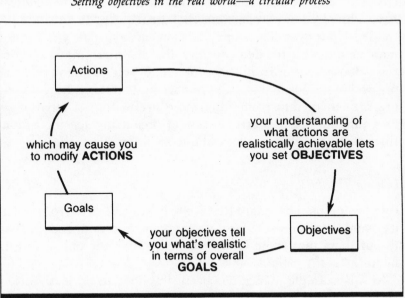

them by senior management with little or no opportunity for consultation. However, on the specific level of strategic goals for individual accounts, most managers can and do control the objective setting process. Setting, revising, and refining account objectives is the first step in developing account strategy.

An Action Framework

We said that account strategy, and the strategy coaching derived from it, required two things:

- Clear account objectives
- An action framework

We've explained what we mean by clear account objectives. Now let's turn to the idea of frameworks that help translate account objectives into workable actions.

First, let's be a little more precise about what we mean by an *action framework.* If you accept the logic of our argument so far, then it follows that *specific actions to advance the sale* are at the heart of any practical account strategy. But our focus on specific actions can create its own set of problems. In a typical account you may well have a hundred or more actions that are required to advance you towards your overall account goal. The more specific you get, the more actions you have to consider. Big picture thinking, in contrast, doesn't suffer from this problem. If you've literally dozens of specific actions making up your account strategy, how do you organize them into something more useful than a terrifyingly long random list? It's this process of organizing specific actions that we mean when we talk about an *action framework*.

Using a Timeline

By now it must be evident that we're greatly attracted to simplicity—and there's no simpler way to organize account actions than to put them into some kind of timeline, like the one shown in figure 5.7.

In this example, which has been simplified to fit neatly into a small diagram, it's easy to see how the timeline serves to organize the various sales actions. Of course, there are much more sophisticated versions of timelines. Instead of a single column for sales actions, we've seen examples with multiple columns. One column, for instance, might contain sales actions for the manager, one for the account salesperson, one for technical support, and so on.

The timeline is one example of what we mean by an *organizing framework*. Before we look at a different example, let's be a little more specific about the three characteristics of any good organizing framework.

The framework organizes sales actions in a logical way: The most noticeable characteristic of our example framework in figure 5.7 is that it takes fourteen separate sales actions and puts them into a meaningful sequence. In doing so, the timeline framework has transformed a list into a plan. This is the most obvious function of any organizing framework.

The framework links sales actions to the customer's decision process: A less obvious characteristic of an effective framework is that it should *link* sales actions to the customer's buying process. Our illustration in figure 5.7, for example, starts on the left-hand side with

FIGURE 5.7
A timeline for organizing account actions

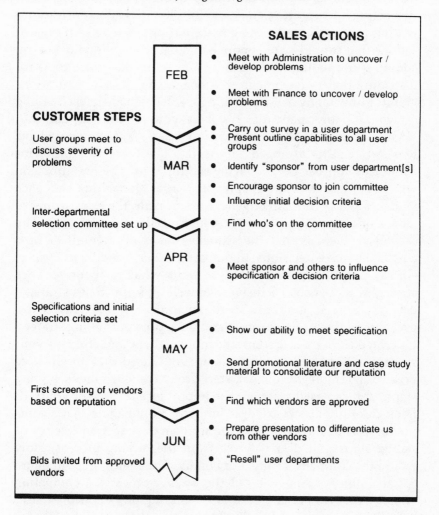

a series of steps that the buying organization is likely to go through in arriving at a decision, then links these through the timeline to the selling steps. Why is this link so important? Surely, what really matters is clarity about the *selling* steps, not about the customer's buying process. On the contrary. A selling strategy that is out of step with how the buyer makes decisions will invariably fail. Too many sales strategies, and the timelines derived from them, are about the selling process alone. As a result the sales actions are laid out in a sequence of selling steps like suspecting, prospecting, making initial visits, demonstrations, writing proposals, and closing presentations. We've seen organizations that should be old enough and big enough to know better adopt selling sequences like these and build them into tools for managing their sales pipelines. Managers in these organizations monitor how many actions their people have made in each selling category. "How many demo's have you set up this month?" "Why haven't you sent out any proposals?" "I see you only have two initial visits arranged for April." There are two problems about this approach to managing selling steps. The first problem, which we discussed in chapter 2, is that the selling sequence manages *activity*, not effectiveness. As a result, the sales sequence may work in smaller sales but usually fails in larger ones. The second problem is that the sequence takes no account of how customers make decisions. In our book *Major Account Sales Strategy*, we say some very nasty things about what happens to sales strategies that focus exclusively on selling steps. Sales strategy, despite the name, is about how the customer buys. The better you understand the buying process and the more your selling strategy is derived from buying steps, the more realistic and effective your strategy will be. That's why we are convinced that an effective organizing framework must start from the customer's buying steps. You can easily test out the importance of this for yourself. Look carefully at our example in figure 5.7. Imagine that a competitor was selling to this cusotmer using a traditional series of selling steps that didn't derive from the buying process. How would the competitor fare? Very badly. The selling steps in figure 5.7 all influence some step of the buying process. A competing strategy that isn't anchored into the buying process will, at best, be a hit-or-miss affair. We don't think that there's much place for the unfocused spray-and-pray approach to selling strategy we see in many organizations that use generic frameworks that don't correspond to how their individual customers buy.

The framework establishes Key Intervention Points: Another important characteristic of a good strategic framework is that it shows managers where they need to intervene in the sales process. One of the real problems in strategic coaching is timing. Every manager has his or her own version of sad tales that start, "If only I'd known in time, I could have . . ." How do you, as a manager, know when the sale is coming to a critical strategic point where your intervention can make a unique difference? One of the functions of a strategic framework is to alert you in advance to points in the sale where your intervention matters. We call these critical junctures Key Intervention Points—or KIPS for short. A KIP is a point in the sales timeline where your intervention is likely to influence the success of the selling effort. Your intervention may be in the form either of selling or of coaching. In chapter 3 we discussed some of the principles for deciding how and when to become involved in the selling role. In terms of the coaching role, the Key Intervention Points are:

- Where you can, through your coaching, influence the seller's strategy in a way that can alter the direction or the success of the sale.
- Where your coaching can help the seller's learning by, for example, increasing the seller's understanding of some element of account strategy.

An illustration of how a strategy framework can incorporate Key Intervention Points is shown in figure 5.8.

In this example, the KIPS are added to part of the basic timeline from the previous example in figure 5.7. How useful is this concept of KIPS? We've worked with many managers who, initially, have honestly wondered why we bother to make such a fuss about it. "I do that anyway," said one. "I don't give it a fancy name, but I intervene in the sale whenever any of my people gets into difficulty or finds something they can't handle." This manager, and many like her, are missing an important point. Strategy isn't about reacting to situations after they happen. Strategy is about intervening *before* your people encounter problems that might damage their sales efforts. The value of the KIPS concept is that it encourages managers to think about when and how to intervene before problems have a chance to arise. Try it. Draw a timeline of one of your sales. Set out the selling actions and then ask yourself where the Key Intervention Points are where your intervention will make a difference. One manager from a chemi-

FIGURE 5.8

Putting Key Intervention Points into the timeline

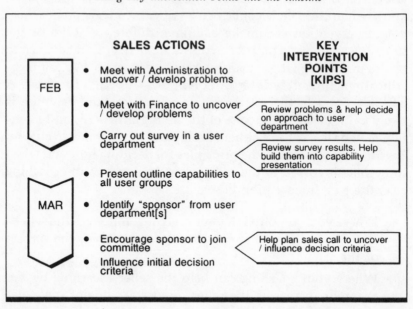

cal company, who had initially claimed he was much too busy to try such a fanciful exercise, reluctantly agreed to try out the KIPS concept. Three months later he told us, "It's worked better than I expected because it's actually *saved* me time. I now realize that I was spending too much time firefighting, trying to put out flames my people were lighting in their accounts. Now I'm much more in the fire prevention business."

An Alternative Way to Create Timelines

Timelines have many advantages as organizing frameworks for your sales strategies. However, their main strength is also their principal disadvantage. The main reason why timelines are so useful is that they help you link your selling actions to the customer's decision process. That's fine if you know in advance what the customer's decision process is likely to be. But, often:

- You don't have a clear idea of the steps the customer will go through in making the decision.

- Detailed steps will vary so much from customer to customer that you have to go back to square one and start again every time you set up a timeline for a new sale.

For these reasons, timelines can appear to be a lot more effort than they are worth. Is there some way to capture the usefulness of timeline strategy planning without these disadvantages?

The Generic Buying Framework

Years ago, when we were first working with timelines, we had a good answer to the question of how to set up a timeline when you don't have an understanding of the customer's decision process. Most people, we argued, spend too much effort in setting out their initial sales strategy and not enough effort in revising it as circumstances change. So, the first time round, just *guess* the customer's decision steps. Later, when you have better information about the decision process, revise your timeline accordingly. In some ways this was sound advice. People *do* spend too much time in worrying about details of their initial strategy. It's smart to think of your first attempt at a timeline as an initial approximation that can be completed in a few minutes. The initial laying out of any sales strategy is far less important than the updating and revision that should inevitably happen as the sale unfolds, circumstances change, and better information becomes available.

However, to be honest, we knew there was a flaw in our good advice. It's fine to tell people to guess the customer's decision steps, but what if that guess is wrong? All the sales actions and Key Intervention Points derived from the wrong guess will also be inaccurate and the whole exercise will become a meaningless waste of time. "Isn't there some way to avoid this guesswork?" managers would ask us. "Can't you show us some ways to set out these buying steps so that we don't just pull imaginary steps out of the air at random? Give us a starting point." We had to admit this was a reasonable request. It would certainly make the process of constructing a timeline much easier if there were some broad generic buying steps that could be used as a plausible first approximation in the timeline until better information came along. Fortunately, our research into the buying process, described in our book, *Major Account Sales Strategy,* gave us just such a simple generic framework for starting the timeline.

Figure 5.9 shows an outline of these generic decision steps. From the customer's point of view, most decisions go through three broad buying phases.

Recognition of Needs: In this first phase the customer's main interest and activity lie in deciding whether problems exist that need to be solved through some purchase of a product or service. If you could see inside the head of a hypothetical customer during this phase of the buying process, you'd find questions like, "How do we know this problem is big enough to justify action?" "Do we need to change our present methods?" or "What's wrong with the way we're doing it now?" All these questions are about *needs.* The first phase of any buying decision is for the customer to recognize that needs exist at a level of seriousness that justifies action. Once

FIGURE 5.9
A generic strategy framework for customer decision steps

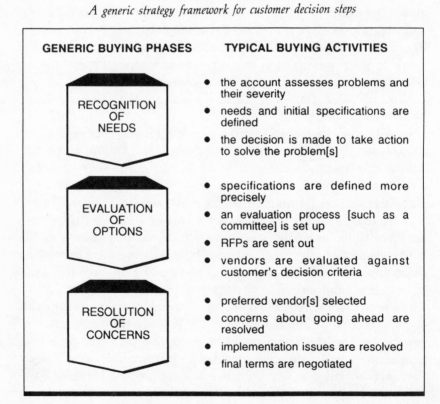

GENERIC BUYING PHASES	TYPICAL BUYING ACTIVITIES
RECOGNITION OF NEEDS	• the account assesses problems and their severity • needs and initial specifications are defined • the decision is made to take action to solve the problem[s]
EVALUATION OF OPTIONS	• specifications are defined more precisely • an evaluation process [such as a committee] is set up • RFPs are sent out • vendors are evaluated against customer's decision criteria
RESOLUTION OF CONCERNS	• preferred vendor[s] selected • concerns about going ahead are resolved • implementation issues are resolved • final terms are negotiated

the decision to take action has been reached, the buying process moves into its next phase.

Evaluation of Options: In this second phase of the buying process, the customer's main interest lies in making valid choices among alternative ways of meeting the need. Again looking into the head of our hypothetical customer, in this phase we'd find questions like, "Which competitor offers the best value?" "Does the extra quality of their product outweight its additional cost?" or "Is speed more important to us than compatibility?" The common thread among these questions is that they all try to make judgments that help the customer choose one option rather than another. Once the customer has chosen a preferred option, then the purchasing decision enters its next phase.

Resolution of Concerns: In this last purchasing phase before the decision, the customer has to cope with last minute worries and concerns. In some sales cycles, this last phase may be a nonevent. Having chosen the preferred option, the customer may be ready to go ahead and sign the contract. However, most really large sales involve the account in a degree of perceived risk. Questions arise in the customer's mind such as, "What if it goes wrong?" "How shall I explain it to my boss if they don't deliver as promised?" or "Suppose their aftersales service isn't as good as they say—what am I going to do?" The common link here is risk. In large decisions, individuals within the account who are responsible for making the purchase often feel under great personal pressure and have real fears and reservations about making the final decision.

These three phases provide a simple generic framework that can be used as a starting point for creating a timeline. As your knowledge of an account increases, you can refine this generic framework into an increasingly specific picture of how the account is making its decisions. In this way, your initial outline of customer decision steps, on which your timeline is based, will be a whole lot better than guesswork.

Generic KIPS?

If there's a generic framework for how customers make decisions, then it follows that there might also be some fairly generic points in the decision process at which a manager can usefully intervene to help the sales strategy. The possibility of generic KIPS is an interesting one. If there are certain points at which it's generally helpful to intervene in the sales strategy, then it becomes possible to develop tools to help managers coach sales strategy at each of these points. We'd like to close this chapter with an example of three strategy coaching tools, one for each of our three phases of the buying process. These tools are designed to help with common strategic coaching problems that arise during this phase of the decision.

A KIPS coaching tool for the Recognition of Needs Phase: A common strategy coaching issue during the early part of the sales process

FIGURE 5.10
Three KIPS tools for strategy coaching

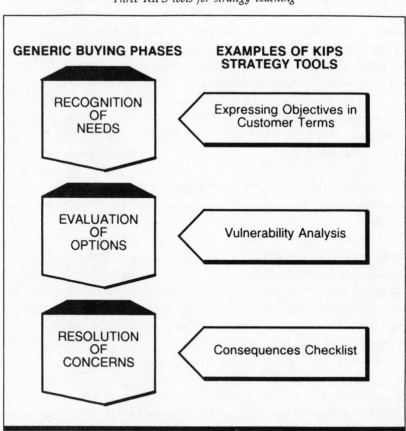

is how to best help people with the transition between their overall objective setting and their specific sales actions. Take a typical sales objective like "to upgrade the customer's present system by installing a new model 7865." Some salespeople, given an objective of this kind, have no difficulty in translating the objective into specific sales actions such as, "convince the customer that the existing system can't cope with the increased load from the reorganization," or "show that the model 7865 will save money by allowing invoices to be processed in-house." But, for every salesperson who can take an objective and easily turn it into sales actions, there are three or four others who have real difficulty linking objectives with actions. In our experience, the salespeople who find it hardest to make this transition are those who tend to think of their objectives in terms of what *they* want to achieve in the account, rather than what the customer wants to achieve. Because they don't see their objectives in customer terms, these salespeople don't see how the customer will benefit if the objective is achieved. An objective that doesn't do anything for the customer is clearly difficult to express as a sales action. To help with this problem, we've designed a very simple KIPS tool that lets a manager coach a salesperson to translate sales objectives into something more actionable. An example of this tool is shown in figure 5.11. It's based on a very simple premise. For an objective to be realistic and actionable, the customer must solve a problem when the objective is met. Think about that for a moment. For example, if the objective is to place a new system, then that objective will only be achievable if the new system solves one or more customer problems. A system that doesn't solve a problem contributes nothing to the customer, so there's no reason for the customer to install it.

The usefulness of thinking about objectives in terms of the problems they solve for customers can be seen by comparing the left and right halves of figure 5.11. On the left, objectives like "to sell an optimization study" or "to sell a disaster recovery system" do nothing to help the seller think about the actions needed to make the sale. In contrast, the right hand side, because it is expressed in customer terms, readily suggests sales actions. A clear understanding of the problems you can solve for customers is a necessary first step in any successful sales strategy. We've

FIGURE 5.11

Expressing objectives in problem-solving terms

Objective I would like to achieve	Problems the CUSTOMER would solve if I achieved this objective
To sell and conduct a network optimization study	• helps VP MIS plan strategy for new applications • lets bank identify potential cost reduction areas
To develop and manage a turnkey implementation plan for installing and commissioning a new network	• MIS wants a network plan but is too busy to develop their own • planned approach will help MIS fight "quick fix" demands from users
To sell a customized network training support package	• easier changeover to the new system • greater acceptance from operators and staff
To sell a disaster recovery system	• 24-hour backup system would have prevented data losses bank suffered in last year's flood • system will reduce pressure on MIS to improve data security

found that this simple little tool is a useful way to help people begin to express their objectives in problem-solving terms. Next time you have an objective-setting session with one of your people, try it out. Get them to list each of their sales objectives for the account. Then get them to express each objective in terms of the problems it would solve for the customer. Finally, ask them to plan a sales call where they will help the customer understand the potential seriousness of the problem and the value of solving it.

This example of a KIPS tool is one that is useful at the start of the selling cycle. Our next tool is designed for a Key Intervention Point right in the middle of the selling cycle, when competitive pressure is at its strongest.

A KIPS coaching tool for the Evaluation of Options Phase: During the

Evaluation of Options phase, the customer is comparing competing alternatives and trying to decide among them. We describe
this process in detail in our book, *Major Account Sales Strategy.*
Where should a manager make a strategic intervention during
this middle part of the cycle? As one manager put it, "The best
strategy is to wait until your people screw up. Then turn the clock
back a few hours and catch them just in time to prevent them
screwing up in the first place." We couldn't agree more. Although
we don't have the manager's ability to reverse time, it's clear that
it's better for strategic coaching to help people *avoid* problems
than to solve problems that have become messy and difficult. The
most difficult problems in this phase of the cycle are those that
occur because a competitor is hurting you by successfully ex-
ploiting their strengths or exposing your weaknesses. In other
words, the difficulty arises because you are competitively vulnerable. Many salespeople don't see this vulnerability coming until
it's too late to adopt an effective counterstrategy. It's a valuable
strategic coaching intervention if a manager can help people see
vulnerability in advance, and plan how to counter it before the
vulnerability has a chance to seriously damage the chances of a
sale. Figure 5.12 illustrates a simple KIPS tool for helping people
analyze competitive vulnerability. Here's how it works:

- The seller first lists the criteria that the customer appears to
  be using to make the decision. In this case, the factors that
  may be influencing the decision are cost, quality, after sales
  service, and flexibility.

- Next, the seller stack ranks these criteria in terms of their
  importance to the customer. As the left hand scale of figure
  5.12 shows, flexibility, in this case, is crucial, whereas aftersales service is incidental.

- Then, in the center scale of the diagram, the seller rates the
  customer's judgment of how you rate on each of these criteria. For example, in this case the customer rates you as very
  strong in terms of after sales service.

- Finally, the seller rates how the customer sees the competitor
  in terms of the criteria. In this case, the competitor's aftersales service is seen by this customer as weak.

FIGURE 5.12
Vulnerability Analysis

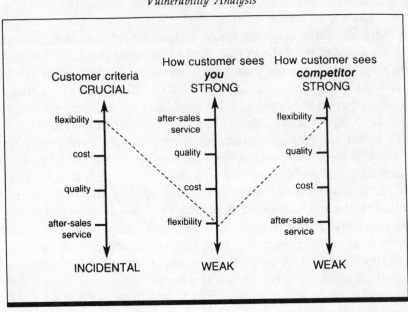

If a "V" shape appears when you connect the rating levels of a criterion across the three scales, then you are vulnerable and you need to plan a competitive response to counter the vulnerability. In this example, flexibility is the area of greatest vulnerability: the competitor is strong, you are weak, and flexibility is crucial to this customer. The attraction of Vulnerability Analysis is its simplicity. It's the easiest way we know to summarize, on a single piece of paper, the key factors influencing the decision. Over the years, many hundreds of the managers we've worked with have used Vulnerability Analysis and found it a helpful strategic coaching tool.

A KIPS coaching tool for the Resolution of Concerns Phase: As a final example of a strategic coaching tool, we'll turn to the end of the decision cycle. Here, just before the decision, the customer is likely to be concerned about the risks involved in going ahead. However, as we explained earlier, that's not true in every sale. In some cases the customer feels perfectly comfortable. In others,

FIGURE 5.13
Checklist to predict consequence issues in an account

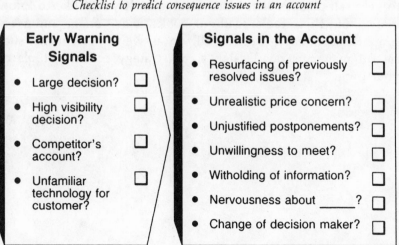

Early Warning Signals

- Large decision? ☐
- High visibility decision? ☐
- Competitor's account? ☐
- Unfamiliar technology for customer? ☐

Signals in the Account

- Resurfacing of previously resolved issues? ☐
- Unrealistic price concern? ☐
- Unjustified postponements? ☐
- Unwillingness to meet? ☐
- Witholding of information? ☐
- Nervousness about _____? ☐
- Change of decision maker? ☐

perceived risks may be at such a level that they prevent the customer from doing business with you. We call these perceived risks "Consequences." Consequences often lurk under the surface. The customer who, for example, feels afraid to decide in your favor because her boss might prefer a competitor, may be reluctant to tell you about it. However, unless you can get these issues out in the open and resolve them, they are likely to work against you behind the scenes. But how do you know whether a Consequence issue exists? After all, as we've said, in some sales there are no Consequences. In others they loom beneath the surface like icebergs waiting to wreck your sales effort. A simple strategic coaching tool to help people with Consequence issues is a checklist like the one in figure 5.13. Using this checklist, seller and manager can assess whether Consequence issues are likely to be present and can develop strategies accordingly.

Other Strategic Coaching Tools

The three examples we've covered here should illustrate what we mean by "strategic coaching tools." There are dozens of other tools—some simple, some very sophisticated—that can help a manager to analyze what's happening in an account and to help salespeople plan better strategies. If you'd like to know more about these tools, read our books, *SPIN*® *Selling* and *Major Account Sales Strategy*. Better still, do as we've seen many successful managers do. Design some strategy coaching tools of your own.

6

THE SKILLS OF COACHING AND THE COACHING OF SKILLS

How to Develop Your People's Skills

When two hundred managers in Xerox Corporation opened their mail one Monday morning, each found an unexpected little gift. Inside every one of the plain envelopes was a large Band-Aid with instructions that read, "Managers' Emergency Coaching Kit: tape firmly across the mouth if you are suffering from an inability to stay quiet during coaching calls." We had sent this "kit" as a not so gentle reminder to managers that the cardinal sin of skills coaching is trying to both coach and sell in the same call. Research in Xerox, which we've described more fully in chapter 3, showed that one key difference between effective and less effective skill coaches lay in the way that they handled selling and coaching roles. Less effective coaches tried to combine both roles. They would go out with their people on sales calls with the intention of coaching. Typically, as the call progressed, they couldn't resist *helping* the sale by adding a little selling of their own. In most cases, if their intervention had any impact, then the customer

175

would want to draw them into the conversation and the call usually ended with the manager doing the selling. Why do we see that as such a sin? Isn't it smart for managers to intervene in calls if, by their intervention, they increase the chances of making a sale? Unfortunately, the answer is no. Selling and coaching just don't mix. Each is a difficult and skilled task that requires a manager's full attention. Trying to combine selling and coaching in a single call usually means that neither is done well. That's one reason why our coaching research in Xerox had shown that effective coaches chose their calls carefully. On some important calls, where their selling skills could make a unique difference, they decided to sell and not give even a moment's thought to coaching. On other calls that were more routine, they coached and took no part in the selling.

It's not just the difficulty of combining two complex skills that makes us warn managers not to mix selling and coaching. In a study carried out in a multinational technology company, we investigated salespeople's perception of those things their managers did that they felt most positive or most negative about. Right at the top of the list of negatives came "taking over the call during joint sales calls to my customers." Nothing else that managers did created such negative reactions from their people. By separating selling from coaching, a manager can minimize this potential negative. The salespeople in our study didn't resent their manager selling, provided it was clear in advance that the manager's sole purpose in the call was to sell. What they complained about was having their own selling undermined by their manager's unexpected intervention.

You might argue, surely there's such a thing as a *helpful* intervention? If, for example, you were making a coaching call and you realized that the selling was going badly so that the salesperson was getting into difficulty, wouldn't your salesperson be grateful to you if you stepped in and saved the call? In theory perhaps, but not in practice. One of the Xerox sales managers we worked with had a nice way of explaining the practical difficulties of intervention in calls. "My mistake," he told us, "was that I thought I was helping. Now I realize I was only hurting my own credibility. If I took over a call as soon as it started to get into trouble, then I could usually save it. But if I took over a call in time to save it, the sales rep wouldn't realize that it was going wrong. So, afterwards, the rep would say to me, 'Why did you take over? I was doing fine.' On the other hand, if I waited long enough for the sales rep to see that the call was in trouble, it was usually too late to save it. So we'd lose the sale. Afterwards, because I'd lost the sale, it was hard to talk about how the sales rep had gone wrong. My credibility was shot."

Not only can intervening in the call put the manager's credibility at risk; it can also hurt the credibility of the seller, which is one reason why salespeople resent their manager's intervention. From the customer's point of view, a manager's involvement in the call is often interpreted as a lack of confidence in the salesperson. As we saw in chapter 3, it's important that managers sell in a way that builds the stature of their salespeople in customers' eyes. Intervening in sales calls, particularly if that involvement is clearly an attempt to get the calls back on track, can signal to the customer that you have little confidence in your salespeople. For these reasons we suggest that the first principle of skills coaching should be:

> *Sell or coach, but don't try to combine selling and skills coaching in the same call.*

Mercifully, because strategy coaching normally takes place away from the customer's office, the selling/coaching dilemma doesn't usually arise.

Setting Up the Right Conditions for Skill Coaching

We've said that skills coaching involves traveling with salespeople and observing them in actual sales calls. Because that's a key difference between skill and strategy coaching, it's easy to focus all skills coaching attention on the sales call itself. That would be a mistake. Good skills coaching starts well before the call. Here are some of the things you should think about before you ever enter a customer's office to coach one of your people.

Who should I choose for skills coaching? In the last chapter we said that a key skills coaching principle is that it's initially better to coach fewer people in greater depth than to spread yourself thin by superficially coaching your whole team. That raises the important question, "If I can't coach the whole team at one time, then whom should I choose?" Although there are no fixed rules, we've found the following guidelines useful:

- *Average performers:* Although your top performers can certainly benefit from skills coaching and will usually welcome feedback on their selling skills, we suggest that you don't start with them. They are already producing results and they have less need for immediate help. We generally wouldn't start with poor performers either. It will usually take a lot of your time to coach a poor performer to a point where there are visible results. For every hour of coaching time that you spend, you'll usually get the fastest payback from working with average performers. For this reason, we usually recommend that coaches start with their average performers, moving to their high and low performers later.

- *Volunteers:* If you have any people on your team who are anxious to be coached, then give them priority. A person who wants, or asks for, coaching will be more motivated to learn than someone who has been pressed into it. There's the added advantage that, if you haven't done much coaching before, a volunteer will be much more tolerant if your initial coaching is less than perfect.

- *Recently trained people:* If any of your people has recently been through a skills training program, then he or she is likely to be a good candidate for skills programs. Skills learned during training decay rapidly unless they are systematically practiced. Coaching provides an ideal way to encourage practice of new skills in a systematic and organized way.

What kind of calls should I set up for skills coaching? One reason why many managers find coaching difficult is that they go out on sales calls that are unsuitable for skills coaching.

As figure 6.1 illustrates, when salespeople arrange joint calls with their managers, they naturally tend to set up calls that are important or difficult. Often, they have the expectation that

FIGURE 6.1
What kind of calls?

Your people will set up	But, for coaching, you need
• closing calls	• calls earlier in the cycle
• tough selling situations	• safe selling situations
• calls with high business potential	• calls with moderate business potential
• calls where you will sell for them	• calls where they sell and you coach

their manager will take an active selling role. These high-profile calls are usually unsuitable for coaching. So, before you go out with your people for skills coaching, ask them to set up calls like the ones in the right hand side of the table. Ask for calls that are

- *Early in the selling cycle:* because that allows you to coach the crucially important skills of uncovering and developing customer needs. If you can help your people develop better skills for handling the early part of the selling cycle, then the whole sale will be built on a more solid foundation.
- *Safe selling situations:* because, if it's a tough call, then all your attention needs to be on how to handle the customer, not on coaching. What's more, a tough call isn't the place for your people to try new skills.
- *Calls with moderate business potential:* because, if the call has really high business potential, your focus should be on getting the business, not on developing skills. Conversely, if the call has very low business potential, it's unlikely to give good skill practice opportunity.
- *Calls where they sell, you coach:* because, as we saw earlier, it's important to separate your selling role from your coaching role. Consequently, the ideal call is one that you would ex-

pect a salesperson of this experience level to handle adequately without your intervention.

How do I explain my coaching role to the seller? It's important, before you begin skills coaching, that you and your salesperson are clear about what's going to happen and what the skills coaching role means. In particular, explain that skills coaching isn't some kind of evaluation or test. Your primary role is to *help*. One very effective way to demonstrate this is to sit down with your seller before the call and plan it together. By actively helping in the planning, you can demonstrate that you want to help the call succeed—you're not an *examiner* who is there to assess and criticize the call. There are other aspects of your coaching role that you may need to explain. For example, if the seller isn't expecting you to keep out of the selling role during the call, you'll be in trouble unless you've discussed this in advance. Here's how one salesperson from an office products company described exactly this problem. "The first time my manager came with me on a skills coaching call, I just didn't know what to expect. I thought she would be doing the talking, so I just sat in front of the customer and waited. It turned out that she was expecting me to explain why she was there. The customer must have realized that we hadn't got our act together." Don't let that happen to you.

How do we explain to the customer that I'm there as a coach? The key principle here is to keep your explanation simple. We've seen managers and their salespeople get into real difficulty through too detailed and too complex an explanation. A couple of sentences is all you need, so that the customer understands you'll not be taking an active part in the selling; but your couple of sentences are important ones. If the customer doesn't realize that the salesperson is in charge and that you are there as an observer, then you're risking confusion and awkwardness.

In general, we recommend that you get your salesperson to do the explaining. This is because

- It establishes that the seller is in charge of the call, which makes it easier for you to sit back and observe.
- If you begin the talking, then you may find it harder to disengage yourself and take up your observer role.

So, before you enter the customer's office for your first skills coaching call, position your coaching carefully. By choosing the right people to coach, setting up the right kind of calls, and setting the right expectations with both salesperson and customer, you can greatly increase your chances of creating the right conditions for skills coaching.

Use An Effectiveness Model

Good skills coaches invariably have a clear idea of what an effective performance looks like. Before you coach, you must understand what kind of behaviors you are trying to develop by your skills coaching efforts. It's for this reason that we've included a chapter on effectiveness models and how to create them. You may choose to develop a model of your own using Contrast Analysis or Performer Analysis. Alternatively, you can adopt models developed by other people, such as researchers like us. However you decide to do it, a crucial starting point for skills coaching is to be clear about the detailed behaviors that make a salesperson effective. With a model of effective behavior you know what to look for during sales calls. What's more, the clearer and the more specific your model, the easier you'll find it to communicate to your salespeople.

Even if you don't feel able to go through all the steps needed to develop an effectiveness model, *do*—at a very minimum— travel with your best salespeople before you begin any skills coaching. Watch them in action. Think about what they are doing differently. Try to describe these differences in terms of the behaviors they use. You'll be surprised at the difference this will make to the effectiveness of your skills coaching.

Skills Coaching: A Question of Style

Some excellent strategy coaches we've worked with have been, at best, mediocre skills coaches. That's because strategy coaching and skill coaching each demand different skills. It's quite possible to be good at one without being good at the other. We once worked with an outstanding strategy coach whose salespeople dreaded his skills coaching. The qualities that made him so good at strategy were a ruthless intellect, merciless analytical ability, a deep understanding of purchasing procedures, and an extraordinary creativity which allowed him to out think his competition. Unfortunately, when it came to skills coaching, his abilities were much less evident. In strategy coaching, his capacity to analyze complex problems and devise creative solutions meant that anyone with a really tough problem tended to seek him out because he was such a powerful strategic thinker. It was a different story when it came to skills coaching. Far from seeking him out, his people avoided him and came up with elaborate excuses to escape skills coaching from him. Sitting in on several of his skills coaching sessions, we were able to see why. It wasn't that he was deliberately unhelpful. On the contrary, his strong analytical skills let him make lots of potentially useful observations about how his people could sell more effectively. His problem wasn't substance, it was *style.* There was something about the way he coached that created barriers to learning and prevented him from developing the skills in his people that he genuinely was trying to improve. But "style" is a slippery word. It's hard to pin down. When people talk about a difficulty with style, it's a fair bet that they mean something's wrong but they haven't a clue what it is. Watching this coach in action, that's exactly how we felt. Here was this sincere and clearly talented manager who was entirely failing to improve his people's skills. Why? What was going wrong? At the time, we weren't at all clear. Since then we've watched many hundreds of managers in action during skills coaching. We've a much better idea of what goes wrong and how to prevent it. We can now be more precise about what we mean by an effective coaching *style.*

Where Skills Coaching Goes Wrong

There are four common mistakes that managers make during skills coaching. Each of these mistakes is relatively easy to prevent. By recognizing and avoiding them, skills coaching becomes easier and more effective. Let's look at each of these mistakes, why they happen, and how to prevent them.

Mistake 1: Underestimating salespeople's discomfort: Skills coaching is much more threatening than strategy coaching, both for seller and for coach. One reason, as we've seen, is that skills coaching centers around a sales performance in the customer's office, with all the attendant pressures that the customer's presence creates. Another reason is that the coaching is about *skills*—about the sales behavior that's being used in calls. Salespeople know that their behavior during calls is being watched and analyzed by their manager. Inevitably, this tends to make them feel self-conscious and it's likely to distract them from their selling. Consequently, most salespeople feel that they sell less well during coaching calls than they do when they are alone with the customer. This can create acute discomfort for salespeople. Put yourself in the seller's shoes. Here you are in a sales call with your manager present watching you at work. Clearly, you'd like your manager to be impressed, but as the call progresses, you feel uncomfortable and you become awkwardly aware that your selling isn't up to its usual standard. You feel increasingly self-conscious and the smooth flow of the call starts to disintegrate. As you fight to get the call back on track, you wonder what your manager must be thinking—and that thought distracts you still more. After the call, as your manager prepares to review it with you, you're likely to feel discomfort about your performance and resentment over the whole idea of skills coaching.

It's not only the seller who is likely to be uncomfortable. The manager who has just watched a sales call that, to put it kindly, was a long way from perfect will also feel unhappy. "Should I have intervened?" the manager will wonder; "did I do the right thing to keep quiet? Are all this person's calls this bad?" With thoughts like these, when manager and seller sit down to review the call, skills coaching may be off to a perilous start.

Too many managers spring straight into discussion of skills at this point, without taking into account that both parties may be feeling awkward about what went on in the call. It's a serious mistake for a coach to underestimate the degree of discomfort that a salesperson may be feeling. Over and over again we've seen coaching start off on the wrong foot. It's particularly likely to go wrong if the coach, frustrated by the call, decides to let that frustration show by starting with negative comments about how the call was handled. Good coaching demands a careful creation of receptivity at the start of the discussion. When we're training coaches, we suggest that there are two simple steps they should take to help the coaching get off to a good start.

- *Acknowledge pressure:* Let the seller know that you understand how difficult it is to make a call with a coach present. Say things like, "I always felt uncomfortable when my boss came out with me because I sold better when I was on my own," or "It's tough to sell when someone's watching you. . . ." By acknowledging that your presence has made selling harder, you reassure your people that you won't judge them badly if they haven't been at their best. We've seen this simple reassurance diffuse potential resistance more effectively than much more elaborate introductions. So we advise coaches, particularly if they haven't been skills coaching in the field with this salesperson before, to start by acknowledging the pressure that the coach's presence creates.

- *Pick out a positive:* We're all of us much better at seeing what's going wrong in sales calls than what's going right. We once set up a small experiment to demonstrate this. We made a videotape of a sales call that was specially designed to have an exactly even balance of both good and bad points. We then asked experienced sales managers to watch the tape and to pick out any points about the selling that struck them as worthy of comment. We were careful to be very neutral in our instructions, reminding the managers that they could pick out both good points and bad points. When we analyzed managers' comments, we found that 82 percent of comments were about the *bad* points in the tape. They said things like, "He shouldn't have ignored that objection," "He wasn't listening," or "The customer didn't want to hear all those features." Only 18 percent of comments were positive or neutral. Most sales calls, rather like our videotape, contain a mixture of things that were effective and things that weren't. Yet we're naturally more attuned to seeing the ineffective. We see faults, we see things we would have handled differently, and we see mistakes. Inevitably, this tends to color the coaching we give. It's much easier to coach by focusing on the very visible negatives than on the positives that we may be less skilled at seeing.

Because of this, we advise coaches to start their coaching by picking out, and mentioning, something positive that happened during the call. We do this for two reasons. The obvious reason for picking out a positive is simply that the discussion begins on a positive note. There's a more subtle reason too. If coaches know they will be starting the discussion by picking out a positive, then they will be looking for that positive during the call. In this way, by alerting coaches to look for something positive we can counterbalance our natural tendency to see too many negatives.

Mistake 2: Forcing the coach's opinion on salespeople: The next common mistake stems from the difficulties of handling a skills coaching role that requires the coach to keep quiet during calls. Many managers find it frustrating to sit silently through sales calls quietly taking notes. They itch to say things. Thoughts pile up inside them and, as soon as they are out of the customer's office, the dam bursts. They can't wait to give their opinions about the call and how it was handled. They say things like, "You need to work on your product knowledge," or "What you should do is find out more about customer needs." Let's assume, for a moment, that these conclusions are accurate. What's wrong with starting with conclusions like these? It's an issue of acceptability. A manager would never dream of offering conclusions to a customer in the first minute of a call. Even someone with mediocre selling skills knows that you don't start a sales call by saying, "What you need is our product." To do so would mean almost certain objections and rejection by the customer. Yet, with alarming frequency, that's exactly how managers behave while coaching salespeople. They begin with the equivalent of "What you need is. . . ." It's not good selling and its not good coaching either. Just as a customer will resist and raise objections if you offer your products too soon, so salespeople will resist your coaching message if you start with conclusions. Their resistance easily leads into argument and, before you know it, coaches find themselves forcing their opinions on their salespeople. It's a common and a serious coaching mistake.

How can coaches avoid this mistake? The easiest way is to treat a skills coaching discussion as if it were a sales call. Use your selling skills. What do you do when you sell to customers? You ask questions. And asking questions is just as powerful a technique in skills coaching. Instead of starting with your conclusions about the call, ask questions like, "How do you feel about the call?" "Did you meet your objectives?" "Did the call go as you'd expected?" or "If you were making this call over again, what would you do differently?"

Coaching should never become a confrontation between you and your salesperson about what happened—or what should have happened—during the call. Coaching through questions is the surest way to avoid an unproductive clash of opinions.

Mistake 3: Overloading salespeople with too many points: Most skills coaching would be twice as effective if it covered half as many points. Take, as an example, this gem we recorded during our coaching research:

> . . . and we've agreed that you jump in much too quickly with product details, so in future you're going to cut back on the product area . . . that means offering details later in the call . . . and when you do talk about the product, be sure it's benefits not features . . . which brings me to another thing: you've got to focus on applications more. That means using the banking applications package. Even more important you've got to work on your questions. Next time I'm with you I want to hear a lot more open questions. And sometimes, I notice, you don't wait for the customer to answer, so hold back more. Whatever you do, don't ask those double questions we talked about. And I know it's good to take notes, but don't let it lose you eye contact with the customer, which happened here. Keep eye contact and use a lot more of positive nonverbals like smiling and nodding.

Pity the poor recipient of this torrent of advice. It would be hard enough, working under the pressures of the average sales call, to put just one of these lessons into action. A rare person—and, believe us, it *is* a rare person—might be able to execute two of these lessons in the same call. Nobody we've ever met could simultaneously put all nine of this manager's points into action. The problem here is one of gross overload. Yet it's easy to see why a coach would behave this way. It seems, somehow, that the more lessons you can extract from a call, the better your coaching should be. It's hard for a coach who comes out of a call brimming with good advice and insights, to hold back from dumping them all on the unfortunate seller. Here again, there's a parallel to selling. One of the most common faults of less experienced salespeople is an irresistible urge to tell the customer *everything* about the product. In selling, you soon learn that more isn't necessarily better. Customers quickly become confused and overloaded with too much product information. It's the same in coaching with one additional complication. When you coach, you're not just giving information. You're asking the salesperson to carry out the difficult additional step of translating the information into selling skill. All the evidence suggests that people learn new skills slowly and in small increments. It's perilously easy to overload people with too many points. In fact, this is the most common of all errors in skills coaching.

How can a coach control this natural tendency to cover too many points during coaching? We find that the concept of a *Priority Behavior* is helpful here. When we're training coaches, we ask them, in each coaching session, to pick out *just one* behavior for the seller to work on. This we call the Priority Behavior. From all the potential opportunities for improvement that the coach has observed during the call, the Priority Behavior should be the one key behavior or skill that, if executed more effectively, would most help the seller perform better. By focusing their coaching on this single behavior, managers can greatly speed skills learning. Many of the managers we've worked with have initially been doubtful about our claim that skills learning is much faster if you coach just one behavior at a time. They accept that people are easily overloaded but feel that it's realistic to coach two or three behaviors at once. The idea of working on a single behavior sounds inefficient and unnecessary. Surely, they argue, we'll get faster change if our people are working on several behaviors at a time, getting a little more skilled at each. If you don't believe our claim that it's actually faster to develop skills one behavior at a time, try it out for yourself in your coaching. You may find yourself pleasantly surprised, as many of the coaches we've trained have been, at how much more quickly your people learn skills when you focus your coaching on one priority behavior.

Mistake 4: Failure to follow-up: Our fourth and final common mistake isn't unique to coaching. Of all managerial weaknesses, one of the most epidemic is poor follow-up. Whether we're talking about coaching, delegating, goal setting, or simple day-to-day management, persistent and systematic follow-up is an essential—if tedious—ingredient for success. Coaching suffers particularly badly when it comes to follow-up. Many coaches clearly don't see the important role that follow-up plays in the success of their efforts. Managers who, for example, would never dream of letting a reporting system drift unmonitored, seem quite happy to leave coaching lessons to somehow implement themselves. We once worked with a sales manager in a large communications company who was especially proud of the meticulous attention he gave to following up on projects. In his office, he proudly showed us a whole range of project management software and tickler files that he had specially configured to let him follow up on every conceivable detail of systems installations under his control. On his desk, set in a perspex block, was the motto, "Control the details and the big picture will be yours." Here, without doubt, was a true believer in the supreme power of detailed follow-up, but when we started to discuss how he coached one of his people, it was a different story. "Yes," he told us, "I went out on some calls with her a couple of months ago and I thought she was too technically centered so I suggested that she practiced asking customers more questions about business issues." "How is that working?" we asked. "Oh," he replied, "I assume she's doing it OK." "Assume?" we queried. "Well, she's bright," he responded, "so I suppose that she's been working on it during the last two months." It was clear that he hadn't given a moment's thought to following up on his coaching visits. Yet he would have been the first to criticize any fellow manager who allowed a single day to go by without following up the progress of a customer installation project.

When we're working to develop coaching skills, we urge managers to give special attention to the issue of follow-up. We suggest that any coaching session should end with an agreed *practice plan* which has two components:

- *Specific goals:* The plan should set a goal in the form of a specific behavior that needs to be practiced together with a time period in which the practice will take place. So, for example, manager and seller might agree that during the next two weeks the seller will practice the Priority Behavior of asking questions to uncover customer problems with the existing system.

- *Specific follow-up:* The plan should specify how and when the coach will follow up in order to ensure that the specific goals are being met. So, for example, manager and seller might agree that by Wednesday the seller will make a list of some questions that could be asked to uncover these problems and will meet with the manager to review the list. Then, two weeks from today, the manager will spend another day in the field with the seller helping the seller plan one or more calls, observing how the seller is using these questions during the calls, and giving feedback afterwards.

Good follow-up is, of course, time consuming. It's tempting for a busy manager to try to save some of this time by cutting coaching follow-up to a minimum. This is a false economy. Without adequate follow-up, behavior change—if it happens at all—will be minimal.

A Coaching Model

Let's now combine the common mistakes and what to do about them into a coaching model, illustrated in figure 6.2

This model takes each of the four common skills coaching mistakes and, in its place, suggests an action that will allow the manager to avoid each one. We find it a very simple, but very effective, skills coaching model. We should point out that books and programs on coaching abound and that there are dozens of alternative coaching models you might choose. We happen to like this one a lot because it combines two very important virtues. First, it's simple. In our time we've designed some extraordinarily complex coaching models. Consequently, we really know what we're talking about when we say that simplicity is a great virtue. The second reason why we like this model is that it was designed to solve common real-life coaching problems. Again, if we go back to some of the earlier models we've been associated with, we have to confess that these models were designed more as an elegant way to coach than as a practical answer to managers'

FIGURE 6.2

Coaching model that addresses common coaching mistakes

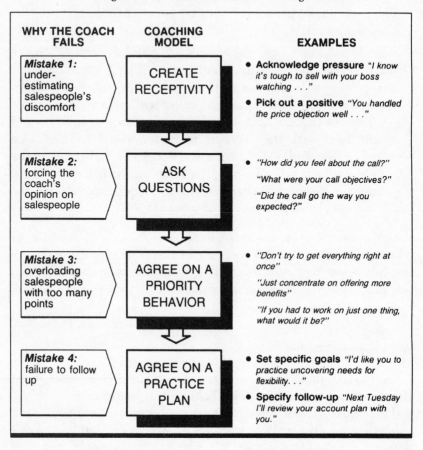

coaching problems. However, if you've been brought up to coach to a different model, if you're comfortable with your model, and if it brings you results, we're not suggesting that you should drop it and adopt ours. What matters is that you adopt some kind of a systematic coaching process. Which kind is a matter of preference. In deciding whether our model is appropriate for you, it's useful to ask yourself the question, "Do I ever make any of the common coaching mistakes?" If your answer is yes, then we think you'll find our little model a helpful way to avoid these mistakes in the future and make your skills coaching more effective.

7

FINDING THE RIGHT CARROT

Motivation and Performance in the Major Sale

Sales force motivation is a hot topic for many chief executives. In a survey of CEOs who were members of the Young Presidents' Organization, we found that 55 percent of them were actively implementing measures aimed at increasing the motivation of their salespeople. Some of these CEOs felt that sales force motivation was the single most powerful method available for increasing sales productivity. We interviewed one CEO whose company manufactured and sold electrical goods and lighting fixtures. He told us, "I've tried everything you could possibly imagine for improving my sales. I've even tried some things you might prefer not to imagine. I've spent hundreds of thousands on things like tracking systems and selection tests. But now I've found the ultimate—and I mean the ultimate—sales productivity tool." He paused to let our curiosity build a little. Then he went on, "The best $10,000 I ever spent in my life was on a motivational speaker. He spent three hours in a hotel room talking to my sales force and at the end of it he had them so fired up that I thought the hotel was going to burn down." We'd heard this kind of enthusiasm before and we were skeptical. "Yes, Tom, but what did it do to your sales?" we asked. "It was amazing," he replied, "I've been able to track *at least* a million dollars in extra sales from that one meeting. Not bad for a $10,000 investment!" We remained doubtful. Over the years we had investigated dozens of enthusiastic claims for sales performance miracles, only to find that the actual productivity gains were nonexistent or dubious.

This doubt must have shown in our faces. "I know you don't believe me," he sighed, "I'm used to that. Nobody believes results this dramatic. But they're true all the same." At that moment we were interrupted by his secretary, who came in to announce the arrival of a visitor. Tom was delighted. "I've got a witness," he told us. "Here's Jack, and he'll confirm everything I've said." Jack, it turned out, was chief executive of a company that designed and installed large commercial swimming pools. He was a nonexecutive director of our CEO's board. "Tell them Jack," Tom urged, "it *was* a million dollars we got from that motivational session, wasn't it?" Jack was a little more cautious. "Well," he began carefully, "sales certainly increased dramatically. And, yes, we had upwards of a million more in revenue than the same period last year. And I guess that most of the salespeople believe the session really made a big difference for them. But . . . " he paused for thought, "Oh hell, Tom's right. This guy sure had them so motivated there wasn't a mountain they couldn't climb."

We detected some reluctance from Jack. "You sound only half convinced." we prompted him. "No, don't misunderstand me," he told us, "I think that the motivational session was great and that it brought amazing results for Tom's company. In fact, I was so convinced that I got the same speaker to come and do a similar session for us. I was expecting the same sort of results but our session bombed." Further questioning revealed that Jack's sales force certainly liked the motivational speaker, although without quite the same fervent enthusiasm that Tom's folks had shown. The problem was that results didn't show the expected increase. Neither Tom nor Jack could explain why. "Maybe the guy had an off day," was Tom's only suggestion. We had a different explanation. It was the same old story we'd seen so many times before, but from a different angle. A technique that was spectacularly successful in one company had failed in another. And, surprise, surprise, it turned out that the two companies had a different size of sale. Tom's company sold low-value products in single-call sales—and here there seemed a direct link between motivating the sales force and increasing sales productivity. In contrast, Jack's organization was involved in a classic high-value, major sale. And, as so often happens, what worked well in small sales failed entirely in more complex ones.

Efficiency and Effectiveness Again

To some extent, the concepts of efficiency and effectiveness we discussed in chapter 2 help explain why so many attempts to increase motivation, such as the use of motivational speakers, are more successful in small sales than in large. As we've seen, it's generally true that efficiency has a greater impact on performance in small sales. Most motivational tools—whether speakers, prizes, or incentive payments—have a greater influence on efficiency than they do on effectiveness. In other words, most motivational tools are better at encouraging people to work harder than to work smarter. By paying you twice as much, or by firing up your enthusiasm, we can motivate you to work harder. We can get you to make more calls or work longer hours, and as a result, we can increase efficiency. But can we pay you to work smarter? Can we motivate you to be more effective? It's not so easy. A powerful motivational speaker may get salespeople enthusiastic enough to work harder than ever before. However, that enthusiasm doesn't translate so readily into working smarter.

Theories of Motivation

A simplistic view of motivation, based solely on the *working harder-working smarter* model would suggest that motivation is a valuable management tool in small sales but has little or no role in improving major sales performance. Fortunately, that's not true. There are motivational tools and techniques that allow a manager to improve the performance of major account salespeople. Unfortunately, these methods are more difficult than the simple motivational techniques that are provided in the standard tool kit most managers have received from sales training. To understand how to motivate salespeople in major sales, we'll have to begin by looking more closely at motivational theory and how it has been changing in recent years.

Motivation theory today is a sophisticated, complex, and sometimes confusing field. Perhaps it's this complexity that has kept motivation research during the last twenty years from becoming better known.

Yet, unless you have at least a passing acquaintance with modern motivation theory, it's hard to understand the issues involved in motivating salespeople in the major sale. So, before we get down to practical tools for motivating, let's take a brief diversion into modern motivational theories. The motivation chapter of almost every book on management summarizes the older work of Maslow and Herzberg, so we needn't repeat that material here. However, there's one of the older theorists, David McClelland, whose work is less well known than it deserves to be.

Need Achievement Theory

McClelland's work on need for achievement, carried out in the late 1950s, contains several interesting points for sales management. Unfortunately, in common with so many other motivation theorists, McClelland couldn't resist adding a little piece of unintelligible jargon to complicate an otherwise lucid account. He used the term N-Ach to describe the need for achievement. So a high N-Ach individual is a person having a strong need to achieve, while a low N-Ach individual has a weak need for achievement. McClelland predicted that high N-Ach individuals would seek out jobs in sales. High N-Ach people have certain recognizable characteristics. They show distinctly similar patterns of behavior, and their outlook on life has clear similarities. For example:

High achievers like tasks of moderate difficulty: Very easy tasks bore them because they don't provide enough challenge. The fact that high achievers get bored without a challenge is hardly a startling new discovery. Most managers would have predicted it without any difficulty and without the need for research. However, most managers would also have predicted that high achievers would enjoy challenge, so that the harder the task the better they would like it. And that prediction would be wrong. McClelland showed that salespeople high on N-Ach chose tasks of moderate difficulty. In contrast, those low on N-Ach were less likely to choose moderately challenging tasks. McClelland devised an ingenious little test to demonstrate this. It's a test we've had a lot of fun with and, because it's easy for you to try out for yourself, we'll describe one version of it here. We used this version some years ago with Liam Gorman of the Irish Management Institute, and whether due to the test or the Irish whiskey we were using to help make our observations more accurate, a memorable time was had by all. You'll need a dart board and darts. Ask the salespeople to come into the room one at a time. Give each person three darts. Tell them they can stand as close or as far from the dart board as they wish. Their task is to throw the three darts to be as near to the bullseye as possible. Most people are momentarily thrown into confusion at the idea that they can stand *anywhere.* Some of our subjects chose to stand a couple of feet from the board, some chose to stand further away. At the extreme, one salesperson stood inches from the board and pushed the darts in as if they were thumbtacks. Another terrified us by trying to throw the darts from over 50 feet away with great oaths, greater force, and even greater inaccuracy.

Sure enough, McClelland's predictions about task difficulty were nicely demonstrated. The high N-Ach salespeople—who had scored high on need achievement tests—tended to stand a *moderate* distance from the board. If their first dart succeeded, then they stood back a little further. If it failed, then they moved in closer. Low N-Ach scorers, on the other hand, usually stood very close like our thumbtack exponent, or unrealistically far back like our forceful but inaccurate maniac. What has this got to do with sales motivation? Be patient. As Liam explained to the puzzled salespeople helping us in our experiment, it will get clearer when it gets clearer. For now, let's conclude that people with high need achievement will selectively choose tasks of moderate difficulty.

High achievers set realistic goals: Associated with their preference for tasks of moderate difficulty, high N-Ach people tend to set realistic goals in line with their abilities and skills. They don't, for example, dream of maybe becoming CEO one day. Instead, they think about how they can progress into sales management within three years. They don't aim to double their sales, they plan a realistic 15 percent increase over last year. Goal setting—or, at least, goal setting measured in terms of sales volume—is generally easier for salespeople in small sales. One of the difficulties of the large sale is that business doesn't come in the same steady stream characteristic of the smaller sale. Realistic goal setting can be tougher in major sales and high achievers may need some help, particularly when they are new to major account selling.

High achievers seek and use feedback: McClelland found that high N-Ach people sought feedback on their performance and used that feedback in order to improve. So, he suggested, those jobs that provided plenty of feedback—or had tangible, measurable results—would be particularly attractive to those with high N-Ach. Right at the top of his list of attractive occupations, McClelland put selling. From his point of view it was an ideal occupation for the high need achiever. Performance was easily measurable, there was plenty of feedback from customers and from sales results, goal setting was encouraged by most sales managements.

Unfortunately, McClelland was working at a time when nobody was thinking much about the differences between large and small sales. In small sales, he was right. There *is* feedback from results, but how about the larger sale? It's not so easy to see how you're doing by looking at this week's sales volume. In fact, in very large sales, there will be long periods where salespeople are starved of sales results and customer feedback. If McClelland is correct, high N-Ach individuals easily become demotivated without constant feedback on their performance. There's an immediate implication here for sales managers. To keep your people motivated, you must find other ways to measure their performance and provide them with feedback. Your high N-Ach people may look to *you,* rather than customers or sales results, as the source of an important component of their motivation.

High achievers take personal responsibility for success: One of the reasons McClelland suggested that high achievers would seek out jobs in selling was that sales jobs allowed individuals to take responsibility for their performance. High N-Ach people like to feel in control of their own success. If they win, they want the credit—if they lose, they are happy to shoulder the blame. High achievers may therefore be more comfortable working alone than working in a team.

Again, we see a difference here between small and large sales in terms of need achievement. In small sales it's more common for salespeople to be working alone. Increasingly, in large sales, salespeople are members of a team. In the small sale it's easy for successful salespeople to compare their sales figures with those of others and to feel that they, and they alone, won that business. In the large sale it's much harder for salespeople to see the link between their own efforts and results.

Conclusions from N-Ach Theory

What lessons can we draw from McClelland's work on need achievement? Two important conclusions stand out. First, using the N-Ach concepts, it's possible to create an *achievement climate*—a set of conditions that let you arouse or release an individual's need to achieve. In this way you can create an environment that will allow high need achievers to succeed and will encourage others to adopt the behaviors used by high achievers. So, for example, a manager can

- Provide tasks of *moderate difficulty,* making sure that people realistically assess challenge and, in particular, that they don't take on tasks too difficult for them where possibility of failure is high.

- Help people set *realistic goals,* so that their expectations in terms of such things as sales volume, or how long it's going to take them to penetrate an account, are realistic and achievable.

- Provide *feedback* to people on how they are doing. This feedback can take many forms. For example, a manager can help people develop clear account strategies so that progress can be assessed against the strategy plan. This not only provides feedback, it can also be a valuable exercise in setting realistic goals. Going out with people on calls and coaching their selling skills is another valuable form of feedback. We, and members of our research team, traveled with thousands of salespeople, watching their selling skills in action for our book *SPIN® Selling.* During our research we found, over and over again, that successful salespeople in the larger sale showed great interest in having us travel with them. Many of them regretted that their manager didn't come out with them on calls as often as they would like and that they didn't get enough feedback on how they were selling. High need achievement people welcome feedback and a good manager must try to provide it.

Once Again: Large Sales Are Different

The second conclusion we can draw from McClelland's work is that, yet again, the distinction between small sales and larger ones is all important. In motivational terms, small sales can provide the right achievement conditions for high N-Ach people without very much action on the part of sales managers. As McClelland himself pointed out, high N-Ach people gain satisfaction from jobs in sales because these jobs give lots of feedback on performance and they allow people to take personal responsibility for their achievement. As we've seen, that's true in smaller sales but rarely true in major sales. In small sales, the job itself may provide the right conditions for high achievement. A high N-Ach person can derive job satisfaction and perform well in smaller sales without any action on the part of sales management. In other words, the job motivates even if management doesn't. However, that's not true in major sales. The job doesn't intrinsically provide motivation. In major sales, there's often a lack of feedback, it's harder to set realistic goals, its difficult for salespeople to feel complete individual responsibility for their success or failure. Under these conditions, sales managers become the critical link in maintaining motivation.

What's New in Motivation Theory?

Since the classic theories of Maslow, Herzberg, and McClelland, there's been a lot of further work in motivation which hasn't yet worked its way into books on sales management. At the risk of oversimplifying a very complex body of research, we can group current motivation theories into four main types.

Need Theories

Need theories of motivation attempt to explain motivation level by examining those factors within an individual that energize, direct, or stop behavior. Most ideas presented by the classic thinkers on motivation, such as Maslow, Herzberg, and McClelland, are examples of need theories.

If you measure the importance of a contribution by its space in textbooks or the hours of management training time devoted to it, Maslow and Herzberg are certainly the major contributors to Need Theory. However, as we've seen, David McClelland's work provides some of the most useful and practical insights about motivation for sales managers.

FIGURE 7.1

Theories of Motivation

THEORY	WHAT IT SAYS
Need Theory	Motivation results from factors (such as the need for self esteem) within an individual that energize, direct, or stop behavior.
Equity Theory	Motivation is influenced by a desire to achieve fair and equitable treatment relative to others.
Expectancy Theory	Motivation requires three conditions: • *Expectancy*: the belief that effort will result in performance • *Instrumentality*: the belief that performance will be rewarded • *Valence*: the value of the reward to the recipient.
Attribution Theory	Motivation is influenced by people's desire to understand why they succeed or fail.

Equity Theories

Equity theories of motivation have focused on motivation from the perspective of the social comparisons people make between themselves and others. While Need Theory suggests that our behavior is most influenced by inner needs and drives, Equity Theory sees our behavior as influenced by a desire to achieve fair and equitable treatment relative to those around us. Equity Theory distinguishes between two different ways people make comparisons between themselves and others—outcomes and inputs. Outcomes are those things that are the results or outcomes of work, such as pay, prestige, or fringe benefits. Inputs are the efforts required to produce the outcomes, such as hours worked, qualifications, and the degree of effort expended.

Equity Theory predicts that people will become unhappy when they compare themselves with others and find that inputs or outputs don't match up fairly. So, for example, some airlines recently adopted a two-tier pay structure, giving newly hired staff less pay (outputs) for the same work (inputs). Equity Theory would predict that a whole heap of motivational trouble would result from this two-tier system—a prediction that has been accurately borne out in the airlines. What's more, while the airlines are hoping that the demotivating effect of this inequity will be short term and will go away once everyone gets used to the new system, Equity Theory predicts that the demotivating effect of the inequity will continue and will have a devastating effect on long-term employee motivation.

Equity Theory raises several issues for the sales management of major sales. Its most important message for sales management is about the powerful motivational value of perceived fairness. And that doesn't only mean the fairness of decisions themselves. It's also equally important that the *process* by which decisions are made is seen to be fair.

Expectancy Theory

Expectancy Theories are broader in scope than Need Theories or Equity Theories. It's harder to summarize Expectancy Theories because they exist in many different versions, the best known ones being those of Vroom and of Porter and Lawler. Put very simply, Expectancy Theory states that people are motivated to work when they expect they will be able to achieve the things they want from their jobs. Most versions of Expectancy Theory suggest that motivation is the result of three different beliefs that people have:

- Expectancy: the belief that a person's efforts will bring about the desired result or performance. For example, a salesperson may operate on the *expectancy* that putting effort into planning sales calls will bring more sales. Under these conditions the salesperson will be motivated to plan. However, a salesperson who doesn't expect that the planning effort will bring results, will not be motivated to take planning seriously.

- Instrumentality: the belief that the desired result or performance will be rewarded. To continue our example, the salesperson who plans sales calls with the expectation of making more sales will believe that more sales will be *instrumental* in getting them more income, more status, or more reward. Motivational problems will arise if the link between performance and reward becomes unclear. For example, if the compensation system becomes so complex that salespeople can't see the link between their sales volume and their paycheck, then the compensation system no longer motivates them.

- Valence: the perceived value of the rewards to the recipient. For a reward to be motivating, the salesperson must see the reward as valuable. So, going back to the example, we could imagine a sales manager setting up a sales contest with a case of whisky as the prize. To a nondrinking salesperson in the team, the reward has little value and therefore isn't likely to stimulate performance. The contest, for that individual, has failed to motivate.

An obvious consequence of Expectancy Theory for sales management is that a successful plan to motivate salespeople requires attention to all three components: expectancy, instrumentality, and valence. So, to take another example, if you hope to motivate your people to produce a sales strategy plan for each of their key accounts, you must have

Expectancy, so that your people see that their strategic planning will bring them more sales.

Instrumentality, so that they see the link between more sales and rewards.

Valence, so that the rewards matter.

If any of these three motivational components is absent, your motivational attempt is likely to fail.

Attribution Theory

The fourth class of motivation theories, Attribution Theory, offers some interesting insights into the difficulties of motivating in the major sale. It agrees with the previous theories that people are motivated to maximize their rewards. However, Attribution Theory adds a new twist. It suggests that people are motivated to understand *why* they succeed or fail. We've included this theory because it has been used by some motivation researchers to help explain why it's easier to motivate people to sell harder than to sell smarter. Let's explore this by looking at three motivational measures that have been used to understand the harder vs. smarter distinction. These are:

- *Persistence,* which means working for a longer period of time. Highly motivated people won't easily be discouraged and will keep trying even if they meet some failure or rejection. To increase their chances of success, many people will attempt to alter their level of persistence. They will say to themselves, "I mustn't be discouraged. Perhaps if I stick with it, I'll succeed." So persistence becomes one of the strategies people use to turn their perceived failure into success. And, of course, persistence can be influenced by management or by the reward system. You can motivate your people to be more persistent.

- *Intensity,* which means working harder, faster, or more intensively. A motivated person is likely to work harder than a less motivated person. Altering the intensity of effort is a common strategy people use to help themselves be more successful. "I'll increase my success by working harder," say those people trying to understand why their performance isn't succeeding as well as they would like. "I'll make more calls. I'll try to set up more appointments." Reward systems can, and do, influence the intensity of an individual's efforts. However, going back to what we said about the relationship between selling harder and success, it's clear that salespeople who changes the *intensity* of their efforts will be more likely to succeed if they are involved in small sales than in large.

- *Choice,* which means that people are motivated to choose one type of activity over another. When attempting to understand and increase their successes, people will often alter their choice of activities. So the salesperson who says, "I'll try a different approach with this customer," is using *choice* as a means of understanding what succeeds or fails. While choice *can* be influenced by management or by the reward system, choice is generally harder to alter than persistence or intensity. That's because neither persistence nor intensity involve doing anything new. Persistence is altered by doing the same thing as before but doing it for longer and doing it despite discouragements. Intensity means doing the same thing but doing it harder or faster. Choice, on the other hand, involves doing something new or different. And, because that involves a step into the unknown, it's harder for people to achieve successfully. In sales performance at least, the limiting factor which makes choice a difficult option is that most salespeople are confused about what choice to take. Confronted with failure of their selling skills, for example, they don't know what they should do differently.

Let's go back to our earlier case of the motivational speaker. He motivated the low-end sales force very effectively. How did he do it? He gave people a dynamic shot in the arm that greatly increased their enthusiasm. Looking at this newly found enthusiasm in terms of *intensity, persistence,* and *choice,* it's easy to see why the speaker was successful. Enthusiasm alters *persistence,* so a really enthusiastic person keeps trying and will be less easily discouraged by rejection. Enthusiasm also greatly alters *intensity*. The sales force, full of enthusiasm, would work harder. They would make more calls, they would telephone more suspects and prospects. How did their enthusiasm influence the third component of motivation, *choice?* Chances are that the speaker did little to influence choice which, as we've seen, is much more difficult to alter. In the small sale, where we've seen a direct link between activity levels and sales success, there's a good chance that altering persistence and intensity would increase activity and lead—as in this case—to better sales results.

Now turn to the unimpressive impact of the same speaker on the high value salesforce. What was different? In high-value sales, neither *persistence* nor *intensity* has much impact on success because selling harder is so much less important than selling smarter. Enthusiasm alone doesn't do much to alter the *choice* component of motivation. To make the swimming pool sales force more successful they would have to behave differently. They would have to gain new skills and plan new strategies. They would have to know what to do differently and how to do it before the *choice* element of motivation could come into play. That's a tall order to achieve in a three-hour motivational session. No wonder the speaker failed.

Long on Words, Short on Meaning

From this brief overview, you may have concluded that underneath all the complex terms like *valence* or *instrumentality*, motivation theory isn't really saying very much. If that's your conclusion, then you're in good company. That interesting and thoughtful writer on management, Charles Handy, wrote in his book *Understanding Organizations*,

> Having got this far in an overview of motivation theory, the reader may perhaps be experiencing, as I did, a sense of disappointment with much of the work in this field.*

*Charles Handy, *Understanding Organizations* (New York: Penguin, 1982).

In preparing material for this book, we've certainly found ourselves sharing some of that disappointment. We've sifted through hundreds of thousands of words in order to find a few practical nuggets of advice on how to motivate salespeople. Sometimes, particularly on days when we'd read a dozen or more arid technical papers, we've been on the verge of giving up on motivation entirely (which, as the theorists would undoubtedly tell us, means that we saw our task lacking in expectancy, instrumentality, and valence!). However, there *are* nuggets to be found buried deep in the vast body of motivation research. Despite all the jargon, and the overly complex statements of the obvious, several of the conclusions from motivation theory have profound implications for how to manage the major sale.

The Three Big Questions

Most sales managers are acutely aware of the important role they can play in motivating their people. However, in our experience, managers are often uncomfortable about the nuts and bolts of how to motivate. Over the years, we've worked with literally thousands of sales managers. When we've been running manager training sessions, for example, it's a certainty that at question time several managers will raise issues about motivation—even if the session is about a different topic such as selling skills or major account strategy. Some of these motivation related questions come up again and again. In particular, there are three big questions we're asked so often that we've come to call them the *big three*. Expressed in a wide variety of ways, these three most frequent questions are:

- What sort of targets should I set to motivate my people?
- What's the role of money, and of other incentives, in motivating better sales performance?
- What motivational tools can I use, particularly ones to help me motivate in complex or major account sales?

How do the theories of motivation we've discussed help us answer practical questions like these? Let's look at each question and see whether current motivation theories offer any helpful insight into these important but difficult issues.

Setting Targets

There's a common belief among sales managers that the higher you set the targets, the more salespeople will achieve. There are plenty of well-documented cases which appear to support the idea. Here's a typical example. A new sales manager was appointed to head a sales force of twenty people in a thermoplastics company. Before the appointment, the sales target had been $25,000 per month. The new manager came from an aggressive competitor and was convinced these targets were too low. "The first thing I did," he told us, "was to *double* sales targets to $50,000 a month. Within three months, business had increased by 30 percent." Many other sales managers have described to us similar dramatic sales increases following drastic upward revision of sales targets. For instance, the head of a small electronics company making programmable remote controls told us that during the last year he had increased sales targets each quarter by 15 percent (that's equivalent to a 75 percent annual increase) and that his people had exceeded the target each time. "My one concern," he told us, "is that I should have asked for twice that."

Stories like these sound convincing, but can they be trusted? Would, for example, *your* people's sales volume rise 30 percent if you doubled their sales targets? Our experience suggests that you've got to treat the links between targets and performance with great caution. In the first case we quoted, for example, there's no doubt that the targets were doubled and that, shortly thereafter, sales increased by 30 percent, but on closer examination, we found that the manager had introduced other sales productivity tools such as telemarketing support and increased advertising. There's no way to establish what role, if any, target setting played in getting the 30 percent increase. When we looked closely at the second case, where targets were increased by 15 percent each quarter and sales went up in proportion, the evidence seemed more convincing. There were no significant changes in advertising levels, sales support, pricing, or other obvious factors to account for the increase. On the face of it, here was a case where there was a direct link between increased targets and increased sales. However, when we looked at the performance of competitors we found that they too had experienced a dramatic upsurge in business. The market was expanding fast and—with or without increased targets—sales were on the rise. Again, we couldn't establish a direct link between targets and sales.

Although, from examination of dozens of cases like these, we've not been able to find any irrefutable evidence linking targets to sales, that doesn't mean that the link doesn't exist. Motivation theory suggests that if there's a link between target setting and sales, it will be most likely under conditions such as:

- *Sales are small and simple:* As we've already seen, working harder is more likely to bring results in small sales than in sales that are large and complex. An increase in targets— providing it's a realistic increase—may cause people to work harder in small sales. However, as Expectancy Theory points out, even in small sales there must be a clearly perceived link in salespeople's minds between effort and results or an increase in targets won't motivate.

- *Existing targets are too low:* Clearly, there will be some cases where a sales force has been set targets that are unrealistically low, but who decides whether a target is realistic? The normal state of affairs, in most of the sales forces we work with, is that senior management firmly believes targets are too low while the sales force is equally vehement that they are too high. Who's right? Many senior managers have a simple way to answer that question. As the sales VP of a Fortune 100 company once told us, "If in doubt, always set the target too high. That way you're safe. If it turns out the target was achievable, then you've won because you get higher performance than anyone expected. And if it turns out that the target *isn't* achievable, you haven't lost anything." As we'll see in the next section, there's a fatal flaw in his logic. For us, the measure of whether an existing target is too low is whether opinion leaders in the sales force will accept a higher target with no more than a token gesture of resistance.

- *Targets are realistic:* Motivation theory would strongly challenge the VP's assumption that if you set targets too high, you haven't lost anything. From the perspective of most theories, an unrealistically high target will not only fail to motivate, it may actively demotivate and lead to poorer performance. N-Ach Theory, as we saw, emphasizes the importance of *realistic* goals for high achievers. Setting targets at a level salespeople feel to be unrealistically high will have a devastating effect on high achievers. Equity Theory predicts that if salespeople feel the targets are unfair they will lose motivation. An unrealistic target also violates one of the basic tenets of Expectancy Theory. The concept of *expectancy,* you'll recall, was that motivation requires the performer to see the link between effort and results. If the target is so high that the performer doesn't believe the result is achievable, then this all-important link breaks down. "Why should I even try," thinks the performer, "because there's no way I can meet a target like that." So, in terms of current motivation theory, the fail-safe concept of when in doubt always set high targets is questionable. On the other hand, if the target is realistic, then it *will* have a motivating effect. As a manager, it's important to remember that your own perception of whether a target is realistic doesn't matter. For a target to motivate it must be seen as realistic by the *performer.*
- *People are involved in the setting of their targets:* There's evidence that people are more motivated—and they perform better—if they are actively involved in setting the goals and targets they are expected to achieve. Whenever possible, involve your people in any target setting. You'll get greater commitment and better performance as a result.

In summary, then, we advise managers to be cautious about the assumption that setting higher targets will automatically lead to higher performance. We warn them to be particularly careful not to make that assumption if their people are involved in larger and more complex sales. Targets *can* motivate, although many of the claims linking target setting to dramatic sales increases are doubtful at best. In terms of motivation theory, targets that motivate must, above all, be seen by salespeople as realistic and achievable.

The Role of Money as a Motivator

The questions managers ask us most often are about the role of financial incentives as motivators. These questions come in a variety of forms: "If I pay more, will my people perform better?" "How much of my people's remuneration should be in the form of bonuses?" "Should I compensate salespeople for sales profitability rather than for sales volume?" or even the most basic question of all, "Does money motivate?" Readers will probably by now be able to predict that our answers usually start with, "It all depends . . . ," and continue with, "The rules are different for larger sales." As it happens, these are pretty good answers. The role of money as a motivator is complex and still the subject of great debate among the so-called experts. That's another way of saying that it all depends. And the rules *are* different for larger sales. Let's consider some of the issues involved in the motivational impact of money:

Money doesn't make people smarter: Slightly oversimplifying the points we made in chapter 2 we can say that one of the key differences between large and small sales is that success in small sales can come from working harder but that success in large sales almost invariably comes from working smarter. Money, like other forms of motivation, is much better at helping people work harder. If we pay you enough, we can almost certainly get you to put in longer hours or make more calls. In other words, we can use money to motivate you to work harder, but that's where the effect of money stops. Even if we offered you an extraordinary seven figure bonus, we couldn't—through payment alone—make you smarter or more skillful. Because of this, there's a clearer link between money and performance in those sales where effort is more important than skill. In large and complex sales we've seen no evidence that performance can be directly increased by paying people more.

Does this mean that a low-end sales force should be paid entirely on commission while a high-end sales force should be paid a flat salary? Alas, it's not quite that simple. Money may not motivate smarter performance but it does do two other important things:

- It lets you recruit good salespeople.
- It helps you keep your high performers.

These are not trivial points as Eastman-Kodak found some years ago. Their copier division competed directly with IBM and Xerox. Partly because of their concern that the Kodak sales force should be highly professional, the division decided to pay salespeople a flat salary rather than commission. "This way," they told us, "our people won't have any incentive to sell customers equipment they don't need." We had to sympathize with their motives. The copier industry at that time was notorious for get-rich-quick salespeople who pushed unnecessarily expensive equipment in order to maximize their commission. Unhappily, Kodak's policy had unintended side effects. Some of their top performers looked across the street and saw Xerox salespeople who were making more than twice as much as they were. It hardly needs Equity Theory to predict that this was highly demotivating and an irresistible temptation for top performers to jump ship and go to work for Xerox. Kodak's payment system lost them some top talent. Worse, they couldn't replace these lost stars by recruitment. We talked to a top ex-IBM copier rep who had interviewed for jobs in both Xerox and Kodak. "I preferred Kodak," he told us, "but in the end I went with Xerox because I figured I could make double." So, although money doesn't motivate smart performance—and by paying your existing sales force more you are unlikely to get higher sales—money does have a very important performance role in keeping your best people.

Lack of money demotivates: Extra money may not bring smarter performance, but as Herzberg pointed out, lack of money can and does cause demotivation. So, just because paying additional money may not improve sales results, you shouldn't assume that performance will remain unaffected if your compensation packages are uncompetitively low. The Kodak example is an extreme case in point. As the Kodak case shows, the most dangerous effects of low pay levels come when your high performers leave and your compensation structure means that you can't afford to replace them.

Compensation systems must be simple: When we're asked about whether profit, or margin-based, compensation systems are better than those that are volume-based, we usually answer with a particularly elaborate form of our favorite "it all depends . . ." reply. In theory, at least, margin-based compensation is a better way to reflect the performance of salespeople in the major sale. That's especially the case when the salesperson has negotiating authority, either over purchase price or over the other factors that can affect margins, such as support, training, and ancillary services. By compensating people on the basis of the profitability of their sales you can encourage salespeople to keep their selling costs down and to work for higher margins business. That's the theory. The practice, unfortunately, is not so easy. There's a fundamental motivational rule about compensation systems. A compensation system ceases to motivate if it becomes too complex for people to understand. We once worked with a computer sales force. They had built a sales compensation system of unimaginable complexity. Salespeople were compensated according to seven different profit contribution measures, some of which varied seasonally. In addition, if installed equipment was removed by the customer, this was charged against salespeople's future compensation. The amount of this charge was determined by factors such as the length of time the equipment had been installed, the presence of certain competitors in the account, and the customer's stated reason for having the equipment removed. In addition there were a number of group bonuses with plus and minus elements based on such things as the company's stock price. As one of the salespeople confessed, "I never know what to expect when I open my paycheck. At first I used to spend hours each month trying to figure it out. Now I think of it like I think of rain—you know it's going to come sometime, but there's no way to tell when it will come or how much you'll get." Clearly a system like this no longer had any motivational effect because people were unable to understand how their performance was reflected in their paycheck.

There's a difficult trade-off here. On the one hand, a good compensation system should reflect a salesperson's true contribution—which the computer company's system tried to do in amazing complexity and detail. On the other hand, motivation theory suggests that a good system must be simple, so that salespeople see a direct link between their effort and their reward. In achieving a system that accurately reflected contribution, the computer company lost simplicity and ended up with compensation that didn't motivate.

What's the ideal balance between accuracy and simplicity? We've a strong preference for erring on the side of simplicity; but we would be the first to admit that our dislike of complex systems is for reasons that go beyond their failure to motivate. We've seen too many sales managers who have tried to use complex compensation plans as management techniques for controlling the sales force. Any compensation plan will fail if it becomes a substitute for good sales management. Xerox Corporation, for example, used to put enormous effort into devising ingenious compensation plans, using their best talents to figure out a way to use compensation to direct and control the sales effort. Salespeople, in response, put equal ingenuity into finding ways to defeat the plan. We were running a training program for a group of top Xerox salespeople during the week when the latest compensation plan was announced. Our group asked for a two-hour break on the day of the announcement so that they could read the plan and, as they put it, "come up with counter strategies and battle plans." When we returned to the class after the break, the walls were covered with calculations and slogans, including the memorable, "In the corporate jungle, those that sell the beans are destined to eat those that count them." Compensation plans make poor management tools because they invariably lead to this kind of antagonism. Our advice is to keep your compensation system as simple as possible.

Compensation must be perceived as fair: We don't need to quote Equity or Expectancy Theory to make the simple point that a compensation system must be fair, but what do we mean by *fair?* That's a much more difficult issue. Flat salaries, as we saw in the Kodak case, are perceived as unfair by high performers who feel that the lack of incentive payment means that all their extra effort and achievement goes unrecognized. Low performers, in contrast, usually find straight salary to be much fairer than incentive compensation. There's no such thing as absolute and objective fairness, it's all a question of perspective. No compensation system will be rated as equally fair by all its participants. However, there are ways in which compensation systems can be used to avoid or soften some of the common issues that give rise to perceptions of unfairness. For example, in large sales, salespeople may have a couple of very big orders each year, with lean periods in between when little is happening in terms of sales. A system that is heavily based on incentives may mean that one person in a sales team earns very little while a colleague who has just landed a large sale is gloating over a fat commission payment. The perceived *unfairness* of this can be softened by compensation that spreads payment to prevent extreme peaks and troughs. A word of caution here: the positive motivational effect of greater fairness can be lost if the compensation smoothing process becomes too complex so that salespeople no longer understand the link between compensation and sales results.

Nonfinancial Incentives

We've seen that the motivational role of financial compensation in larger sales is, to say the least, a complex issue. Fortunately, for many sales managers, financial compensation policy is decided at levels above them and isn't directly their problem. Nonfinancial incentives, on the other hand, are more often under the control of sales managers themselves. What do we know about the motivational impact of nonfinancial rewards? How far do competitions, prizes, plaques, certificates, and other forms of recognition actually motivate people? There's fierce disagreement among those sales managers we've worked with. Once, during a sales conference of one of the world's largest software companies, we saw this issue disintegrate first into disagreement and finally into the nearest thing to a fist fight that the Waldorf-Astoria Hotel allows on the premises. Why did people get so upset? It was at the end of a session on sales quotas, and the president had asked his sales managers an innocent throwaway question, "Should we give out plaques or some similar recognition to salespeople who meet these quotas?" His national sales manager replied first. "I don't think so," he said. "We're a professional sales force and I hope we've gone beyond that sort of thing. Plaques on walls are more appropriate to car dealers than to a high-level sales force like ours". One of his regional sales managers, who was from IBM, spoke up with an opposite view. "In IBM people worked their tails off to get those things," he said; "they were great motivators—what you had on your wall was more important than what you earned." Another regional manager spoke up. "In my last company we had a VP of sales who came from Xerox. He tried to introduce sales awards. The whole idea bombed because salespeople just threw the stuff away. Last I heard he had a cupboard with 500 wooden plaques in it collecting dust." Gradually, others entered into the discussion and it quickly became heated. On one side were those who said that nonfinancial incentives had been as powerful as—or more powerful than—financial rewards. On the other side were those who could show instances where nonfinancial incentives had failed or where they had been seen by the sales force as cheap gimmicks. When everybody had become indecently worked up about the issue, the president turned to us and invited us to comment. The points we made in these less than ideal circumstances were

It's the culture that motivates, not the award itself: Both sides in the debate were right. In the culture of an IBM, a piece of paper—or a little wood and plastic plaque—can have a profound effect on people, their self-esteem and their motivation, but that's not because of the piece of paper itself. The impact comes from what the paper symbolizes *within the IBM culture.* Take away that culture and the paper is worthless. We've seen ex-IBM managers fail dismally in introducing IBM style nonfinancial incentives to their new organizations. They fail whenever they think that the awards themselves have some intrinsic value. Those who succeed in introducing incentives of this sort are the ones who focus on building a culture in which the awards merely act as symbols. So, a manager who introduces nonfinancial incentives without first building a culture where the incentive has symbolic value will achieve nothing. It's like the cyclist who, seeing how much faster cars travel than bicycles, and knowing that cars run on gas, goes to a filling station and tries to put fuel in his bicycle. The fuel is no good without an engine. The engine that provides the power for nonfinancial incentives is the sales culture. The awards themselves are like fuel—useless without the engine.

Looking at awards as symbols helps to prevent another mistake many managers make when considering nonfinancial incentives. We once worked with a soft drinks company that ran a contest for its major account salespeople with a car as a prize. Because the company sales culture didn't put much value on sales contests, there was little enthusiasm from the sales force. Senior management's answer was to offer a *bigger* car and they seemed genuinely astonished when this didn't raise enthusiasm either. Putting twice as much fuel in your bicycle doesn't give it an engine. Larger prizes don't automatically have greater impact than smaller ones. Our advice is not to focus on bigger and better prizes, or on ever more expensive and elaborate plaques. Instead, put your effort into building a culture where modest awards are recognized and valued by your management and salespeople alike as symbols which, in your culture, are associated with sales excellence.

Well-designed incentives don't just interest top performers: Many nonfinancial incentives, particularly those where there's a "grand prize," are designed to have only one winner, which is a mistake. Ninety percent of the sales force, realizing they aren't going to win, immediately switch off and the prize fails to motivate them. The other 10 percent, who are the top performers, show more interest, but because they are top performers, they are usually highly motivated even without the prize. Consequently, the prize has a minimal motivational or performance impact. In contrast, really effective award programs try to involve as wide a group of salespeople as possible. This may mean many smaller prizes or having separate competitions for different levels of experience and performance. Most effective sales organizations try to build this principle of widening the net into their whole performance system. IBM, like many other successful sales forces, sets its quota levels so that 70 to 80 percent of people will make quota. It's the same basic reasoning. A quota, like a prize, will only act as an incentive for people if it's seen as achievable.

Motivate as a team if you sell as a team: Most large sales involve a team effort. It can be really demoralizing for other members of the team, such as analysts, technicians, specialists, or support people, to see the salesperson taking all the credit and winning the awards. If your people sell as a team, try to motivate them as a team. Make sure the support people share in any recognition. Try to bring the team together by your incentives, not split them apart.

YOU may be the biggest nonfinancial incentive: In small sales, results can provide day-to-day motivation, even if the sales manager doesn't, but in larger sales where results don't come every day, the sales manager has a more important part to play. Most sales managers find it odd to think of themselves as a form of nonfinancial compensation. However, in motivational terms, that's just what sales managers are. Like other forms of nonfinancial compensation, sales managers give recognition and reward to their people. Through skills and strategy coaching, and by using the right motivational tools, managers can make a powerful impact on their people's performance. We've seen from Expectancy Theory that people lose their motivation when they can no longer see the link between their actions and the sales results their actions bring. Major sales often require actions in the form of calls spread out over a period of many months before salespeople see any tangible results in terms of orders. During this period, the role of sales managers is to provide a motivational substitute for the regular orders that give motivation to salespeople in smaller sales.

Tools for Motivating in the Major Sale

What motivational tools are available to help managers in major sales? We've seen that motivational speakers, incentive payments, and most other motivational tools that generate enthusiasm to work harder, are much more effective in small sales than in large. Orders are possibly the best motivators of all, but as we've said, in larger sales orders come too infrequently to be used as day-to-day motivation. So what can a manager do? Some of the tools we discussed in the chapters on skill and strategy coaching also have a motivational purpose. Let's look at some of these tools in a motivational rather than a purely coaching context.

Motivation theory suggests that there are several reasons why it will be harder to motivate people in major sales. One reason is the difficulty of goal setting. N-Ach Theory emphasizes the importance of setting realistic goals. In small sales that's relatively easy. Targets can be very specific, measurable, and realistically achievable. For example, the week's target in a typical smaller sales operation might be six sales or $15,000 sales volume. What's more, the goal can easily and quickly be modified downwards or upwards as circumstances warrant. So if a salesperson consistently achieves the goal, then future targets might be raised to, say, seven sales or $18,000 sales volume. In contrast, goal setting is harder in the major sale. In extreme cases the order may be upwards of a year away and its size unknowable. How do you set goals that motivate? We've seen that simply setting efficiency goals, such as making fourteen calls a week, can be counterproductive. Clearly major sales need some alternative tools to help with goal setting. Another motivation problem for the major sale is raised by Expectancy Theory. As we've seen, in large sales it's hard for salespeople to see the link between their performance and their results. A call made today, even if brilliantly handled, may not bring any visible results for months. Under these conditions, salespeople may be unable to see the connection between performance and results.

In a small sale, the outcome of a sales call is obvious and evident: you take the business or you don't. Successful calls are those that result in Orders, unsuccessful calls are the No-sales where the customer turns you down. It's easy to tell which is which and, in the classic one-call sale, there's nothing in between. The regularity and ease with which salespeople achieve Orders means that there's a very visible and motivating link between performance on the call and its result. That ceases to be the case in larger sales where, frequently, less than 5 percent of calls result in an Order or a No-sale. Most calls in major sales result in an Advance or a Continuation. An Advance is where an action is agreed on that moves the sale forward. In contrast, a Continuation is where the sales discussions will continue but no action has been agreed on.

At first sight, the concept of Advances and Continuations doesn't seem to have immediate relevance as a motivational tool. We first introduced the idea to provide ourselves with technical success measures for research into sales effectiveness models. We didn't see any practical application for sales managers and we certainly didn't see any motivational possibilities. In fact, during training sessions with sales managers, we only mentioned the idea as a throwaway comment. However, we were surprised at the impact the idea had on many of the managers we worked

FIGURE 7.2
Outcomes of sales calls

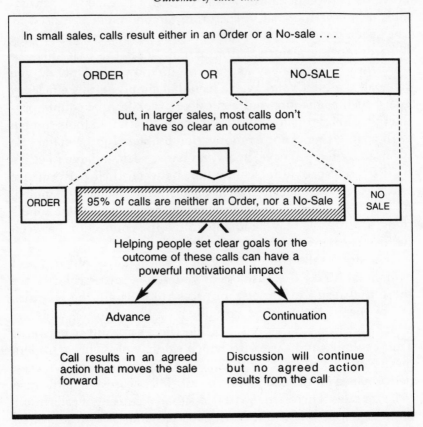

In small sales, calls result either in an Order or a No-sale . . .

ORDER   OR   NO-SALE

but, in larger sales, most calls don't
have so clear an outcome

ORDER   95% of calls are neither an Order, nor a No-Sale   NO SALE

Helping people set clear goals for the
outcome of these calls can have a
powerful motivational impact

Advance   Continuation

Call results in an agreed
action that moves the sale
forward

Discussion will continue
but no agreed action
results from the call

with. People would call us months later to let us know how the
Order-Advance-Continuation-No-sale distinction had been the most
useful single concept of the dozens we'd shared during the program. Naturally, when the idea turned out to be more useful than
we had anticipated, we asked ourselves why. From discussions
with sales managers, we found that many of their people had real
difficulty setting goals. By helping their people plan Advances,
managers were able to help in goal setting for calls. What's more,
when people achieved the planned Advance—such as gaining
access to a higher customer level, arranging a site visit or running
an evaluation test—they came away from the call with a feeling
of movement and progress. In this way, by using the concept of

Advances, managers were able to provide their people with two necessary motivational components. First, the component that N-Ach Theory emphasizes, by planning Advances they were able to help with realistic goal setting. They could help their people set achievable intermediate goals to move the sale forward. The second motivational impact from planning Advances was that the link between present actions and future results became clearer. As one sales manager in Honeywell told us, "My less experienced people used to just keep making calls in the belief that if they called often enough then something might happen down the road. By introducing them to the idea of Advances, I helped them see how what happened in the future was directly tied in to getting some forward movement right now in the next call." Although the Honeywell manager didn't know it, he was using a central concept of Expectancy Theory—the motivational importance of establishing the *link* between behavior (what happens on the call) and results (the potential sale those many months away).

Motivation in the Major Sale

The motivational impact of the *Order–Advance–Continuation–No-sale* distinction rests, as we've seen, on two main motivational concepts:

- Helping people set *goals* that are realistic and that enable them to work smarter, not just harder.
- Helping people see the *link* between their behavior and the ultimate sales result.

Several of the other tools we've mentioned in earlier chapters also embody these concepts. The Key Intervention Points (KIPS), described in chapter 5, are examples of tools that help people in goal setting and linking behavior to results. The tool for expressing objectives in problem-solving terms, for example, helps people set specific goals in realistic customer terms. Vulnerability Analysis℠ helps people see the link between their sales behavior, how the customer evaluates decisions, and the outcome of the sale.

Goals and *links* are fundamental and important concepts, not just for motivational tools, but also for the motivational impact of managers' own behavior. If you've ever been fortunate enough to work for an outstanding sales manager, you've probably experienced what a difference it makes to work for someone who helps you set clear, achievable, and specific goals. If your manager did a good job of motivating you through the discouraging steps of the major sale, think back to exactly how your manager achieved that motivation. Most major account salespeople, when asked about sales managers who really helped their motivation, use phrases like, "helped me see what I needed to do differently," "showed me how to make things happen," or "made me feel I was getting somewhere in the account." In other words, the outstanding motivator showed people the *link* between their behavior and results.

Finally . . .

In this chapter we've seen how the majority of motivational techniques are more effective at encouraging people to work harder than at helping them work smarter. For this reason, most classic motivational tools, like motivational training and incentives, have a more powerful effect in small sales than in large. However, we've also seen how there *are* some motivational tools that do help people's performance in the *working smarter* area that's so important to success in the major sale. In particular, from our survey of modern motivation theory, we've singled out two important dimensions that are crucial to success in motivating major account salespeople. These two dimensions are *setting of realistic goals* and *demonstrating the link between behavior and results.* You can predict the effectiveness of any motivational tool by asking how well it operates on each of these dimensions. Will the new incentive payment system, for example, motivate people to perform better? Not unless it has an impact on how people set *goals* or it helps people see the *link* between their behavior and results.

As researchers' understanding of the major sale grows, there will be an increasing number of tools, such as the *Order–Advance–Continuation–No-sale* concept, that will help managers in goal setting and in linking behavior to results. But, even with the development of new and better management tools, the most important single motivational influence on the major sale is the sales manager. In the small sale there are motivators that can sometimes have a powerful impact equal to a good manager. The outstanding motivational speaker, a steady stream of orders, or the compensation system—factors like these can greatly influence people's motivation to work harder and more successfully in the small sale. In the large sale, however, it's the manager who has by far the greatest impact on motivation. Through coaching of skills and strategy, through goal setting, through helping people see links between their behavior and results, a good manager motivates people to work smarter. No payment system and no motivational tool can equal the impact of a good sales manager.

8

MANAGING A CHANGING SALES FORCE

A Sales Effectiveness Case Study

In this final chapter we want to take the ideas we introduced earlier in the book and show how to put them into practice. To do this we've created a case study. It's a fictitious case, being a composite of events from a half-dozen actual clients we've worked with. To keep things simple, in this case we'll be dealing with the problems of just one sales manager. However, in real life, we usually find ourselves working with *groups* of sales managers implementing strategies to increase sales effectiveness across the whole sales organization. We mention this in case you feel that having two experts ganging up on one poor manager is our normal mode of operation. It's not. In real life we would be more likely to have a dozen managers participating in the conversations and plans we describe. One other thing: our case study will focus on issues that managers typically face when they try to improve sales effectiveness. We're not concerned here with showing—as case studies tend to do—that we can provide some clever answers. Instead, we want to give you a feeling for some of the difficulties and uncertainties that a sales manager must overcome in trying to build sales effectiveness.

222

The Client

Our client is Pat Brown, a newly appointed sales manager for Particle Control Inc. Pat is new to the company. In terms of sales experience, Pat has been in sales for about ten years, starting as a territory sales rep with Texas Instruments. After four years with Texas Instruments, Pat moved to Honeywell, selling control systems for residential and commercial use. Before accepting this new position with Particle Control, Pat had two years as a sales manager at Honeywell, again in the residential and commercial control systems market. There are some similarities between Pat's old marketplace and the market served by Particle Control, which was one reason why Pat felt confident about being successful in this new job. In this case study, we shall begin working with Pat two months into the new job—just long enough for Pat to see that things are going to be a little more difficult than they first seemed. We'll be meeting with Pat once a month for the next nine months to help increase the sales effectiveness of Pat's people and to advise Pat on some strategies for improving sales performance.

Particle Control Inc.

To understand Pat's problems, you'll need a brief overview of Particle Control Inc. and its products. The company makes and installs dust control equipment for a variety of industrial applications. Their sales force has three primary product areas:

- *Electrostatic Dust Precipitators:* These are relatively simple devices which are installed into existing commercial and residential air ductworks to reduce dust in the air. Precipitators cost from $1,500 to $4,000 depending on the model. The precipitator sale is a typical simple sale. The sale can often be completed in a single call. There's usually only one customer involved in the decision. It's a "box" sale in that, apart from some simple wiring and mechanical work, the precipitator just plugs into existing ductwork and isn't part of a specially designed dust control system. Five years ago, the precipitator market was Particle Control's core business. However, with a number of new competitors entering this market, and margins becoming increasingly eroded, the company believes that precipitators will soon become a commodity item. Consequently the company strategy is to move away from precipitators during the next few years and to concentrate on its other products. When Pat was hired, the company explained the mission of sales managers as, "to move us away from the precipitator business and get us into the systems area where the margins are sustainable." At the moment, just over 70 percent of Pat's sales volume comes from precipitator sales.

- *Particle control systems:* The company is pinning its future hopes on building the market for larger particle control systems. These systems are built in to dust free environments, such as electronics assembly rooms, medical facilities, and scientific research laboratories. Systems, even the simpler ones, generally cost upwards of $50,000. A large system, including installation, could well exceed a million dollars. Internal company jargon calls these systems PACS. That's the term we'll be using in our discussions with Pat. Unlike the precipitators, which can be sold in a single call, it takes nine to twelve months of hard work to sell a PACS. And, as you'd expect, decisions to install a PACS are usually made by customer committees and require technical justification to specialists such as architects and engineers. Strategically, Particle Control would like to see at least 60 percent of its future business coming from PACSs, where the profit margins are excellent and there's little competition. However, because the sales force has so far failed to penetrate the market, only 20 percent of present business comes from PACSs sales. These poor sales alter the economics of the systems business. At present it's running well below capacity and is losing money. Pat's most urgent priority will be to increase sales in this systems area.

- *Consulting and design:* The third area of Particle Control's business has grown almost by accident. In order to support the PACS systems business, the company has set up a technical group consisting of particle scientists and design engineers. Customers have approached Particle Control for technical advice and the head of the design unit, who is rather entrepreneurial, has responded by selling consulting services. To the surprise of management, the design function—which had been thought of as an expensive, but necessary, overhead—is now the most profitable part of the business. All consulting sales so far have been handled by the design engineers themselves. However, management believes that this profitable business could be greatly expanded if the sales force were to take over responsibility for selling consulting services. This has not yet been finalized, but the decision is expected soon. If management decides to give responsibility for consulting services sales to the sales force, Pat will face another major challenge. None of Pat's salespeople has ever sold consulting services before. Will the services sale involve the same effectiveness skills as product sales? Can the sales force handle this business area successfully? Pat doesn't know.

Our Initial Perspective

Before our first meeting with Pat, we'd formed some tentative opinions about where the trouble lies and what to do about it. It's often the case, when a sales force is asked to sell both high- and low-end products, that the low-end products get disproportionate attention from the sales force because they are easier to sell. It's not an easy problem to handle. We anticipate that Pat will find it hard to divert salespeople's attention to the systems products.

An initial conversation with Particle Control's VP of Sales has convinced us that there are some other problems too. Because we want a free hand, we've asked for—and been given—an unusual assurance from the VP. It's an assurance we often ask for when we're working with groups of sales managers. Pat, like most sales managers, is under a heavy burden of reporting paperwork. We've explained to the VP that we'll be putting some extra demands on Pat's time. So that Pat can cope with the demands we'll be making, we have obtained the VP's agreement that reporting requirements will be kept to a bare minimum during the coming months. With some reluctance, the VP has also agreed to be flexible over other managerial controls such as targets.

To keep our case study as realistic as possible we're putting it in the form of extracts from our discussions with Pat, adding only minimal editorial comment.

From the Initial Meeting: May 17th

NEIL: . . . Pat, what's *your* diagnosis of why your people don't seem to be able to sell these PACS systems?

PAT: Well, I think it's a combination of things. PACSs are certainly tough to sell. My people think our systems products are overpriced.

DICK: Do you think that?

PAT: It's hard to say. No . . . not really . . . I think price is an easy excuse.

NEIL: How far do you think that selling low-end precipitators has taken your people's attention away from the systems products?

PAT: Quite a lot. My folks are much more comfortable selling the precipitators. It's a simple sale, most of them have been selling precipitators for years. Yes, "comfortable" is the word.

NEIL: Yet they know that competition is increasing at the low end. Are they *really* comfortable?

PAT: Well, maybe I should say they are less uncomfortable with precipitators than with systems products.

DICK: So, left to themselves, they focus on quick precipitator sales at the expense of the more complex PACS products?

PAT: That's the problem, yes.

NEIL: And what has management done about it?

PAT: When it was clear that the PACS systems weren't selling, they brought in a call reporting system and set call targets for PACS calls. Everybody had to make at least seven PACS sales calls per week.

DICK: Let me predict what happened. You got lots of resentment, lots of faking of call reports, but nothing positive in terms of sales. Would that be accurate?

PAT: You've obviously seen this kind of thing before. I don't want to be disloyal to my management because I agree with what they were trying to do. But, so far as I can see, the call reporting system brought us nothing but trouble.

NEIL: And it's still in operation?

PAT: Yes.

NEIL: The good news is that we've got your VP's permission to suspend the call reporting system for several months while we work with you on sales effectiveness.

PAT: That *is* good news. What's the bad news?

NEIL: The bad news is that in its place will be a lot of hard work for you.

PAT: That's fine by me if it gets results. What do you want me to do?

NEIL: Before we talk about what we think you should do, let's hear *your ideas.* After all, you've been living with the problem and I'm sure you've given it a lot of thought.

PAT: I'm not sure that I have any answers though. Here's how I see it. Call reporting isn't working right now because, for some reason, people are fighting it. But the *principle* is right. We've got to find a way to push up the call rate. But call reports aren't the way to do it because they are a form of *punishment.* If only we could give people a *reward* for making calls, then that might solve the problem. I don't know if we could do it, but suppose we gave people additional payment—some extra bonus for every extra systems call they made. That way we could push the call rate up to an acceptable level.

DICK: What would you guess to be an "acceptable level"?

PAT: Right now we're targeting seven calls a week and actually getting about five. If we could double that—get the call rate up to at least ten calls a week—then that should make a big difference to our sales.

NEIL: Pat, it sounds like you're saying *more calls equals more sales.* If we could double the call rate we'd get double the sales. *Are* you saying that?

PAT: Not double exactly. But more calls *must* lead to more sales, so I think that's where we should start.

DICK: Pat, in our experience, there's very little relationship between call rates and sales in systems selling. Before we decide what to do about call rates, can I ask you to check something out? How many people have you on your team?

PAT: Nine.

DICK: And are any of them selling these PACS systems successfully?

PAT: Two of them are doing moderately well. The others don't seem to be getting anywhere at all.

DICK: Then take those two who are your best performers. I'd like you to go back into their call records for the last six months. Find out how many calls they've been making compared with your other folks. If they've been making more calls than the others, then perhaps you're right—we need to push up call rates.

PAT: I've not looked at their records, but I imagine they *must* be making more calls—otherwise how are they making more sales?

NEIL: It doesn't always work that way. That's something you should check out before we take any action.

DICK: There's something else you should check out. Talk to your folks and see how *they* explain the problems with your systems products. Obviously, the first answer you'll get is "price." But try to get past that. Get them to talk about all the barriers they're facing and bring a list we can talk about at our next meeting.

NEIL: And one other thing, get your people to write down their call objectives for, shall we say, the next five systems sales calls they intend to make. I think that might prove interesting reading.

PAT: Sure, I can do that . . . but . . . well . . . isn't there some *action* I can take?

NEIL: You're impatient about all this data gathering?

PAT: Hey, I *am* a sales manager. I'm always impatient . . .

Following the meeting, we reviewed what we had learned from Pat. As we suspected, Pat was a fairly typical sales manager. Although the call reporting system wasn't working, Pat didn't question the old *more calls = more sales* formula. We felt that at this stage it was important for Pat to collect some data to test this formula. For reasons we discussed in chapter 2 we expected that, in the systems sales, there would be little evidence to support Pat's belief that pushing up call rates had led to more sales. Dick felt that it was also important at this stage to hear what Pat's people had to say about the problems of selling PACS systems. Even if we didn't get any startling insights from Pat's people, we might get a useful indication of any psychological barriers or ingrained attitudes (if any) that Pat would have to face in building greater sales effectiveness. Finally, Neil was anxious to find what sort of call objectives people were setting. In our experience, people who are unsuccessful in major sales often have some difficulties in setting realistic call objectives. By collecting some data on call objectives, we hoped to assess how well Pat's people were moving forward in the selling cycle. Pat, clearly, was hoping for immediate action and felt some impatience at all this data collection.

From the Second Meeting: June 3rd

DICK: Pat, last time we asked you to look at three things:

- testing out the *more calls* = *more sales* formula by seeing whether your top performers were, in fact, making more calls than your less successful people

- Finding your folks' explanations of why PACS systems are proving so hard to sell

- Collecting some examples of call objectives for us to discuss

That's a lot of stuff. How did it go?

PAT: It took more time than I'd expected, but I've got some material in each of the three areas. Where would you like to start?

NEIL: Let's begin with the call-rate issue. As I remember, you have two people out of nine who are moderately successful in selling PACS systems. How do their call rates compare with the others?

PAT: I'm real surprised. When you asked me to check this out, I thought it would be a waste of time because I just *knew* that they would be making more calls. But when I went back into the call records for the last six months, I found the opposite. These two are actually making *fewer* calls. Yet they are my most successful systems salespeople. I can't understand it.

NEIL: It often happens that way. In major sales making more calls rarely leads to more sales.

PAT: But there's something here I don't understand. I've got one person who *is* making more calls than anybody else—and she has the highest sales of precipitators. So—in her case at least—making more calls *does* mean more sales.

DICK: But, Pat, she's selling precipitators, which are low-end products. In small sales, there's often a very clear relationship between calls and sales. The *more calls* = *more sales* formula can work. What you've found is that the things which make people successful in small sales often don't work in large ones.

PAT: But what do I do now? Do I tell people to make *fewer* systems calls? That doesn't make sense—and anyway, management would kill me if I did that.

DICK: No, we're not suggesting that your people should make fewer calls. The issue here is one of working harder or working smarter. Pushing up the call rate is a way of making your folks work *harder.* What you've discovered is that, in the PACS sale, working harder isn't enough. Your strategy has to shift. You've got to find ways of helping people work *smarter,* helping them get the most out of each call.

PAT: That's easy to say, but how how do I do it?

NEIL: Yes, that's the problem, isn't it. We all understand how to work harder because that's just doing even more of what we're already doing now. But working smarter is about doing something *differently*—and you're right, that's a whole lot more difficult. Perhaps that leads us into the next topic. Your people obviously need to work smarter. What's their explanation of what's going wrong?

PAT: Why they aren't making systems sales? Like I told you at the last meeting, price is the first reason they always come up with.

DICK: But you tried to get underneath price? You tried to find some of the other issues?

PAT: Yes. We discussed this as a group at one of our Monday morning team meetings. I noted down some things people said. For example:

- "You know where you stand when you're selling precipitators. It's a clean sale and you can see results. But PACS sales take months and you don't have any way to tell how you're doing."

- "After a while, when you're not taking orders and not making any progress, you get discouraged."

- "With precipitators you're dealing with one customer but with PACS there're committees and consultants. You can't find the decision maker."

Those are fairly typical comments.

DICK: There's a common thread here. Your folks all seem to be saying that they haven't got a sense of *direction* or of movement in their PACS sales.

PAT: I think that's true. One of them said, "I just make calls and hope something's going to happen."

NEIL: It often happens, when people have worked in a small sale marketplace, that they feel lost and directionless when they try to adjust to making major sales. We'll be able to get a better feel for that when we look at the other piece of data we asked you to collect—the call objectives that your people have been setting.

PAT: I've brought them along. You asked me to get my people to write down their objectives for the next five systems calls they intended to make. Here they are.

NEIL: (reads) "To develop a better relationship," "to collect data," "to build relationships," "to understand more about this customer's business," "to get to know the customer . . . ," oh dear, oh dear.

PAT: Why do you say, "oh dear"? Surely there's nothing wrong with building relationships?

NEIL: Absolutely not. That's what selling at this level is all about. Don't get me wrong, Pat. I'm not disappointed because your people are trying to build relationships. I'm groaning because they see relationship building as their only call objective. *Every* call should build relationships. But having relationship building as a call objective is like saying that your objective is "talk to the customer"—it doesn't tell you anything specific about what the call is trying to achieve. The other objective I don't like to see— for exactly the same reason—is "collect information." Every call collects information, so that's hardly an adequate call objective. I'm disappointed that these objectives your people have set don't have much of an action orientation.

PAT: That's not really surprising. As you said, they don't have much sense of direction in these systems calls. If people can't see where the sale is heading, then no wonder their call objectives are kind of vague and wishy-washy.

DICK: But which is chicken and which is egg? Is it that your folks don't have a feel of where the sale is going—so they don't know what objectives to set? Or is it that they are setting poor objectives—so calls tend to go nowhere?

PAT: Frankly, it's a bit of each. If I could help them set better objectives, then I think that would give them some feeling of movement and progress. But it's not just a question of call objectives. There's also a motivational issue. Most of my people just don't feel motivated to sell PACS. They're discouraged. They've had a lot of failures. I think maybe I should deal with the motivation problem before I worry about call objectives.

NEIL: Call objectives and motivation may not be separate issues, Pat. We've found that objective setting is one of the most powerful motivational tools for managers in complex sales.

DICK: Remember the idea of *Advances* and *Continuations* that we talked about earlier? We explained how you could motivate people and help them get a better sense of direction by working with them to set objectives that get an Advance.

PAT: Yes, I remember that an Advance is an action to move the sale forward, like getting access to a higher level in the account, or having the customer come to a demonstration site.

NEIL: And a Continuation is where another meeting will take place but where no *action* had been agreed to move the sale forward. Look at these examples of objectives your people have set. Will they lead to Continuations or Advances?

PAT: ". . . get to know this customer better," ". . . start to build a relationship with people in Engineering," . . . well . . . they aren't *directly* Advances. But they could lead to an Advance indirectly, so I guess you *could* call them Advances.

NEIL: Don't kid yourself, Pat. Objectives like those have "Continuation" written all over them. An objective that would get an Advance might be something like, "Get agreement from Engineering that Particle Control will be included on the Approved Vendor list," or "Get architect to visit Adipose Corporation's clean room to see one of our systems in action."

DICK: Let's talk about how you can get more Advances from your calls, Pat. Why don't you

- Use your next team meeting to explain the idea of *Orders, Advances, Continuations,* and *No-sales* to your folks. Then get them to brainstorm a list of Advances that they can realistically achieve from PACS systems calls.

- Ask them each to set an objective that will get an Advance for two of the systems calls that they will be making during the next week.

- At the team meeting the following week, ask everybody to describe their two calls. Ask each of them things like

  - *What was the Advance you were trying to get?*
  - *Did you succeed?*
  - *Did setting an Advance as your objective alter the way you approached the call? How?*

PAT: I'll be very happy to do that because I can see some benefit in terms of sales. To be honest with you, I wasn't so happy after our last meeting when I just ended up with a list of questions but no answers.

NEIL: I hate to disappoint you, Pat, but I'm going to add another question to your list. When you go out with your people, I'd like you to watch their selling very carefully. At our next meeting I want us to talk about selling skills and how to improve them. So the question is, "Can you see any weaknesses in your people's selling skills?'' Don't try to answer now. In fact, I'd like you to watch your people sell as if you've never seen them selling before. Clear your head of any preconceptions. Try to take a fresh look at each person. As we won't be meeting for another five weeks, you should be able to watch each of your nine people, shouldn't you?

PAT: No problem. I'll be out with each of them at least three or four times.

Reviewing the meeting, we had mixed feelings. We were pleased with the outcome of Pat's analysis of call rates. Pat's own data showed that top performers were making fewer calls than the rest of the team. That was psychologically important. No amount of persuasion from us would have made Pat question the *more calls = more sales* formula; but because Pat's own data showed that, in this case, more calls *didn't* mean more sales, we were able to shift the issue away from selling harder towards selling smarter. Pat readily accepted this and agreed that we should focus on the sales effectiveness area. We were also pleased that Pat clearly saw that although selling harder—or making more calls—seemed to work in low-end precipitator sales, PACS sales required a different strategy.

We were less happy when we read through people's call objectives that Pat had collected. They made dispiriting reading. They lacked that sense of movement and action that we would expect from successful salespeople. Privately, we were a little concerned that Pat seemed satisfied with objectives like these. However, Dick's suggestion for using team meetings to brainstorm Advances, and for reviewing call objectives, had given Pat something actionable that could provide a constructive first step for Pat in building better systems selling skills.

From the Third Meeting: July 17th

PAT: . . . and working on Advances turned out to be a whole lot easier than I expected. I thought the idea would be useful but I also thought people would find it hard to understand. Some did at first, but as soon as we'd brainstormed a few examples, the idea sort of came clear.

DICK: So they set better objectives?

PAT: *I* think so. And they do too. At the meeting where we reviewed the calls, people were saying how much it helped them to have a clear idea in advance of where the call was aiming to go. And another thing. You're right. It *is* a motivational tool. I was out with one of the team on a call last week. He said, "I think this is helping me see where these systems calls are going—and that makes me feel a whole lot better about them."

DICK: Any problems?

PAT: Not with the idea of setting better call objectives.

DICK: But . . . ?

PAT: Well, I'm not sure how to put this, but . . . I guess that what I've done so far is give people an appetizer. They liked it, but it's just made them hungry for the main course. It's a start . . . but I sense there's a lot more to do before we'll see better systems sales results.

NEIL: You're right. You've just made a start. But it sounds like a good start, and that's encouraging. The issue now is where to go next.

PAT: I've been thinking about that. I believe that my people don't have any sense of account *strategy*—and that's their main problem now. You don't need strategy to sell low-end products like precipitators, but unless you have some idea of what an account strategy looks like, it's impossible to sell systems. Earlier you showed me a whole range of tools for managing strategy. And I picked up some other tools and ideas from reading Neil's book, *Major Account Sales Strategy.* I think that the logical next step is to put some of those strategy tools into action.

NEIL: Logical, yes—practical, no. A word of warning here, Pat. Over the years we've seen too many sales forces rush in to improve their people's strategy without first working to get their fundamental selling skills right. Unfortunately, without a firm bedrock of selling skills, strategy is just so many words. I can sympathize with your impatience to begin building some strategy competence, but I would urge you to get those bedrock selling skills right first. That's why, at our last meeting, I asked you to go out with each of your people and look closely at how they were selling. What did you find?

PAT: Well . . . it's hard to say.

DICK: Because it's difficult to assess skills?

PAT: Yes. And . . . well . . . I didn't really get a chance to watch them all.

DICK: Why was that?

PAT: The calls I went out on weren't really suitable for watching how people sell.

DICK: Not suitable?

PAT: I found I was out on calls where I had to do all the selling. In practical business terms I didn't have any choice. We're way below target and I can't afford to waste opportunities. So, what happened was that I had to take over calls. I could try to kid you and say I watched all my people sell—like I told you I was going to do—and most of them don't seem to have good selling skills. But the truth is I did the selling. I'm sorry.

NEIL: No Pat, don't apologize. We're grateful that you're being so frank with us. But now, let me be equally frank with you. I think you may be caught in one of the worst traps that a sales manager can fall into. It goes like this. Results are bad, so there's a lot of pressure on you. You go out with your people and you find they aren't selling well. So, rather than let a potential sale slip away, you jump in and take over the selling. Before long, your salespeople *expect* that you'll do their selling for them, so the moment a call looks difficult, they pull you in to take over. And customers get used to dealing with you and they also expect you to remain involved. Soon, you're spending so much time in selling and customer follow-up that you don't have any time to invest in improving your people's skills. So, as a result, they get even more dependent on your selling, which means you have even less time to develop them, which makes them yet more dependent, and so on. Does that sound familiar?

PAT: I've got to admit, that's exactly what's happened.

NEIL: You've got to break out of it. And that means you'll have to do less selling and more managing.

PAT: That's easy to say, but I'm not in a position to cut down on my selling. You know how bad our results are and I can't just sit there and let one of my people lose a potential sale.

DICK: Pat, when you're there in the call it can become the center of the universe and all your energy gets focused on how to make this one particular call succeed. But think of it this way. While we're talking—right now, this minute—you've got people making systems sales calls, right?

PAT: Yes, maybe there're two—possibly three—systems sales calls being made by my people as we speak.

DICK: And you're not there in any of them. The fact is, you can only be in a very small percentage of calls. So the role of supercloser isn't really going to be workable.

PAT: I recognize that, but what do I do instead? Do I stop selling entirely?

DICK: No. Just the opposite. You've got to sell where it counts most. At the moment you're selling in almost every call. Because of that, you're stretched very thin. So you've got to focus your own selling effort where it really counts—where your selling will make a unique difference. Give *more* selling attention to the few calls that really matter. That way, you'll free up some time for coaching.

NEIL: The first thing is to decide in advance whether you are making a call to sell or to coach. If it's a sales call, as Dick says, it should be one where your selling will make a unique difference in getting the business. If it's a coaching call, then it should *not* be one that needs your selling to succeed. The ideal coaching call is one which—in theory at least—your salesperson should be able to handle without you.

PAT: I don't go out on many of those.

NEIL: That's the problem. Because you've taken a sales role, your people only involve you in calls where they expect you to sell. By definition, those will be the tougher calls.

DICK: So you'll have to break out of that by asking your folks to set up some relatively routine calls—preferably early in the sales cycle—so that you can see them in action in the kind of call they make routinely when you're not with them.

PAT: I can set that up. But what exactly should I be doing during these coaching calls?

NEIL: We said earlier that you should start by making sure that your people have the fundamental skills needed for effective systems selling. Research suggests that the key basic ability in high-level selling is understanding customer problems and developing needs. That requires questioning ability. Earlier we showed you some models for assessing questioning skills. You can find some other questioning models in my book *SPIN® Selling.* I suggest you start there.

PAT: That's going to be a big job with nine salespeople.

DICK: Pat, I suggest you don't try to work with everybody at once. Skill building takes time. It's much better to coach a few people in depth than to superficially coach your whole team.

PAT: I'm glad about that. I was wondering how to handle all nine. But if, say, I was to work with three or four, then it gets a lot easier.

NEIL: Can I suggest three people initially as a maximum. If you find you've some spare time, once you get into the coaching, you can take on a fourth person. But it's better to start with fewer than to start with more and find you have to drop someone.

PAT: Have you any suggestions for picking someone?

DICK: There are some principles you should follow. For example, it's usually better to start with average performers than with your top people or your poorest performers.

PAT: That surprises me. I can see that it might be smart to leave my top performers alone. After all, they are doing OK without my help. But I'd have thought I should start with my poorest performers. They are the ones who need it most.

NEIL: Possibly. But they are also the ones who will take longest to improve. We've found that a little time spent with average performers can make a big difference and, in the long run, can free up more time for you to spend later with problem people.

We weren't surprised to find Pat caught in the trap of doing too much selling. Fortunately, unlike some managers, Pat was very willing to recognize the problem and to take action to correct it. In this case study we suggested that Pat just go out and do some coaching. In real life, we would want to give much more support to managers we were working with. For instance:

- Pat might need some help with coaching skills.
- We would need to help Pat decide what behaviors to look for during coaching.
- If Pat's people turned out to have a real skills deficiency, we might suggest some off-the-job sales skill training as a more economical way to begin developing the basics, followed by on-the-job coaching from Pat.
- We would certainly encourage Pat to draw up a detailed action plan of coaching activities so that coaching became part of the managerial routine and not an isolated event.

Pat left this meeting enthusiastic about coaching and ready to begin a coaching program with the three chosen people. Good skills coaching, however, is very hard work—both for manager and salespeople. The early stages of skill development are usually frustrating and painfully slow. In consequence, we anticipated that some or all of Pat's enthusiasm would evaporate during the coming weeks. In fact, we deliberately chose the date of the next meeting, about three weeks later, to come at the point where we thought Pat's enthusiasm was likely to be at its lowest. We anticipated that Pat would need a shot in the arm to revitalize the coaching effort.

From the Fourth Meeting: August 7th

PAT: . . . so I think I must be doing something wrong. Two of the three people I'm working with seem to be selling *worse* now than when we started. They really seem discouraged, and to be honest, I don't feel so great about the coaching myself.

DICK: Pat, do you play golf?

PAT: Yes

DICK: And you've taken lessons from a professional?

PAT: Yes, I have.

DICK: And, after you've taken a lesson, is your next round better or worse?

PAT: In my case, usually worse.

DICK: Why do you think that is?

PAT: I guess it's because I'm trying hard—maybe too hard—to do what the pro has told me, so other bits of my game go to pieces. I kind of get self-conscious about what I'm doing and that interferes with my game.

DICK: So, if you're worse after a lesson, why take lessons at all?

PAT: Well, in the end—if I keep practicing what the pro says—my game gets better. And I think I know what you're going to say next. You're going to say that my people are just like I am after golfing lessons. They *have* got worse, but you think it's only temporary.

DICK: Doesn't that sound plausible?

PAT: Yes, but the point is, I'm being measured by results and I can't afford to spend all this effort to make my people sell *worse.* You guys will get me fired.

NEIL: Pat, it's time we talked to you about the discussions we had with your VP. I don't need to tell you, your boss wants results and wants them quickly.

PAT: Yes, that's why I'm surprised that he's given you such a free hand. He's kept off my back over call reporting and he's given me a lot of latitude lately. What did you do to him?

NEIL: It wasn't anything we did. You see, your VP understands one very important fact about selling. It's called "sustainable competitive advantage." Let me explain. It takes years of effort to build a really skilled sales force. But, once you've built it, a first class sales force may be one of your strongest advantages over competition. In the past, most organizations tried to get ahead of competition through product design and manufacturing. The right product could put them literally *years* ahead of competition. But, in today's fast moving technologies, new products can be outdated in months. It's getting harder to sustain your competitive advantage through products alone. Organizations have learned to design and manufacture products on a much shorter cycle. But it still takes *years* to build a strong and effective sales force, and as you've seen with your own team, it's not an easy task. So, any company that succeeds in creating real sales effectiveness may have a competitive edge that puts them years ahead. There's no doubt about it—and your VP understands this well—that building an effective sales force is one of the most sustainable areas of competitive advantage.

DICK: Let me give you an example, Pat. During our meeting, your VP told us of the days when he was selling for one of IBM's competitors. He had cheaper products with superior features, but he had a tough time establishing competitive superiority because he didn't have IBM's sales force. He told us that, in those days, his definition of managerial heaven was "an organization with our products and IBM's salespeople." He knows it's going to be difficult to build a top class sales force in your systems business, but he sees that if he succeeds, he's giving Particle Control an important and sustainable competitive advantage.

PAT: That's reassuring, providing he understands that I'm working hard even if it doesn't show up yet in the numbers.

Sales effectiveness *is* hard work—and it's a great deal harder unless there's strong top management support. It's no accident that we had prior meetings with Pat's VP before we started this project. If, during these meetings, we had felt that the VP was unenthusiastic about going ahead, we would have withdrawn. Notice that, for the VP, sales effectiveness was about "sustainable competitive advantage"—which is the primary goal of competitive strategy. In recent years, an increasing number of theorists have been making the point that companies depend too much on products and marketing strategy to provide competitive advantage. In the future, they suggest, the *soft* people areas, such as sales and customer service, may become a much more sustainable source.

From the Fifth Meeting: September 7th

PAT: . . . I'm now starting to see some real progress in terms of people's selling skill. And I think I'm using my own time much better as a manager. I only get involved in a selling role in those calls where I really do make a unique difference. When I'm out on calls, I've been consciously trying to strengthen my people's position with the customer. That's made customers rely more on my salespeople and less on me. As a result, it's freeing me up to do more coaching and I've started with two more of my folks.

DICK: That's a very positive picture.

PAT: I'm glad you talked me into working on selling skills *before* starting on strategy. The people I've coached on skills will be much better at putting strategy into practice. If I'd worked with them on account strategy before skills I think it would have bombed. Even if we'd come up with great strategies I don't think people could have executed them.

NEIL: And now, you think you have some people who are ready to start work on account strategy?

PAT: Ready and waiting. Where do we start?

NEIL: What would you say is your people's weakest area in terms of strategy?

PAT: They really aren't very effective at handling competition. I don't think they've got a clear enough understanding of our strengths versus competitors' strengths. Because of that, they don't position our PACS systems to best advantage.

DICK: Suppose you were sitting down with one of your people who was right in the middle of one of these competitive sales, what would the two of you discuss?

PAT: Our strong points and how important it is to really emphasize them to the customer. And I'd try to help my person see where we are weakest and come up with a strategy for compensating for our weak areas. That's harder to do.

DICK: Would it be useful to have some tool for looking at competitive strengths and weaknesses?

PAT: I've tried that. We introduced a kind of competitive analysis questionnaire last year. It was a lot of paperwork—and it took hours to fill in. I don't think it was very useful and people hated it.

NEIL: I'm on their side. I hate paperwork too. There's a lot of material out there that's called strategy but it's really no more than very tedious and elaborate form filling. If you need more paper than the back of an envelope, then forget it. Any useful strategy tool must be one sheet of paper at the most.

PAT: I'm relieved to hear you say that. But competitive strategy is complicated. I'm not sure that one sheet of paper can give you enough detail to be useful.

DICK: Let me give you one example of a simple tool that's very useful for analyzing and discussing competitive strengths and weaknesses. It's a diagram that gives you a very simple visual way to see how you stand against competitors. First you list the criteria that you think the customer is using to make the decision. So, for example, take a competitive sale you're concerned with right now. What are the criteria—things like cost or quality—that the customer is using to judge you and your competition?

PAT: Cost is always one. But there are other factors too. For example, speed of installation is crucial in this case where the customer's trying to set up a clean room production process and get it into operation before others in their market. And in terms of installation speed, we have a longer installation time than some competitors. The customer's an engineering company, so they give some weight to technical specifications. Our strong point is maintenance support, but they don't seem too concerned about that because they are an engineering company and they have a good maintenance capability of their own. We're stronger than competition in terms of maintenance, weaker on installation speed but, well . . . it's a bit complicated to explain.

DICK: Pat, would it help to explain it in terms of a simple diagram like this one?

FIGURE 8.1
Vulnerability Analysis

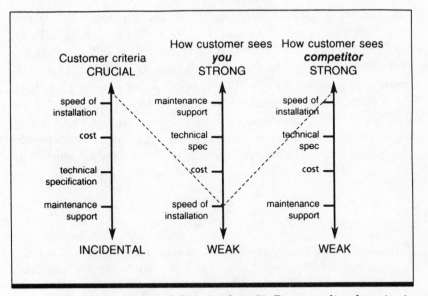

We call this Vulnerability Analysis℠. First you list the criteria the customer is using to decide between you and a competitor, estimating which criteria are most important to the customer and which are incidental. Then you rank yourself as you think the customer sees *you*, using the same criteria. Finally you rank how the customer sees the competitor in terms of those criteria. Whenever you find a "v" shape—in this case it would be installation speed—you know that you're vulnerable and you need to develop a strategy for handling this vulnerability.

PAT: That's neat. I can see it would be a helpful little diagram for talking with my people about where we stand in the account.

NEIL: There's a lot more you can do with very simple tools like this one. Let's talk about some others . . .

At this meeting we started to introduce Pat to some simple strategy tools like those described in our book *Major Account Sales Strategy*. The key here *is* simplicity. We want to avoid complex compilations of account data and, instead, provide quick and easy tools to help manager and salesperson communicate about what's going on in the account. During the next two meetings we introduced Pat to other tools of a similar type. Under some circumstances we might also encourage Pat to bring the sales team together for formal training on strategy tools and how to use them. We can skip over these meetings because, by this point, Pat—like most sales managers working on similar sales effectiveness projects—was making steady and uneventful progress.

At this stage, Pat's work on sales effectiveness seemed to be on track and progressing well. Of course, with a selling cycle for systems products of six months or longer, it would still be some months before we finally had tangible sales results to reward Pat's efforts; but we could now start to look forward to those results with some confidence. However, this wouldn't be a realistic case study of a sales organization without an unexpected complication, just when things seemed to be going right. The complication came in our eighth meeting with Pat in early December.

From the Eighth Meeting: December 12th

PAT: . . . in case you haven't heard, management has finally decided that from January 1st, the sales force will be selling consulting services in addition to the other products. My team has been chosen as a pilot and I'd like some advice.

NEIL: These consulting services originated in design engineering. Who has been selling them so far?

PAT: The consultants themselves. It's been a profitable little business. I suppose you could say that the *supersalesman* has been the head of Design but the others—five of them—have all played a part.

DICK: So why change a good thing?

PAT: Opportunity, I suppose. I think our president feels that if five people who weren't even trained to sell can be so successful, we'll have a real money maker if we give consulting services to our whole sales force of three hundred.

NEIL: What does your head of Design think?

PAT: I think he's very positive. He wants to see more Design services sold, but he's not sure whether the sales force has the technical knowledge to handle a consulting sale.

NEIL: He could be right. In service sales, particularly sales of consulting, it's hard for the customer to separate the service from the person selling it. So if the salesperson isn't credible, neither is the consulting service. That *does* suggest a need for a high level of technical competence.

PAT: I think some of my people *are* very technically competent. They've learned a lot about design from selling the PACS systems. My worry isn't technical ability. It's something different. It's . . . well . . . I'm not quite sure what it is.

DICK: Selling skills?

PAT: Not exactly. I've just got an uneasy feeling that this is a different kind of sale. I can't pin it down, but I'm sure there are important differences between selling consulting services and selling PACS systems. Everyone's acting as if design consulting will be so easy it will almost sell itself. I can just hear top management saying that if engineers can sell it—and they haven't even been trained to sell—then the sales force will be able to sell it standing on their heads. But something tells me it won't be that easy.

NEIL: Pat, my gut feeling goes along with yours. I really suspect that this could be harder than people think. But you'll need more than an uneasy feeling to convince your senior management. Here's what I suggest you do. Remember Contrast Analysis, that you read about in chapter 4? I think that would be a very useful technique for you here. You said that the head of Design was very positive?

PAT: Yes. I'm sure he would do anything he could to help us.

NEIL: Get him to help you to complete a Contrast Analysis. Remember the steps we went through in the example in chapter 4? First you should describe the customer's decision steps. Are they the same as for the PACS sale or not? Then you should describe the selling tasks that you expect salespeople to perform to influence each customer decision step successfully. For example, does the consulting sale require selling tasks such as making technical presentations or cost justifications? Finally, for each of these selling tasks specify the behaviors needed for a future performer to be effective. *How* does an effective performer make a technical presentation, for example? By going through this sequence you'll get a better picture of what an effective consulting sale will look like.

DICK: And once you've done that, you can look at how well you think your present performers would handle the sale. If you come up with some serious gaps, then we should talk more about them at our next meeting.

Reviewing this meeting, we found we both shared Pat's uneasy feeling about the consulting sale. In our case, we had many years of experience working with consulting and service organizations to give us a foundation for our unease. The consulting sale *is* different. For example, when you sell consulting services, you design your *product* as you sell it. From your discussions with potential clients you must collect accurate information that lets you understand client problems and, from your understanding, to design appropriate solutions. In the classic product sale, in contrast, the product has already been designed before you meet the customer. Your solutions are relatively fixed. What this means is that consulting sales put even greater demands on excellent questioning skills than product sales. Poor questioning skills can lose product sales. But with consulting sales, the consequences of inadequate questioning skills are worse. Not only are sales lost but, through asking poor questions, you may sometimes make the sale and end up designing the wrong solutions—with consequent damage to reputation and profitability. The PACS sale that Pat's people had been struggling to master, like any systems sale, contains some elements of the consulting sale. Although the hardware is a fixed product, the particular configuration is a unique solution designed for the specific customer. However, unlike the consulting sale, there *are* fixed and tangible hardware elements. We weren't convinced that Pat's people would find it easy to handle the *pure* consulting sale, where there was no hardware.

There was another difference in emphasis between product and consulting sales that we feared might prove difficult for Pat's people. In a typical product sales force like Pat's, there's a strong ethos and reward system aimed at getting the business. In successful consulting organizations, there's usually an equally strong emphasis on *avoiding* certain types of business—business, for example, where you can't add value, where you haven't a solid professional competence, or where you can't achieve worthwhile margins.

From the Ninth Meeting: January 5th

PAT: The head of Design and I did the Contrast Analysis, as you suggested, and I think we've come up with several areas where I feel people will need help.

DICK: Did you find that Contrast Analysis helped you get a bit clearer about what was troubling you?

PAT: Yes. And it showed us both some things we'd not thought about before.

NEIL: Such as?

PAT: Let me give you an example. The head of Design convinced me that good selling in his area wasn't just a question of getting the business. An effective performer would also keep clear of certain types of business that customers might try to give us. A good illustration is ductwork. Design gets lots of requests to design ductwork—which is business that we don't really want to take. It's got low margins and it takes up a lot of design resources that we could use working on particle control applications. But customers want help in ductwork design and they get upset if you turn them down. So a key skill for a successful salesperson is learning how to say no without upsetting the customer. My people spend so much time trying to get customers to say yes that they aren't experienced in how to turn business down.

NEIL: Yes, we call that skill *Withdrawing.* Just as you say, it's the ability to turn down *bad* business without damaging your relationship with the customer. There's another kind of selling skill that's particularly important to successful consulting. I wonder if it also came out in your Contrast Analysis. It's called *Rescoping* and it's shown in figure 8.2. As you can see, Rescoping takes a piece of *bad* business and, through discussions with the client, redefines the scope of work in a way that lets you perform it better. So, in your ductwork example, Rescoping might mean persuading

FIGURE 8.2
Three outcomes for the consulting sale

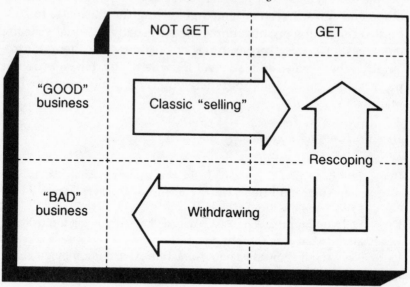

the client to undertake ductwork through internal resources or a subcontractor, while you provide advice on particle control issues.

PAT: We came up with something like that. We said that the effective future performer would need to generate creative solutions that the client hadn't thought of. But I think you're right, what we were getting at was Rescoping.

DICK: So it sounds like you've a much clearer idea of what it takes to be successful in this consulting sale. How clear are you about how to get your people to a point where they can be successful?

PAT: We agreed on a number of things that I think will help us there. For example, during the first three months, we'll team sell with the designers. That way we'll get a lot smarter about what sort of business we should be aiming for. And there're other things we identified that we can do to prepare the team . . .

This was our last meeting with Pat. Three months later, Particle Control decided to split its sales force into two, with one group handling precipitators and two additional low-end products that Particle Control had recently acquired. The other group was dedicated to PACS systems and consulting services. Pat was promoted to Regional Manager of this group and, last we heard, was very successfully taking market share away from competition.

Some Conclusions from the Case Study

As we said at the outset, this case study wasn't intended to provide answers. Its purpose has been to illustrate some of the issues and uncertainties that arise from any real-life attempt to improve sales effectiveness. What conclusions can we draw from the case? Here are some of our thoughts:

- *Sales effectiveness improves slowly and in small increments:* During the nine months we worked with Pat there were no dramatic breakthroughs. We made progress through lots of small steps. And progress was slower—and it took a lot more effort—than Pat had anticipated.
- *Controlling competing priorities is crucial:* We might never have got off the ground if Pat's management had not agreed to ease some of the existing reporting systems so that Pat had time to focus on sales effectiveness.
- *Top management must have an incentive:* The idea of building a sales force that would provide a sustainable competitive advantage at a time when product advantages were getting difficult to sustain was an attractive one to Pat's VP. As a result, the VP had an incentive to support Pat's efforts.
- *A systematic process is essential:* Our efforts succeeded because they were planned as a systematic process over a defined time period. We didn't have the one-shot *event* orientation that often prevents sales training from having a lasting impact.
- *An external catalyst is helpful:* It's unlikely that a sales manager, even one with Pat's talent, could bring about these improvements alone. Some external influence is almost essential as a catalyst for achieving significant changes like the ones described here. But that catalyst doesn't have to be an external consultant such as ourselves. We've seen excellent sales

effectiveness results achieved by groups of sales managers, working together under the guidance of a determined and experienced internal facilitator.

Overall, the message of the case is that sales managers can dramatically improve their people's sales effectiveness. Using simple principles and tools like the ones described in this book, a sales manager can make a real and lasting impact on people's sales performance.

Last Words

That leads us to the conclusion of this book. Sales management, as we see it, is emerging as a sophisticated and exciting profession. Any professional field, as it grows and matures, develops its own technology. That's starting to happen in the sales management area. Sales management is no longer the province of the enthusiastic amateur. Ten years ago we remember sitting in a meeting discussing the redeployment of managers from a company location that was being closed down. When we came to an unfortunate manager who had no internal job offers, one person said, "He hasn't a good enough grasp of finance to take on any key position. And he doesn't understand manufacturing, so that rules him out for a technical job. However, he's a nice guy and he gets on with people, so why don't we make him a sales manager?" The chorus of agreement from around the room told us exactly how people saw sales management. To them, "getting on with people" was about as much professional qualification as a sales manager needed. We would like to think that today, at a similar meeting, participants would show a great deal more professional respect for sales management. And in the future, with the increasing number of new tools and techniques emerging from the work of researchers and consultants like ourselves, we hope that sales management will command ever greater respect from other professional areas of the business world. In this book, we've tried to show that the challenges of managing major sales demand an altogether different level of skill and sophistication from the traditional "crack the whip and make the numbers" philosophy of sales management.

It's our hope that, in some small way, this book has contributed ideas to advance the cause of effective professional sales management. Over the years we've had the privilege of working closely with many hundreds of fine sales managers. We've learned more from them than we could ever describe. They have given us insights that we would never have discovered from years of research. They have given us encouragement and help at times when the way forward seemed bleak. Now, in writing this, we hope to give something back in partial repayment for all we've received.

Appendix

DIAGNOSING EFFICIENCY AND EFFECTIVENESS PROBLEMS

In chapter 2 we described two components of sales productivity—efficiency and effectiveness.

- *Efficiency* is about how to get in front of the right customers, for the right amount of time, at a minimum cost.
- *Effectiveness* is about how to maximize sales potential once you succeed in getting in front of these customers.

Actions to improve both efficiency and effectiveness have an important role to play in improving the productivity of a sales force. However, as chapter 2 explains, it's no good hoping for significant productivity gains from using effectiveness improvement methods if your problem is in the efficiency area. And, of course, the opposite is also true—many sales managers have run into difficulties trying to implement efficiency solutions to effectiveness problems.

How do you tell which kind of productivity problem your sales force may have? In the chapter we suggested a number of methods to help you decide whether you have efficiency problems or

FIGURE A.1

Relationship between calls and sales volume in a high-value capital goods sales force

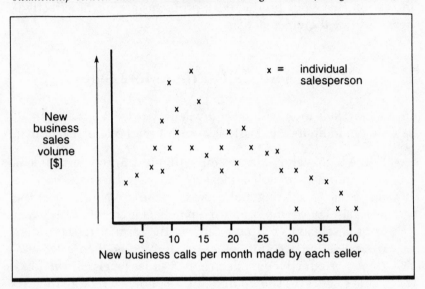

effectiveness problems. Some of these methods were simple rules-of-thumb. For a more precise analysis, you can use the method shown in figure 2.5. First, exclude from your call data all those calls, such as maintenance and routine customer care calls, that don't have a direct sales purpose. You should be left with *true* sales calls. Next plot on the horizontal axis of a graph, the number of sales calls made by each salesperson. On the vertical axis show dollar volume or some equivalent total performance measure for the salesperson. Note that the longer your selling cycle, the longer the time period over which you must collect your data. That's particularly important in terms of your performance measure on the vertical axis. The nature of major sales means that results measured over a short time period have very little meaning. Finally, look at your data (or if you want to be really sophisticated, run some regression analyses). In this example, taken from a capital goods sales force of thirty people, the top five performers all had new business call rates of between seven and fourteen calls a month, compared with the sales force average of twenty-two calls a month. The evidence here doesn't suggest a strong relationship between call rates and success. If an analysis in your company produces similar results, it's a strong indication that your productivity problems are in the effectiveness and not the efficiency area.

When More Calls Bring More Sales

In contrast, let's look at some equivalent data from a classic small sale shown in figure 2.6. First, a couple of methodological points:

- In the high-value sales example (figure 2.5) the vertical axis was confined to dollar measures of new business because inclusion of existing and repeat business would distort the analysis. For example, approximately 60 percent of the average salesperson's business came in the form of repeat orders from existing accounts where factors other than sales efficiency or effectiveness determined order levels. In the low-value sales force shown in figure 2.6, however, more than 90

FIGURE A.2

Relationship between calls and sales volume in the eastern region of a low value office supplies sales force

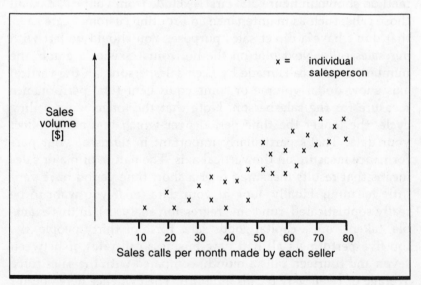

percent of total business was from new accounts. With less than 10 percent of repeat business we thought it unnecessary to break out new business separately from total business volume.

- On the horizontal axis, the number of calls per month, as you would expect in small sales, is much higher than in the earlier example.

In contrast to the earlier capital goods example, you can see that:

- On the whole, high performers were making *more* calls than the sales force average.
- The top five performers out of a sales force of twenty-eight were averaging seventy calls per month compared with an average of fifty-five calls per month for the rest of the sales force.

In circumstances like these there's a much stronger case to be made for the value of actions to increase overall sales force activity levels. Here, the *more calls = more sales* equation may be applicable.

If, as in this example, you find that your top performers are indeed the ones making the most calls, then you've built a good case for putting energy into the efficiency measures described in chapter 2. However, even if your analysis shows that you could gain sales by increasing call rates, be careful that you try to minimize the side effects we discussed in the chapter, such as the focus on small sales or the proliferation of paperwork.

Index